Praise for Stuart Isacoff's

A Natural History of the Piano

"A history written by a pianist and historian with a lively touch and a reach that spans octaves of science, culture and politics."   —*The Dallas Morning News*

"Like listening to a fascinating raconteur who informs and entertains and really knows his stuff. . . . Isacoff's heartfelt history of the piano will make you want to Stop! Read! and then go Listen!"   —*The Washington Post*

"Isacoff follows the piano into the honky-tonk, the drawing room, the middle-class home and the jazz club, tracking the evolution of the physical instrument itself as well as the composers and performers who made the piano an emblem of cultural variety and a laboratory for musical form."   —*The Wall Street Journal*

"Wonderful. . . . The perfect gift book. . . . So layered with anecdote that it reads like a novel or a good biography."   —*Hudson Valley News*

"A big slice of heaven for piano lovers."   —*Booklist*

"An exhaustive and entertaining cultural history of the piano. . . . 'Sparkling discourse' is his aim, and he succeeds. . . . An enjoyable read."
—*The Star-Ledger* (Newark, NJ)

"Fascinating. . . . A rare journey of discovery and delight. . . . Every detail is conveyed with a vivid sense of 'you are there,' and on every page we sense Mr. Isacoff's enthusiasm and lifelong dedication to the art of the piano. . . . This is no obvious retelling of the piano's development. . . . It contains a wealth of information, lavish illustrations, thought-provoking comments, and, most of all, it is a pleasure to read."   —*Clavier Companion*

"Deft. . . . In *A Natural History of the Piano*, Isacoff proves as fleet-fingered as any virtuoso."   —*The Chronicle of Higher Education*

"It's almost like listening to the music as you read Isacoff's relaxed, compelling prose."   —*The Huffington Post*

"A lively, virtually all-inclusive survey of all things pianistic. . . . Isacoff's ability to convey his formidable erudition in the most engaging terms, coupled with his infectious enthusiasm for music of all kinds, make this a charming and highly readable potpourri. Informative fun for every variety of music lover."   —*Kirkus Reviews*

"Engrossing. . . . Witty. . . . Pianists at all levels, music history buffs, and academics will appreciate Isacoff's insights and clever way with words; this is an enjoyable and informative book."   —*Library Journal*

"An encyclopedic and argumentative overview of all things piano. . . . Readers will be impressed . . . by the depth and diversity of Isacoff's research and references."   —*Publishers Weekly*

"Entertaining. . . . Crammed with great anecdotes and mini-essays."   —*The Seattle Times*

"Informative, comprehensive, and conversational. . . . Refreshing. . . . A deft rendering."   —*Choice*

"A dazzling structural juxtaposition from Mozart, Liszt, and Horowitz to Joplin, Tatum, and Jerry Lee Lewis, written with verve and sensitivity. Piano lovers will eat it up!"   —David Dubal, author of *The Art of the Piano*

"Never before have I learned and enjoyed so much about the instrument and its most distinctive practitioners—transcending so many categories of music. Whether the subject is jazz or classical music, the writing is unfailingly engaging and revealing."
—Nat Hentoff

"Every page of this book is filled with the poetry of Isacoff's writing as he outlines the fascinating development of the piano and its effect on music tradition throughout the centuries. The research is of great depth: how Isacoff weaves what he has discovered into a gripping and entertaining narrative is sheer magic. Essential reading for anyone who embraces not only the piano, but music, history, and culture. Bravo, Maestro Isacoff!"
—Frank Brady, author of *Endgame*

"I loved this book. Isacoff tells the story of the piano through every conceivable device and viewpoint. . . . And he never forgets that piano lore includes the highest of high culture as well as the popest of pop. It's a terrifically enjoyable read."
—Sara Fishko, Producer/Host, WNYC

"Supremely informative as well as fascinating and entertaining—highly recommended."
—Vladimir Ashkenazy

"A delight, both informative and entertaining. To borrow the author's categories, I find the writing both melodic and combustible."
—Dick Hyman

"Irresistible! Stuart Isacoff charts the three-century evolution of the world's most popular instrument with insight, love, and wit, garnished with the wisdom of today's foremost masters of classical and jazz."
—Sedgwick Clark, editor,
*Musical America International Directory
of the Performing Arts*

"A great read. . . . Any reader will part with *A Natural History of the Piano* having a renewed appreciation for the complexity and magic of the piano, its music and development, as well as an array of musically sophisticated dinner party anecdotes."
—*Music Reference Service Quarterly*

Stuart Isacoff

A Natural History of the Piano

Stuart Isacoff is a pianist, composer, and critic; he was the found-ing editor of *Piano Today* magazine. A winner of the ASCAP Deems Taylor Award for excellence in writing about music, he is a regular contributor to *The Wall Street Journal* and other publications. Isacoff gives lectures and performances at numer-ous venues, which have included the Chamber Music Society of Lincoln Center and the Metropolitan Museum of Art. He cur-rently teaches at the SUNY at Purchase.

www.stuartisacoff.net

ALSO BY STUART ISACOFF

*Temperament: How Music Became a Battleground
for the Great Minds of Western Civilization*

A Natural History of the Piano

A Natural History of the Piano

The Instrument, the Music, the Musicians—
from Mozart to Modern Jazz, and Everything in Between

Stuart Isacoff

VINTAGE BOOKS
A DIVISION OF RANDOM HOUSE, INC.
NEW YORK

FIRST VINTAGE BOOKS EDITION, NOVEMBER 2012

Grateful acknowledgment is made to the following for permission to
reprint previously published material:

Alfred A. Knopf and Harold Ober Associates Incorporated: Excerpts
from "Juke Box Love Song" from *The Collected Poems of Langston Hughes*,
edited by Arnold Rampersad with David Roessel, Associate Editor,
copyright © 1994 by the Estate of Langston Hughes. Reprinted by
permission of Alfred A. Knopf, a division of Random house, Inc.,
and Harold Ober Associates Incorporated.

The Colorado College Music Press: Excerpts from foreword by John
Cage, included in *The Well-Prepared Piano* by Richard Bunger
(Colorado Springs, CO: The Colorado College Music Press, 1973).
Reprinted by permission of The Colorado College Music Press.

The Library of Congress has cataloged the Knopf edition as follows:
Isacoff, Stuart.
A natural history of the piano : the instrument, the music, the musicians—
from Mozart to modern jazz, and everything in between / Stuart Isacoff.
p. cm.
Includes bibliographical references and index.
1. Piano—History. 2. Piano music—History and criticism. 3. Pianists.
I. Title
ML650.I83 2011
786.209—dc22
2011011557

Vintage ISBN: 978-0-307-27933-0

Author photograph © Michael Lionstar
Book design by Maggie Hinders

www.vintagebooks.com

Printed in the United States of America
10 9 8 7 6 5 4 3 2

To my brother, Dr. Mark Isacoff,
and in memory of my teacher, Sir Roland Hanna

Dashing from one thing to another, or linking them together, he heaped them up—first because he had endless things in his head, and one thing led on to the next; but in particular because it was his passion to make comparisons and discover relations, display influences, lay bare the interwoven connections of culture.

—THOMAS MANN, *Doctor Faustus*,
translated by H. T. Lowe-Porter

Contents

Illustrations

A Natural History of the Piano

CHAPTER 1

A Gathering of Traditions

EVEN AS HIS BODY BEGAN TO FAIL, for Oscar Peterson (1925–2007) the piano remained a lifeline. The instrument had long been a trusted companion—sparking early dreams, conferring a place in the history books, and easing his way in a world of racial strife. Now, at eighty-one, he looked worn out. Arriving at the stage of New York's Birdland in a wheelchair, after debilitating strokes had weakened his legs and slowed his left hand, he struggled to move his heavy frame onto the piano bench.

OPPOSITE
Oscar Peterson
VERYL OAKLAND

Yet, as soon as the keyboard was within reach, even before his torso had completed its fall into a seated position, he thrust out his right arm and grabbed a handful of notes; at that signal, the bass player, drummer, and guitarist launched into their first number. And suddenly there was that sound. He still had it—a musical personality as large as life, steeped in tradition yet recognizably, unmistakably all its own.

For decades, Peterson's technical command and musical instincts had instilled in others the kind of awe and fear he expressed about his idol, the late Art Tatum. He once compared that older piano master to a lion: an animal that scares you to death, though you can't resist getting close enough to hear it roar. (Classical firebrands Sergei Rachmaninoff and Vladimir Horowitz went to hear Tatum perform and came away with the same sense of intimidation.) And that made his comeback all the more difficult.

The Peterson style was always characterized by rapid, graceful, blues-tinged melody lines unfurled in long, weaving phrases with the inexorable logic of an epic narrative; and, equally important, a visceral sense of rhythm, transmitted with fire and snap. Those qualities for which he was renowned—effortless fluidity and clockwork precision—were not merely aspects of his playing; they were the very foundation on which his artistic expression rested. And pulling them off required the highest level of athletic prowess.

At times that evening in 2006, in one of the few scheduled performances on what would turn out to be his farewell tour to the world, flashes of the old brilliance emerged, unscathed by illness and time. Yet the strain was also clear. No matter: playing was for him as necessary as eating and breathing. "That's my therapy," he said after the set, nodding in the direction of the piano as a small smile inched across his half-frozen visage. But in the memorable moments during his set, the large, glistening, ebony Bösendorfer that filled most of Birdland's stage meant something even greater than his personal salvation; for everyone in that room, it became the center of the universe.

I T'S A ROLE the piano has enjoyed for over three hundred years: luring music lovers to Parisian salons to hear Chopin's plaintive improvisations, and to Viennese concert halls for Beethoven's ferocious, string-snapping outbursts. The piano captured the spotlight at Harlem "rent parties," where two-fisted ivory "ticklers" worked furiously to outshine each other, and consoled lonely miners in the California Gold Rush as roving European virtuoso Henri Herz performed his variations on "Oh Susannah" [sic] for them. It comforted thousands of Siberian peasants who never had heard a note of classical piano music until Russian master Sviatoslav Richter brought it to their doorsteps. It is still capable of wowing crowds in concert halls, clubs, and stadiums the world over.

But the piano is more than just an instrument; in the words of Oliver Wendell Holmes, it is a "wondrous box," filled as much with hopes, yearnings, and disappointments as with strings and hammers and felt. It has been a symbol as mutable as the human condition, representing refined elegance in a Victorian home and casual squalor in a New Orleans brothel.

Consider the gamut of emotions, from elation to dread and even to terror, a performer may face in conquering its technical hurdles, as the young woman in Nobel Prize–winner Elfriede Jelinek's novel *The Piano Teacher* learned: "She gathers all her energy, spreads her wings, and then plunges forward, toward the keys, which zoom up to her like the earth toward a crashing plane. If she can't reach a note at first swoop, she simply leaves it out. Skipping notes, a subtle vendetta against her musically untrained torturers, gives her a tiny thrill of satisfaction."

THE CRUELTY OF THE PIANO—*by Piotr Anderszewski*

When I play with orchestra, I sometimes tell myself I'll never play a concerto again. Too many artistic compromises. I only want to do recitals.

When I'm confronted with the extreme loneliness of the recital, the heroism and also the cruelty involved, I sometimes think that I'll never do recitals ever again. From now on I'll only make recordings.

When I'm recording and am free to repeat the work as often as I wish, the possibility of doing better, of giving the best possible performance and where everything can turn against me, the piano, the microphone, and above all my own sense of freedom, I think to myself, I'll never go into a recording studio ever again. It's even more cruel. In fact, the ultimate temptation would be to stop everything, lie down, listen to the beat of my heart and quietly wait for it to stop . . .

[Yet] sometimes I may not want to play at all, but upon striking the final chord, I say to myself, Something happened here. Something that is completely beyond my control. It's as if the audience had co-created something with me. That's life. Giving is receiving.

FROM THE BRUNO MONSAINGEON FILM *Piotr Anderszewski: Unquiet Traveller*

Nevertheless, the piano can also exert an almost mystical attraction, seducing devotees into lifelong bonds. The magic, when it happens, is inexplicable. Even the technicians who maintain the piano's working parts can seem at times like initiates in a mysterious cult. "A tuner makes a good husband," claims a character in Daniel Mason's novel *The Piano Tuner*. "He knows how to listen, and his touch is more delicate . . . Only the tuner knows the inside of the piano."

Those innards are a miracle of invention. With wood and cast iron, hammers and pivots, weighing altogether nearly a thousand pounds—and capable of sustaining twenty-two tons of tension on its strings (the equivalent of about twenty medium-sized cars)—this majestic contraption will whisper, sing, stutter, or shout at the will of the player. Its tones range from the lowest notes of the orchestra to the highest. It has the remarkable ability to express music of any time period, and in any style—Baroque fugues, Romantic reveries, Impressionist sketches, church hymns, Latin montunos, jazz rhythms, and rock riffs. In the process, it makes everything its own.

THE WONDER OF THE PIANO *by Menahem Pressler*

I was recently asked by Indiana University, where I teach, to select a new piano, and I found one that I felt was exceedingly beautiful. I've chosen many pianos over the years, and most of the time there were some colleagues who complained about my selection, saying, "It's not brilliant enough," or "It's not for chamber music," or "It's not for solo performance." It's like when you choose your mate and someone else says, "I would never have married her." But this time it seemed that I had selected the Marilyn Monroe of pianos—everyone loved it.

The other night I was playing the Schubert B-flat Sonata on it, and the piano was like a living soul. This was at the end of the day, and I was very tired. And yet I was reminded of what a happy man I am playing on such a piano. You become elated, invigorated, and inspired . . . all through something built by a factory. It tells me that there is more to life than we can see.

At BIRDLAND, OSCAR Peterson again proved the instrument's enduring power. By the end of the evening he had the crowd on its feet, cheering and whistling. It was a special moment, and the audience knew it, the culmination of a unique career, and a last chance to experience the Peterson style, crafted by melding many of the disparate strands that ran through the piano's history. His artistry encompassed them all.

For dazzling technique, he followed the lessons of the European classical tradition, culled from childhood sessions in his native Canada, first with his sister, Daisy, then with local pianist Louis Hooper and the Hungarian teacher Paul de Marky. He was so serious about his lessons as a young boy that he would practice for up to eighteen hours at a time, he said, on days "when my mother didn't drag me off the stool." De Marky was a good model: he had studied in Budapest with Stefan Thomán, who had studied with the great Franz Liszt—a musical titan of his day and the founder of modern piano technique.

Liszt's phenomenal facility—in trademark rapid-fire passages and streams of double notes, along with other exciting displays, such as the quick alternation of hands on the keyboard (which, he explained, he had taken from the music of J. S. Bach)—created such a sensation that poet Heinrich Heine described him in 1844 as "the Attila, the scourge of God." Indeed, claimed Heine, audiences should take pity on the pianos, "which trembled at the news of his coming and now writhe, bleed and wail under his hands, so that the Society for the Protection of Animals should investigate them." Liszt's musical tricks had made many of the breathtaking

piano feats of Art Tatum possible. (Peterson was so flabbergasted when he first heard Tatum on record that he almost retired on the spot. "I still feel that way," he admitted that evening at Birdland.)

De Marky trained Peterson in that great tradition, and assigned the pianist other staples of the repertoire, such as Chopin's treacherously difficult Etudes, along with the "big, rich soft chords" (harmonies, or simultaneously sounding tones) of Claude Debussy. "Oscar is our Liszt and Bill Evans is our Chopin," commented composer Lalo Schifrin, referring to the popular conception that Liszt conquered the piano while Chopin seduced it.

It's only partly true: the dreamy, impressionist character of a Bill Evans performance does suggest comparisons with the hushed, poetic approach of Chopin, who, according to witnesses, played the instrument using a dynamic range that fell somewhere between a whisper and a murmur. Yet the intricate melodies spun out in an Oscar Peterson solo also owe a great deal to the lyrical genius of Chopin, a composer whose "irregular, black, ascending and descending staircases of notes," wrote critic James Huneker, could "strike the neophyte with terror." And as he taught Peterson, Paul de Marky homed in on Chopin's most important trait. "I don't hear the melody singing," he would tell his student. "The melody is choppy. Make it sing." And so the works of the celebrated classical composers—great improvisers, all—served as his training ground.

Peterson's immersion in classical studies made him an easy tar-
get for some of the jazz crowd. Writer Leonard Feather, using the
pseudonym Prof. S. Rosentwig McSiegel, authored a lampoon
about a technically astounding pianist named Peter Oscarson who
dumbfounded other musicians at a concert by playing a "somewhat
esoteric interlude, a set of quadrilles and French-Canadian folk
songs." But those studies with de Marky put him in good stead for
the artistic heights that would come.

Paul de Marky's classical expertise notwithstanding, he also
encouraged Oscar Peterson's immersion in the jazz canon. "Mr. de
Marky was a very great pianist and teacher," remembered Peterson.
"What I loved about him was that he was not shortsighted. He was
a fantastic classical pianist. But I would come to him for a lesson,
and he'd be playing jazz records"—greats like Teddy Wilson, Nat
"King" Cole, and Duke Ellington. "Their playing served as my
rudiments," he reported.

He was swept into almost instant fame when producer Norman
Granz, visiting Canada, heard him in a live radio broadcast in 1949,
and soon after coaxed him into playing in a Jazz at the Philharmonic
concert at Carnegie Hall in New York. Introduced as a surprise
guest performer, no sooner did he take the stage than, as Mike Levin
reported in the magazine *DownBeat,* the event was stopped "dead
cold in its tracks." According to Levin, "he scared some of the local
modern minions by playing bop ideas in his *left* hand . . . Whereas
some of the bop stars conceive good ideas but sweat to make them,
Peterson rips them off with an excess of power." Reminiscing about
that time, Peterson revealed that he had decided the only way to get
attention was "to frighten the hell out of everybody pianistically."
He did, and the Peterson-Granz partnership was cemented. The
two ended up touring across the continent together, building larger
and larger audiences, while battling the pervasive racial prejudice
they encountered along the way.

That American debut helped Peterson move beyond an early
reputation as an expert in the rhythmically charged, perpetual-
left-hand-motion technique of boogie-woogie. After winning a
Canadian amateur contest in the style when he was just four-

teen, he became known for a while as "the Brown Bomber of Boogie-Woogie," a takeoff on the nickname given to boxer Joe Louis. ("That was RCA Victor's idea, not mine," Peterson recalled with a glint of anger. "They insisted that I do that. As for whatever name they gave me, I'm happy not to remember.")

JAZZ VS. THE CLASSICS

Oscar Peterson was not, of course, the only jazz great with a classical foundation. Even Louis Armstrong, whose sound seemed hatched from the streets and sporting houses of New Orleans without a hint of European influence, spoke of studying the classics as a child in the city's Colored Waif's Home for Boys. "I played all classical music when I was in the orphanage," he recalled. "That instills the soul in you. You know? Liszt, Bach, Rachmaninoff, Gustav Mahler, and Haydn." Pianist Lil Hardin, who eventually married Armstrong, had been a classical-music major at Nashville's Fisk University before she joined the Creole Jazz Band. She found the transition a bit of a challenge, however. "When I sat down to play," she said, "I asked for the music and were they surprised! They politely told me they didn't have any music and furthermore never used any: I then asked what key would the first number be in. I must have been speaking another language because the leader said, 'When you hear two knocks, just start playing.' " She did, they hired her, and her life as a jazz musician was launched.

Leonard Feather was just having a little fun with his "Peter Oscarson" portrait. Yet, even today, it's easy to find "experts" guilty of such silly pigeonholing. Ironically, just at the time the "original instrument" movement in classical music was reaching the conclusion that the quest for absolute stylistic authenticity in the performance of early works was futile, the leadership of Jazz at Lincoln Center in New York was attempting to frame the parameters of "authentic" jazz, as if a sort of purity test were possible. But Whitney Balliett got it right when he wrote that jazz was "the sound of surprise." It thrives on unlimited possibility, not hidebound categories.

Boogie lacks the subtlety and sophistication of the music that later thrust him onto the world stage, yet the ragged bounce and propulsive rhythms that permeated this music were what made early jazz so attractive as it emerged at the end of the nineteenth century from the poor sections of cities like New Orleans, Memphis, New York, and St. Louis—nurtured, wrote James Weldon Johnson in his novel, *The Autobiography of an Ex-Colored Man*, by "Negro piano-players who knew no more of the theory of music than they did of the theory of the universe." What they *did* boast was plenty of what Johnson called "instinct and talent," and the fertile material that rose out of communal songs and dances like the bamboula, which, reported an 1886 magazine article about black culture in New Orleans, "roars and rattles, twangs, contorts, and tumbles in terrible earnest."

This was around the time that Czech composer Antonin Dvořák, during his famous American sojourn, announced in 1893 in the

Louis Armstrong's Hot Five, with Lil Hardin

The Oscar Peterson Trio of the 1950s: guitarist Herb Ellis, bassist Ray Brown, and Peterson

New York Herald: "I am now convinced that the future music of this country must be built on the foundations of the songs which are called Negro melodies." Despite the influence of folk songs on Haydn, Beethoven, and others, few in the "serious music" world paid Dvořák's advice much attention.

But jazz didn't develop from just one source; even in its beginning stages, it was a mixed breed of black and white, the edgy and the sentimental, European classical forms and rambunctious shouts. African-American traditions combined with those brought by the new European immigrants to forge a hybrid art filled with infectious, throbbing rhythms and soul-wrenching melodies—along with familiar dances and nostalgic ditties. As piano music, it first made its way into the parlor as ragtime, combining familiar march styles and sentimental waltzes with new, odd rhythms that skewed the music's usual lilt by placing accents in the "wrong" places. The result was a style brimming with playful hops, skips, and stumbles. As it evolved, this folk art picked up elements of the blues, took on added rhythmic vitality, and exploded into boogie-woogie and swing.

The new sounds had universal appeal. In Chicago, people of all races rushed to hear performers like clarinetist Wilbur Sweatman play his "hot" music, which, in 1906, included his rendition of the schmaltzy concert song "The Rosary," which he executed on three clarinets simultaneously. And Sweatman was no interloper: even the likes of young Duke Ellington happily performed in his band. Ben Harney, a piano player of indeterminate race (who passed for white), reportedly said he learned his jazzy style from an Appalachian fiddler as well as from a black singer he accompanied in Chicago; he quickly became a star attraction in New York, and challenged anyone to find a rag that predated his "You've Been a Good Old Wagon but You've Done Broke Down" of 1895.

Meanwhile, in New Orleans, Jelly Roll Morton (Ferdinand Joseph LaMothe) famously claimed that he had invented jazz in 1902. The region's unique brand of music owed as much to the dancing of slaves in the Crescent City's Congo Square and especially to the town's Creole, Caribbean, and Latin American cultures as it did to Morton's inventiveness. But, as piano great Willie "the Lion" Smith put it, "Jelly Roll was a guy who always talked a lot." (And Morton was also influenced by European classical music; in recorded interviews with Alan Lomax in 1938 for the Library of Congress, he spoke specifically about Dvořák's *Humoresque* and several "light operas" he had heard, and played two piano versions of Verdi's "Miserere"—one remembered from childhood, the other jazzed up in "Jelly Roll" style. "You have the finest ideas from the greatest operas, symphonies and overtures in jazz music," he informed Lomax. Jazz, he said, was an art of the highest quality because "it comes from everything of the finest class.")

James Reese Europe and his band

Then there was Yiddish swing, exemplified by Romanian Abe Schwartz, who arrived on America's shores in 1899. As jazz expert Nat Hentoff has written, Schwartz's band, with its "swooping trombones" and "staccato banjo," featured "a powerful front line of fiddler Schwartz and the magical clarinetist I yearned to be, Dave Tarras."

This burgeoning new musical world wasn't free of the racial antagonism that permeated other layers of American society. But the mix of many influences was arguably as important to jazz's growth as the strut and sass that became its calling card. Before long the sound was influencing music makers of every stripe. Seven-year-old George Gershwin soaked it in from a curb outside Baron Wilkins's nightclub in Harlem, where he sat listening to performances by composer and bandleader James Reese Europe.

Beginning in the early years of the twentieth century and up through the teens and twenties, composers on the other side of the Atlantic such as Claude Debussy, Maurice Ravel, Darius Milhaud, and Paul Hindemith latched on to these sounds and used them to give their compositions a sense of the new. (It's telling that Milhaud titled his early jazz-tinged work *The Creation of the World*.) Back in America, the art was advanced by generations of self-schooled musicians: ragtimers such as "One Leg" Willie Joseph and Eubie Blake; boogie players like Meade Lux Lewis and Albert Ammons; gospel and blues musicians who infused it with their experiences of church and of the hard life; and jazz musicians with names like "Jelly Roll," "Fats," "Count," "Duke," and "the Lion," who injected it with swing, wit, and technical command, while joining their harmonic palettes to those of the Europeans.

OSCAR PETERSON, MY TEACHER *by Mike Longo*

During the 1960s I had the honor of being Oscar Peterson's private student. He and some colleagues had started a school for contemporary music, and though there had to be around fifty students, after about two or three weeks he took me under his wing. From that time on, I saw him three or four times a week, instead of the usual once. He gave me the key to his studio so I could practice on his piano. That was necessary, because he had me practicing thirteen hours a day.

Discipline was the heart of the program. You had to address him and bassist Ray Brown as "Mister," and students were required to wear a tie.

He transformed my playing. I had already graduated college as a piano major, but no one had ever spoken to me about my physical approach to the instrument. I was playing with my wrist down. He had me raise it, and taught me to play without a lot of arm weight. The technique originated with Liszt; it allows you to strike the keys without ever exerting yourself.

He also taught me the true meaning of piano "style," which has to do with developing a personal sound. Think of all the jazz organists, he said, who each have a tremendous number of "stops" at their disposal, mechanical devices on the instrument that change the quality of the sound. Despite that variety of choice, they all use the same ones, so every jazz organist ends up sounding exactly like Jimmy Smith, the jazz master who popularized the instrument. To have real style, he explained, means to create a sound that is instantly recognizable as yours.

So Oscar Peterson didn't let his students play like him—or like anybody else, for that matter. One day I was using chord voicings [particular spatial arrangements of the tones in a harmony] like those of Bill Evans and he yelled: "You know damn well that's not you!" He had a formula for achieving beautiful results at the piano. He called it "the five T's": touch, time, tone, technique, and taste. Of course, he had them all.

Oscar Peterson's rise to the top of the jazz pantheon was based on a formula that embraced all of these elements, brewed over centuries, merging the classical European tradition and the homespun American one. But he focused especially on a common denominator he had found in the approach of all the greats: their refusal to settle for anything less than a full command of their resources. "I never tried to sound like a trumpet or a clarinet," he said, alluding to a common jazz-piano practice of building improvisations from simple "instrumental-style" melody lines accompanied by sparse, left-hand chordal tattoos. "I was taught to respect [this instrument] for what it was: a piano. And it spoke with a certain voice. And that was what I was determined to bring forward." He had always striven, he explained, to be the kind of musician who could take advantage of the entire keyboard, of everything the instrument was capable of producing.

THAT GOAL has been a driving force throughout the evolution of the piano. It pushed Bach to advance his skills of intricate counterpoint to unequaled heights, and Mozart to find ways of bringing dramatic character to wordless melodies. It drove Beethoven to storm the heavens with his unparalleled, turbulent imagination, and sparked powerhouse performers such as Liszt, Paderewski, and Horowitz to conquer the physical limits of the keyboard (along with the hearts of their fans).

The need to discover the piano's full potential spurred impressionist Claude Debussy to produce new, shimmering effects through what he dubbed the "alchemy of sound," and Russian mystic Alexander Scriabin to envision a magical music that would usher in the Apocalypse. It moved bebop's Thelonious Monk to create his odd, angular music, filled with eerie silences that seem like portals to an alternate universe. It was the force behind rocker Jerry Lee Lewis's ripping rock glissandos, and composer Conlon Nancarrow's player-piano experiments, designed to render in real time works that are simply impossible for normal human hands. It encouraged French composer Erik Satie to produce the first minimalist piano music, and American maverick John Cage to create the "prepared piano," in which an array of objects inserted into the instrument's strings creates sonorities reminiscent of Balinese gamelan music.

The impulse to expand music's expressive horizons was responsible for the very invention of the piano over three hundred years ago—and of endless tinkerings, failings, and breakthroughs that transformed it into the giant technological marvel of today. Oscar Peterson's handmade Viennese Bösendorfer grand piano could do anything he asked of it, creating thundering choirs of sound in one moment and producing crisp, delicate chimes the next. Yet it bears only the slightest resemblance to that original small, delicate, and unimpressively soft instrument born in Florence around 1700 on which it is modeled.

This book explores the story of the piano: its players, composers, and inventors, greats and would-be greats, teachers and students, patrons, critics, and promoters—all of whom devoted their lives to its artistry. Together they shaped a fascinating history of the most important instrument ever created.

CHAPTER 2

The Piano Is Born

G EORGE BERNARD SHAW, Victorian England's celebrated playwright, was also one of its crustiest music critics. Working under the pseudonym "Corno di Bassetto" (basset horn), he regularly skewered the greatest figures of his day with the same acerbic wit that animated his plays. Of Brahms's *A German Requiem*, he wrote, it "could only have come from the establishment of a first-class undertaker." But in his 1894 essay about the "religious" fervor that surrounded the piano, he sounded like a true believer. "Its invention was to music," he declared, "what the invention of printing was to poetry."

At the time, it must have seemed as though the sky was raining pianos. By the late nineteenth century, they were everywhere. Hundreds of thousands were being sold each year, in a market that was rapidly expanding, with no end in sight.

There were many reasons. Citizens with social aspirations saw in the decorous home piano a key to future success. Family-minded folks found it perfect as the emotional hub of a household—in D. H. Lawrence's poetic description, a shelter for a child, who could sit under the instrument "in the boom of the shaking strings," while his mother's fingers pressed the little hollows she had worn into the ivories. More practically, it put the experience of great music close at hand, even works from the magnificent symphonic repertoire, which composers like Liszt thoughtfully transcribed for keyboard players.

Just a century earlier, a piano had been nearly impossible to find. Wolfgang Amadeus Mozart, whose piano concertos catapulted the instrument to the center of the musical world, never set eyes on one until he toured Germany in the mid-1770s. By then, half his life had passed. And the piano he came upon at that time was seriously inferior to the ones that Shaw experienced: an instrument still in its infancy, little advanced beyond the primitive version that first appeared in Florence some seven decades earlier.

Even then it was bound for greatness. The piano gave the musical world something for which it had long clamored: a keyboard that offered unhampered musical expression. Most instruments can bellow or sigh, or produce any volume in between. A cello can begin a piece faintly, as if from a distance, and gradually inflate its tones into a surging torrent. But early keyboards could accomplish

A typical harpsichord for the home. Keene Bentside spinet, ca. 1700
MIM/HOLLY METZ

such changes only through clunky mechanical devices that necessarily interrupted the flow of music. They couldn't simply respond to changing finger pressure, the way a piano does: No matter how hard a harpsichord's keys are struck, the instrument's quills pluck their assigned strings at a single, consistent volume, unleashing an unchanging, biting sonority.

The great composer and keyboardist François Couperin, for one, while appreciating the harpsichord's brilliance, bemoaned that limitation. "I shall always be grateful," he said, "to those who, by infinite art supported by good taste, succeed in making the instrument capable of expression." The piano (which doesn't pluck but softly strikes its strings with "hammers" covered in a soft material) was the answer to his plea. By changing the amount of strength she exerts on its keys, a pianist can modulate the instrument's tones, making its sweet, nuanced shades of sound appear to "sing." (The tiny clavichord, which strikes its strings with metal "tangents," had the same ability, but its sound was so diminutive it was impractical as a performance vehicle.)

Despite the need for it, the instrument's creation, in about 1700, was serendipitous, born of the odd pairing of a little-known instrument maker and a dissolute prince. Its official father was a keyboard technician named Bartolomeo Cristofori. But it had a godfather in Ferdinando de' Medici, the Grand Prince of Tuscany. If it hadn't been for the prince's love of mechanical gadgets (he collected more than forty clocks, as well as keyboards) or, for that matter, his poor marriage and roving eye, the piano might not have been brought into existence.

Ferdinando's family had ruled Florence since the thirteenth century, producing popes, a bank of unrivaled power, and an astounding number of artworks commissioned from the greatest painters, including Masaccio, Donatello, Michelangelo, Leonardo da Vinci, and Raphael. Many of Florence's architectural wonders, including the Uffizi museum and the Boboli Gardens, were undertaken by the Medicis. Galileo turned to them as protectors when the church bore down on him, and in gratitude, he named the four largest moons of Jupiter after the Medici children he had tutored.

Of course, the family history also included less savory traits. Ferdinando's shaky marriage was a Medici inheritance: his own mother had fled to Paris to escape his father, and when Ferdinando pleaded with her to return, she sent back word that she would rather next meet his father in hell. Such squabbles never interfered with the clan's talent for lavish display—a quality that Stendhal, the great French writer, suggested was the basis for their ability to rule. They had managed to overcome the Florentines' "passionate love for liberty and implacable hatred of nobility," he claimed, only through the overwhelming aesthetic beauty they had fostered.

Both sides of the Medici legacy, the beauty and the domestic grief, appeared to have played a role in the story of the piano. It began in the winter of 1688, when Ferdinando, looking for temporary escape from his burdens in Florence and not incidentally hoping for a good time, made his way to Venice for Carnival, the annual bacchanalian romp that made good the floating city's name, which was taken from Venus, divine goddess of love and seduction.

As a rule, what happens in Venice stays in Venice. But travel writer Francis Misson attended the festivities that year, and though he expressed shock at what he found, he eagerly offered his readers a metaphorical peephole into the goings-on. The degree of wantonness he witnessed was truly impressive. "They are not satisfied with the ordinary libertinism," he reported of the revelers, noting the universal use of masks to hide everyone's identity. "The whole city is disguised. Vice and virtue are never so well counterfeited."

Apparently, the prince enjoyed himself thoroughly, and likely met Cristofori on his way back home. The timing was fortuitous. Ferdinando, who was, among other things, a keyboardist and musical connoisseur (Handel composed his opera *Rodrigo* for the prince's theater), had recently lost his harpsichord maker and tuner, Antonio Bolgioni, and he needed someone to service his large collection of instruments at his court in Florence. It was probably while passing through Padua that he heard about a talented thirty-three-year-old local instrument builder and technician, Cristofori. When they met, the prince decided to make him an offer he couldn't refuse. "The

Ferdinando de' Medici with his musicians, by Antonio Domenico Gabbiani (1652–1726)

prince was told that I did not wish to go," reported Cristofori some years later; "he replied that he would make me want to." In the end, Ferdinando apparently returned home with two things of significance: both the future inventor of the piano and the venereal disease that would eventually claim his life.

In Florence, Ferdinando situated Cristofori in a large room with more than a hundred other craftsmen. Cristofori grumbled that they created "a deafening noise"; it was not an ideal setting for the tuning and repair of musical instruments. The prince casually dismissed his griping. Over time, however, the two men managed to reach an accommodation, and Cristofori's conditions slowly improved. He received money to rent his own place, along with a loan of furniture and household items. There was bonus pay for tunings at the prince's summer residence, Pratolino. And within two years Cristofori was employing other craftsmen as assistants. For Ferdinando, it turned out to be well worth the added expense.

In addition to servicing the prince's inventory, Cristofori produced a series of original, elegantly made instruments, including such oddities as a small "spinet" harpsichord with its strings placed at an angle, rather than perpendicular to the keyboard, to conserve space, and another covered entirely in ebony. The most astounding design that issued from Cristofori's workshop, though, was an instrument of simple cypress, with a boxwood keyboard. It rested atop a stand of "gilded and shaded" poplar, and sported "a cover of red leather lined with green taffeta, trimmed all around with gold ribbon." What made it special was not the look of the thing, however, but the unusual mechanism inside. Cristofori named it *un cimbalo di cipresso di piano e forte*, "a keyboard of cypress with *piano* [soft] and *forte* [loud]."

That name stuck, with variations: over the centuries it has been called a pianoforte, a fortepiano, or simply a piano. Its importance was monumental. But how did it work?

Cristofori explained his invention in an interview conducted by court poet and librettist Scipione Maffei in 1711; his article and its accompanying diagrams appeared in the *Giornale de' letterati d'Italia*. The secret was a sophisticated apparatus—an "action"— that thrust the hammers against the instrument's strings when the keys were depressed, and then allowed them to fall back immediately into their resting positions so they would be ready to strike again. Pressing the keys with greater force caused the hammers to strike with more energy, bringing about an increase in volume.

Cristofori's "action" was the forerunner of today's mechanism. Since the strings would be under a great deal of tension, Cristofori built a sturdy, double-walled case, separating the vibrating parts of the instrument from those that had to endure the most pressure. (This division continues in the modern piano, which uses a tension-bearing cast-iron frame and a freely vibrating soundboard.)

As with anything new, the instrument had some detractors. Critics complained that its tone was too soft and dull. Maffei defended the invention's sound as being superior to the harpsichord's percussive twang and nasal-sounding aftertone, which could be downright clangorous. An instrument with hammers rather than quills opened up remarkable musical possibilities, he explained, but it required a new, different kind of keyboard technique.

CRISTOFORI'S CONTRAPTION

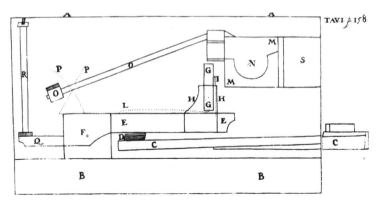

The genius of Bartolomeo Cristofori's piano mechanism (or "action") is that it allows a hammer to be propelled toward a string, strike it, and then disengage, or "escape," from the part that pushed it upward, so it will be ready to strike again. Here is how it works.

As the key (C) is depressed, the intermediate lever (E) is raised. This causes the "escapement" (G) to push the hammer (O) toward the string (A). The escapement then "escapes" from contact with the hammer, thus allowing the hammer to fall back to its resting position. In Cristofori's original design, the falling hammers were caught by a network of silk threads.

When the key (C) is released, the escapement (G), which is hinged and attached to a spring, slides back into its initial position. The damper (R), which had been lowered when the key was depressed in order to allow the string to vibrate freely, returns again to contact with the vibrating string and thus silences it.

Scipione Maffei's diagram of Bartolomeo Cristofori's piano action, 1711

The length of the keyboard was much shorter than those found on pianos today: forty-nine notes, compared with today's eighty-eight. As in later designs, the piano's strings had to withstand greater tension than those of a harpsichord, because even a light hammer delivers more energy to a string than a plectrum will. The earliest pianos were therefore strung with brass wire for the lower tones and steel for the upper ones. The hammers, which today are covered in felt, were made of parchment and glue.

FOR THE LOVE OF HARPSICHORDS

Voltaire declared in 1774 that the piano was a mere "kettle-maker's instrument in comparison with the harpsichord." But harpsichord builders saw the writing on the wall. By the early eighteenth century, they were trying to forestall the piano's ascendance by introducing their own attractive innovations. Jean Marius—whose inventions included a folding umbrella, a collapsible tent, and a method for waterproofing cloth—created a small harpsichord that could be folded for travel. He also produced a keyboard that combined the old and new instruments by using both hammers and quills.

The French Royal Academy of Sciences entertained proposals throughout the eighteenth century for such combinations: bowed harpsichords, harpsichords with organs, harpsichords with pianos, organs with pianos, and even pianos with glass harmonicas. The latter, submitted by a French physician named Beyer, used glass plates instead of metal strings, struck by hammers covered with wool. Benjamin Franklin loved it.

The race was also on to make the harpsichord's sound more pleasing. Jakob Adlung, in his *Musica Mechanica Organoedi* of 1768, declared that harpsichord quills of goose feathers were too soft to produce a good tone, those made of fish bones too stiff, but that raven feathers coated with olive oil were just right. The Parisian instrument builder Pascal Taskin simply used leather quills to produce a "rounder" sound. Bach's biographer Johann Nikolaus Forkel mentioned an instrument built in Rome that went Taskin one better: it used quills of leather *covered* with velvet. "These pieces," he declared, "sound as if softly touched by a sensitive finger and produce a tone combining the sound of a flute with that of a soft bell. In its fine quality of sound this instrument easily surpasses all others."

In Paris in 1776, the celebrated musician and chess player François-André Danican Philidor demonstrated a harpsichord whose upper register used strings that had been "blued"—heated until they turned blue. Philidor had learned of an experiment in England (based on the work of France's royal watchmaker Julien Le Roy) that found such strings richer sounding. He imported an instrument from London so that members of the Royal Academy of Sciences could hear the superior result for themselves. According to the minutes of the meeting, the blued strings "appeared noticeably sweeter."

None of these innovations addressed the piano's great advantage of being able to change volume on the spur of the moment. Burkat Shudi, a young craftsman who had emigrated from Switzerland to London, tried to even the field in 1765 with a "Venetian swell" for harpsichords. In his patent application of 1769 he described it as a shutter device that could be opened and closed on the instrument—like "Venetian blinds," which were patented in London in the same year—to produce shifts in loudness, and Shudi was certain it would make the harpsichord reign supreme. He was wrong. Shudi's daughter, Barbara, married his employee John Broadwood, and in 1790, nineteen years after Shudi's death, the firm of Shudi and Broadwood ceased harpsichord production altogether and devoted its efforts to the making of pianos.

The options of "hammering" or "plucking" were not new; instruments using one or the other approach had been around for a long time. In fact, the harpsichord can be traced to the psaltery, a plucked instrument (using feather quills) with origins in the Far and Middle East, brought to Europe via the cultural-exchange program known as the Crusades. Similarly, the piano is a cousin of the dulcimer, a hammered variant of the psaltery, which uses padded sticks to strike the strings rather than pluck them.

Indeed, around the time Cristofori was putting his new instrument together in Florence, the dulcimer was about to have its moment, thanks to a music and dance teacher named Pantaleon Hebenstreit. In the minds of audiences and instrument makers, Hebenstreit's dulcimer and the piano would become inextricably linked. Born in 1667 in Eisleben, Germany (Martin Luther's hometown), Hebenstreit was fleeing creditors when he settled in Merseburg to become a tutor to the children of a pastor. It was there, with the pastor's help, that he built a giant dulcimer. Soon after, the itinerant teacher and his unusual dulcimer were a musical sensation all over Europe.

Keyboardist and composer Johann Kuhnau (Bach's predecessor as cantor in Leipzig) heard Hebenstreit in Dresden in 1697 and was amazed by both the music and the man's sprightly moves as he played. "Mons. Pantalon [sic] made his leaps, and after he had exhibited his musical treasury of preludes, fantasies, fugues, and all sorts of *caprices* with the bare sticks," recalled Kuhnau, "he then bound the sticks with cotton and played a *partie* [instrumental piece]. Thereupon the Count was utterly beside himself; he led me out of his room toward the hall, listened from a distance and said: 'Why, how can that be? I have been to Italy, have heard what beauty there is in music, but the likes of this my ears have never heard.' "

In Paris in 1705, Hebenstreit so impressed Louis XIV with his virtuosity on the instrument that the king anointed the huge dulcimer with the official title "pantaleon." (It was possibly a double entendre; the term *pantalon* was used in French and Italian comedy for "clown," and thus it might have been a reference to Hebenstreit's puppetlike movements and jumps as he played.)

Charles Burney, the musical diarist, was in Dresden in 1772 and visited a home with a pantaleon. "It is nine feet long and had, when in order, 186 strings of catgut," he reported. "The tone was produced by two baguettes, or sticks like the dulcimer; it must have been extremely difficult to the performer, but seems capable of great effects."

King Louis was not the only one paying attention. Organ builder Gottfried Silbermann developed a successful side business by constructing pantaleons for Hebenstreit. But Silbermann started making and selling them on the side. Hebenstreit discovered the duplicity, and he obtained a royal cease-and-desist order. Once his hands were tied, Silbermann turned his attentions to producing copies of Cristofori's instrument. (German instrument builder Christoph Gottlieb Schröter also confessed that he had found the inspiration for his pianos in Hebenstreit's pantaleon. The dulcimer's sweet, full tones that continue to resonate long after being struck sound more like a piano than like a harpsichord.)

WHO REALLY WAS FIRST?

Bartolomeo Cristofori created a keyboard instrument capable of responding to subtle changes in human touch, but he was not the first to tinker with the idea. From the fifteenth century on, many musicians played a keyboard with hammers called the clavichord. Because of its small size and meager volume, however, it was impractical except in the most intimate settings. Clavichords employ metal hammers, called tangents, to strike their strings, and can therefore produce effects not attainable on a piano. For example, tangents can lightly press against the instrument's strings while they are vibrating, adding expressive fluctuations to the tone.

Well into the eighteenth century, the clavichord had its strong advocates. Composer Christian Friedrich Daniel Schubart praised its superiority over the early piano, calling it "your heart's soundboard," because it is so "tender and responsive to your soul's every inspiration." Indeed, this was the instrument young Wolfgang Amadeus Mozart most prized, and he always kept one near at hand. According to his wife, Constanze, Mozart produced such masterworks as *The Magic Flute* and the Requiem on his beloved clavichord, which now rests in the Geburtshaus Museum in Salzburg.

But there had also been large, pianolike instruments well before Cristofori. A manuscript written around 1440 by Henri Arnaut, a physician, astrologer, and musician working in the Burgundian court of Philip the Good, describes one called a *dulce melos* (literally, "sweet song"). It was rectangular, had metal tangents, and sounded like a dulcimer.

Letters in 1598 from Hippolito Cricca, organist and caretaker of instruments for the Este court in Ferrara, mention another example of an instrument called *instrumento piano e forte* (instrument soft and loud). "When Her Highness of Urbino [Lucrezia d'Este, sister of Alfonso II d'Este] was at the end of her life," wrote Cricca in one letter, "she told me to remove the *instrumento piano e forte*, which was the same one that served her for music, and thus it was removed and taken to lady Laura Turca, and nothing more has been known or heard of it."

What, exactly, was this mysterious instrument? Perhaps it was an example of the illusive échiquier (known in England as a chekker), mentioned as early as the fourteenth century, and possibly named for the resemblance of its black and white keys and square shape to a chessboard? Little is known about it, but in 1360, Edward III of England made a gift of one to King John II of France as he released him from imprisonment. Composer Guillaume de Machaut mentions it in a poem in 1370, and there was an échiquier in the household of Philip the Bold, Duke of Burgundy, in 1385. In 1415, Crown Prince Alfonso of Spain reported that he was having one built.

Cricca's instrument might also have been something like the one invented by the blind fourteenth-century Florentine polymath and organist Francesco Landini. Landini, who wrote the earliest extant keyboard music by a known composer, reported that he had created a new keyboard instrument with "a very sweet sound." The composer called it the Serena Seranarum, which means "the joyous of joyous, the sirens of sirens." It must have been awfully good.

Was Landini's Serena Seranarum similar to Leonardo da Vinci's viola organista, in which constantly rotating friction wheels rubbed against the instrument's strings, creating a kind of orchestra in a box? The viola organista was a descendant of even older designs, of course, such as the tenth-century organistrum and the hurdy-gurdy of the later Middle Ages. In 1581, Vincenzo Galilei, Galileo's father, heard one and said that it sounded like "an ensemble of viols." Such an instrument was actually among the Medici holdings at the time Cristofori served as curator.

Whatever Cricca's instrument was, no one deserved to inherit it more than Laura Turca. A harpist and singer, and an official lady-in-waiting to the duchess at the Ferrara court, Laura was also the romantic inspiration for countless verses by Italy's immortal poet Torquato Tasso. One of her exquisitely decorated harps, the *arpa doppia di Laura,* is still on display in the Galleria Estense in Modena. She and her colleagues Anna Guarini and Livia d'Arco performed daily at court as part of their routine duties. Her marriage in 1583 spurred the publication of two volumes of madrigals celebrating her beauty and her singing. But when she died in 1601, Cricca's instrument with soft and loud was forever lost.

After giving up on the giant dulcimer, Silbermann made several pianos for Frederick the Great, who invited the mighty Johann Sebastian Bach to try them out at his palace in Potsdam in 1747. (Frederick was not only a music lover but also a fairly accomplished flutist, though once when a listener praised the king with the comment "What rhythm!," Carl Philipp Emanuel Bach [1714–1788], one of Johann Sebastian's talented sons—unimpressed with Frederick's sense of time—quipped, "You mean, what *rhythms!*")

Bach had already criticized Silbermann's earliest piano efforts, but the instrument builder took those comments to heart and made several modifications. Composer Wilhelm Friedemann Bach (another of Johann Sebastian's sons) accompanied his father on the visit to Potsdam, and later reported the details: "Gentlemen, old Bach is come," announced the king, who promptly canceled the usual evening court concert and took the composer on a tour of Silbermann pianos. They had been placed in various locations throughout the palace. "The musicians went with him from room to room, and Bach was invited to play extemporaneously upon them at each location," recalled Wilhelm Friedemann. "After he had gone on for some time, he asked the King to give him a subject [a musical theme] for a fugue in order to execute it immediately, without any preparation."

This was a serious challenge. Fugues are complex: they state an initial theme and then, while it is still unfolding, begin it again in another "voice," and then in another, until the texture is dense with segments of the melody all sounding against each other—sometimes combined with other themes as well—in intricate, harmonious counterpoint. Making one up on the spur of the moment is not a task for the weak of heart.

"The King admired the skillful manner in which his subject was developed; and, probably to see how far such art could be carried, expressed a wish to hear also a fugue with six *obbligato* [indispensable] parts," reported the younger Bach. And here is where J. S. Bach finally faltered. Using Frederick's unusual tune to create a six-part fugue on the spot was simply too difficult. Instead, "Bach chose [a tune] himself and immediately executed it to the astonishment of all present in the same magnificent and learned manner as he had done that of the King."

Once he arrived back at home, Bach studiously worked the king's theme into the six-part piece Frederick had requested, adding additional settings, some presented in encrypted form as riddles (such as a canon in which tones become longer as the music progresses, inscribed with the words "May the fortunes of the king increase like the length of the notes"). He bound the entire collection as *The Musical Offering* and dedicated the work to the royal tune-giver.

The king must have been delighted. Certainly his Silbermann pianos could never have been played more stunningly. For the instrument that would eventually rule the musical world, it was an auspicious beginning. Decades would pass, however, before the piano's first stars would emerge to bring its marvels to the public.

CHAPTER 3

The First Piano Superstar

T HE FIRST PIANO SUPERSTAR is still a box-office draw. In
concert halls and annual festivals from Bath to Bethlehem,
Wolfgang Amadeus Mozart (1756–1791) remains an enduring presence. During his 250th-anniversary year, celebrations in New York
seemed nearly as pervasive as the city's riotous traffic and glittery
marquees.

One sultry August evening that season, Lincoln Center's Mostly
Mozart Festival was once again in full gear. Each summer the organization presents operas, recitals, symphonies, and songs, along
with public symposia where academics can churn a kaleidoscope of
shifting portraits: Mozart as angelic prodigy or boorish misfit; tormented soul or comedic genius; pillar of tradition or musical rebel.
His music is far less contentious: in a world predisposed to toppling
icons and deflating masterworks, it is still regarded as something
remarkable, exquisite—perhaps even faultless. "Beethoven, in

*Lincoln Center
at night*
COURTESY OF
LINCOLN CENTER FOR
THE PERFORMING
ARTS

his tumultuous struggles, sometimes reaches to heaven," quipped twentieth-century conductor Josef Krips. "Mozart, of course, *comes* from heaven."

A less misty-eyed observer might draw comparisons between that classical master and more recent virtuosos like Oscar Peterson. They both drew excited fans to small, clublike venues with their fiery improvisations, touching audiences with a musical spirit, as pianist Murray Perahia said of Mozart, "that floats, that searches, that agonizes, that exults." And though the whispers, claps, and shouts heard in a jazz room are as far from modern concert etiquette as a freewheeling revival meeting can be from high-church ritual, the fact is that Mozart often debuted his music in gambling halls, restaurants, and boarding houses, where wagering, eating, and gossiping (sometimes hooting, shouting, and brawling) were the norm. (Well into the nineteenth century, hushed attentiveness at classical concerts was still an unknown convention: old man Liszt himself was once observed yelling bravos from the audience during pianist Anton Rubinstein's performance of Mozart's A minor Rondo.)

On this particular Manhattan evening, however, the location was Lincoln Center's cathedral-like Avery Fisher Hall, and as pianist and conductor Christian Zacharias took his position on stage along with the Mostly Mozart Festival Orchestra to perform Mozart's Piano Concerto no. 20 in D minor, a thick silence settled over the house. The music itself would prove anything but demure. During the Romantic Era, critics considered this work not "heavenly" at all, but demonic; and from its first moments, it's easy to hear why.

The piece begins like a gathering storm. Right from the start, deep-toned cellos and basses seem to groan and howl. Above them, the violins and violas, defying the established pulse, join in a soft, agitated synchrony, like leaves trembling in the wind. As other instruments blend into the thickening texture, Mozart's music crests and recedes in broad waves, until it arrives at a brief moment of stillness—when the piano makes its entrance.

Those familiar with Mozart's opera *Don Giovanni*, written in the same dark key, will find many similarities. Both employ dusky harmonies that hint at terror, along with insistent, jarring rhythms that, in the opera, mark Don Giovanni's descent into hell. Little wonder this concerto was a favorite of that most tempestuous of all composers, Ludwig van Beethoven.

Throughout the opening strains of the music, conductor Zacharias, standing by the keyboard, gestured extravagantly. One moment he folded forward into a crouch, like a hulking predator threatening to snatch the hearts of the violinists; an instant later, he was leaning backward, as if his torso were struggling to remain upright against the blustery winds of the brass section.

But when he finally sat down to begin the piano part, something unexpected emerged—a tender musical narrative of longing and nobility in the face of all that orchestral might. The piano's tones could have represented Odysseus standing resolute against Poseidon's forces, or King Lear striving onward despite the tempest. Yet, there was little doubt that the piano would ultimately triumph over those orchestral masses: its golden sound—warm, bell-like, and strong—easily sang out over all the other instruments as it effortlessly filled the cavernous, 2,738-seat hall.

THE CHALLENGE OF MOZART *by Alfred Brendel*

Let this be the first warning to the Mozart performer: piano playing, be it ever so faultless, must not be considered sufficient. Mozart's piano works should be for the player a receptacle full of latent musical possibilities which often go far beyond the purely pianistic. . . . For example, the first movement of Mozart's Sonata in A minor K. 310 is to me a piece for symphony orchestra; the second movement resembles a vocal scene with a dramatic middle section; and the finale could be transcribed into a wind divertimento with no trouble at all.

In Mozart's piano concertos, the sound of the piano is set off more sharply against that of the orchestra. Here the human voice and the orchestral solo instrument will be the main setters of standards for the pianist.

FROM "A MOZART PLAYER GIVES HIMSELF ADVICE," IN *Alfred Brendel on Music*

This was the Mozart we all know and savor. Yet nothing of this scene would be familiar to the composer: not the size of the concert venue, the audience, or the orchestra—and especially, not the modern Steinway concert grand at the center of it all.

Mozart premiered this D minor Piano Concerto in a guesthouse and dance hall called the Mehlgrube (the "flour pit"), described by a contemporary as having ceilings too low for a good musical effect and rooms too small for a decent-sized crowd. In contrast to Lincoln Center's audience of thousands, there were only about 150 music lovers on hand to hear him.

And though the pianos in that time were smaller and more delicate than our modern version, with a drier, quieter, and more piquant sonority—their clipped, airy tones dying away rapidly, unlike the singing, sustained sound to which modern audiences have become accustomed—at the Mehlgrube, the difference between Mozart's instrument and ours was even more pronounced. Specially commissioned by the composer from the Viennese piano builder Gabriel Anton Walter, Mozart's piano had, besides the usual keyboard for his hands, an extra one to be played by his feet. For the first performance of the D minor Piano Concerto, Mozart played not with two limbs, but with four!

T HOSE INTIMATE EVENINGS in Vienna changed the world. Mozart's concertos marked the awakening of modern concert life, as well as the transformation of the piano from an obscure novelty into an indispensable musical partner. Yet the achievement was in some ways an historical accident: he was in the right place (Vienna) at the right time (the 1780s).

His concerts wouldn't have made an impact in New York, where the spot on which Lincoln Center now sits was untamed woodlands. In the southern part of the island, today the financial heartbeat of the world, stray dogs and pigs picked their way through discarded scraps of food on poorly paved streets. The fledgling American nation was, in fact, just opening to the wider world: a trading ship, the *Empress of China,* had recently voyaged east with the hope of revitalizing an economy devastated by the War of Independence.

As Congress settled in, local politicians were busily passing ordinances for the preservation of civic order, including a law to guard against distempered dogs, and another establishing rooms for the "confinement of lunatic and mad persons." The public protectors were also focused on moral dangers—including those posed by the performing arts. A news item in the *New York Packet* sounded the warning: "A correspondent observes that the infatuation which possesses many of the people of this state for Theatrical Exhibitions is truly alarming . . .

"Alas!" it continued. "The delirium appears to have spread far and wide. And, Strange to tell! The honest, sober Dutchmen of

Albany, who were once distinguished by industry and a laudable parsimony, are now plunging into that very species of luxury and folly which stamps upon the metropolis an indelible stigma. Is it not high time for the considerate inhabitants to step forth and oppose the increasing evil . . . ?"

On the other side of the Atlantic, an infatuation with such "luxury and folly" was already well entrenched. Theatrical troupes were a mainstay of Viennese cultural life. Music could be heard incessantly in restaurants, beer halls, and public parks. And the frenzy for entertainment increased even more as Carnival time approached: balls attracted as many as three thousand partygoers, all crammed into a single theater. "The people were in my time dancing mad," wrote tenor Michael Kelly in the 1780s, noting that at such dances special rooms were prepared just in case all the excitement and jostling caused any pregnant women to go into labor.

This thirst for amusement offered unprecedented opportunities—especially for musicians like Mozart, who had spent a lifetime imploring the powerful (and fickle) rulers of Europe for financial support, with little to show for it. Mozart's parents had begun taking him and his gifted sister, Nannerl, on tour even before his sixth birthday, visiting Germany, France, England, the Netherlands, Switzerland, and, later, Italy. The reception had been wild.

At the time, the world seemed his for the asking. In Rome, Pope Clement XIV bestowed on the teenage Mozart the cross of the Order of the Golden Spur, for having "excelled . . . in the sweetest sounding of the harpsichord." He was only fifteen when Empress Maria Theresa commissioned him to write music for the marriage of her son, Archduke Ferdinand, to Beatrice d'Este, Princess of Modena. The wedding festivities included horse races and nuptials for 150 couples, with dowries supplied by the royal twosome, and an opera by leading composer Johann Adolph Hasse.

Hasse heard Mozart's music and declared, "This boy will consign us all to oblivion." Yet the imperial aptitude for appreciation was erratic—a lesson Mozart would learn more than once. The empress, suspicious of the Mozarts' vagabond ways, even warned her son to be wary of such "useless people." "If they are in your

The Mozarts in the 1780s, by Johann Nepomuk della Croce: Nannerl, Wolfgang, and father Leopold. Mother Anna Maria had passed away in 1778, but her portrait appears on the wall.

service," she explained, "it degrades that service when these people go about the world like beggars."

And so it went, time and again. Despite artistic successes, hopes for financial abundance and a secure future slowly faded over the years. As he grew, Mozart waged his own small rebellions against the indignities, famously refusing at a soiree, for example, to use the entrance specifically assigned to musicians. Now, he no longer had to. Vienna's thirst for artistic diversions prompted a brand-new possibility: to forgo royal patronage and present concerts directly to the public. He went into business for himself.

None of it would have been possible without the political reforms instituted by Emperor Joseph II, who nurtured an atmosphere of political and religious toleration begun by his mother, Maria Theresa. (Of course, Casanova regarded the empress as less than enlightened after she ordered women's skirts lengthened at the bottom and blouses raised at the top. But royal toleration had its limits.)

Joseph liberalized the political landscape further, seizing ecclesiastical holdings to build schools, asylums, and hospitals, and working to eliminate poverty and serf labor. He became the architect of a new, more open society. "No prosecution for morals, and no espionage in private affairs should be maxims of government," he declared. (He even allowed controversial pamphlets to be published and sold, including one called "Why Is Emperor Joseph Not Loved by His People?")

Along with this agenda came an economic lift, and a broadening interest in the arts. The emperor himself played the cello, viola, and keyboard, and founded a National Opera Theater in 1778. During his reign, trios and quartets could be heard in the streets. At a St. John's Day celebration, musicians played from illuminated boats on the Danube.

An anonymous portrait of the young prodigy, 1763

Even music in the churches took on a new level of grandeur. Joseph Richter, in his 1784 *Picture Gallery of Catholic Abuses*, explained that "perhaps the population itself was tired of the eternal, serious sameness. Thus there soon slipped into the church style unnoticed a trio from a menuet, then the thrum-thrum of a symphony, then again fragments of waltzing music, and finally half and whole opera arias."

This new Viennese audience thirsty for the arts was a mix of upper- and middle-class enthusiasts, theatergoers, and ballroom buffs. Some gathered in private salons run by the social elite, like those of Marianne von Martinez and Privy Councilor Franz von Greiner, where Mozart was a constant visitor. Others sought more public venues. It didn't take long for Mozart to form a partnership with producer Philipp Jakob Martin to present open-air concerts and rent space around town for his subscription series. All the while he continued to perform in aristocratic salons at night and teach students in the mornings. His efforts all centered on an instrument that was just coming into its own.

During Mozart's formative years in Salzburg, the piano had been virtually nonexistent. He likely first came into contact with the instrument on a visit to Munich in the winter of 1774–75. But by 1777, he was begging his father to buy a model made by Johann Andreas Stein. "I am glad that Mr. Stein's *Pianofortes* are so good; but they are certainly also expensive," came the reply. At the end of that year, though, the acquisition of a piano had become all but inevitable. Mozart's mother soon wrote from Mannheim that "everyone thinks very highly of Wolfgang, though he plays very differently from the way he does in Salzburg, for there are *piano fortes* everywhere here, which he can play so incomparably that no one has heard the like before." Once he discovered what it could do, its sweet-toned, expressive sound became Mozart's trademark.

THE PIANO GROWS UP

The piano used by Bach underwent rapid transformation all through the eighteenth century. Indeed, Bach hadn't cared for Silbermann's first pianos, but he liked the improved version well enough to use it in public performance. In 1749 he even sold one, working on Silbermann's behalf, to Count Branitzky of Bialystok.

In other parts of Europe, Bach's contemporaries also embraced the new invention. Portuguese King João V was enamored of everything Italian, including the new Florentine instrument, and he purchased several. Composer Domenico Scarlatti gave keyboard instruction to the king's daughter, Maria Barbara, and her uncle, Don Antonio. When Maria Barbara left for Spain in 1729 (to marry the future Ferdinand VI), she brought along as many as five pianos, as well as her teacher, Scarlatti. But even after she left, enthusiasm for the piano continued at court: the very first extant pieces written specifically for the instrument—Lodovico

Giustini's twelve Sonatas for the Keyboard of Soft and Loud Commonly Called the Little Hammers—appeared in 1732 with a dedication to Don Antonio.

Meanwhile, Johann Christoph Zumpe, an apprentice to Silbermann, migrated to England in 1760 (fleeing the Seven Years' War) and there became famous for his small, "square" pianos. Johann Christian Bach used one for London's first solo piano performance in 1768.

However, English and German-Viennese pianos developed along two different lines: the Viennese model, with hammers that faced

Zumpe square piano

toward, rather than away from, the player, was lighter, easier to play, and had a softer tone. (Across the ocean, a Swedish painter named Gustavus Hesselius also began making the first American spinets in Philadelphia in 1742.)

The piano quickly evolved in other directions as well. By the mid-eighteenth century, pianos, like harpsichords, were offering special "stops" to add exotic colors to the instrument's sound. A "lute" stop on a piano, for example, would produce a more delicate, plucked timbre by damping the vibrations of the strings; other sounds available in Mozart's time included "Janissary," or Turkish military band, effects such as bass drum, triangle, and cymbals. A "bassoon" stop placed paper over the strings for a buzzing tone.

Cristofori had introduced a mechanism (operated by hand) in his later instruments that shifted the hammers so that they would strike only one string rather than two—creating a sonority approximated today by the *una corda,* or "soft," pedal. (In 1789, the piano maker Johann Andreas Stein created a mechanism in which the shifting caused the hammers to strike a separate third string, while allowing the normal two to vibrate "sympathetically." He sold the invention outright for 100 louis d'or and a barrel of Rhine wine.)

Silbermann added another wrinkle to Cristofori's device: a hand-controlled lever that lifted the dampers from the strings, so that they would continue to vibrate freely (just as the damper pedal does on a modern instrument). The impetus for installing it might well have been the success of Pantaleon Hebenstreit's dulcimer, whose strings vibrated for quite a long time after being struck. Composer Johann Kuhnau wrote of the splendid effect that resulted when dissonances and their resolutions floated together in the tones produced by Hebenstreit's instrument, "to the great delectation of the feelings . . . The sound diminishes little by little as if from afar, the delightful buzzing of the harmony goes right into the quick." By 1765, the controls for lifting the dampers on pianos were knee levers.

More special effects, faster piano actions, and sturdier frames were just over the horizon.

For his subscription concerts, Mozart's attention was also drawn to the relatively new musical form known as the piano concerto. (The concerto itself had been around since the seventeenth century. It was based on the idea of instrumental forces at odds: an orchestra pitted against a soloist, for example, or a large ensemble vs. a small one. The selection of a piano for the solo role is what made Mozart's concertos unusual.) He knew just what it could do. "These concertos are a happy medium between what is too easy and too difficult," he explained in a letter to his father. "They are very brilliant, pleasing to the ear, and natural, without being vapid. There are passages here and there from which the connoisseurs alone can derive satisfaction; but these passages are written in such a way that the less learned cannot fail to be pleased, though without knowing why."

Like the great operas that would soon follow, Mozart's concertos touched people with a fresh, "Romantic" sensibility, a term defined by literary critic Friedrich Schlegel in 1798: something is Romantic, Schlegel explained, when it sails freely on the wings of poetic reflection, is animated with wit, and embraces everything in life.

Mozart's piano concertos fit that bill: like operas without words, they could laugh and weep and meditate on life's big themes. It didn't hurt that his melodies were breathtaking. An "uninterrupted melodiousness . . . shimmers through his compositions like the lovely forms of a woman through the folds of a thin dress," noted composer Ferruccio Busoni. What's more, these concertos had the remarkable ability to surprise constantly (Schlegel's "wit") while still conveying a feeling of musical inevitability.

Indeed, Mozart took particular pride in his ability to stun his listeners with imaginative twists and turns. In a letter written home after visiting the keyboard factory of Johann Andreas Stein in 1777, he bragged to his father: "Herr Graf, who is Director here, stood there transfixed, like someone who has always imagined that his wanderings from key to key are quite unusual and now finds that one can be even more unusual and yet not offend the ear. In a word, they were all astounded." Many of his works embodied that principle: graceful, innovative, and dramatic, they managed to look backward and forward at the same time. (His Little Gigue for piano, for example, harks back to J. S. Bach, yet bristles with jazzy counterpoint: its melodies dance and leap with a rhythmic punch and modern flavor that almost could have come from the pen of Duke Ellington.)

WHERE HAD Mozart found this winning style? In part, through his travels. He cultivated his lyrical gifts while touring Italy, the birthplace of opera, and reinforced those lessons through his contacts with composer Johann Adolph Hasse and renowned teacher Giovanni Battista Martini. In London, he fell under the influence of J. S. Bach's youngest son, Johann Christian Bach, who had also trained in Italy. Johann Christian, along with such forgotten figures as Philip Hayes, known as "the fattest man in England," and James Hook, a highly successful London piano teacher, wrote some of the very first piano concertos. All had spearheaded the new aesthetic of classical clarity that was quickly overtaking the musical world.

This was a seismic shift in style. During Mozart's formative years, English artist William Hogarth had proclaimed the importance of the "serpentine" line in painting. That idea of a curvaceous line, now transformed into uncluttered, sinuous melody, became the central focus of composition for composers like J. C. Bach and Mozart—replacing the ornate, overwrought approach of the Baroque era with something graceful, transparent, and clean. It became known as the "galant" style. And the soft, warm tones of the piano served as an ideal partner for the approach.

Mozart encountered another formidable influence right in Vienna, through Baron Gottfried van Swieten (1733–1803), the son of Empress Maria Theresa's personal physician. Swieten was an aspiring composer (whose symphonies, reported Haydn, were "as stiff as the man himself"). He had been an ambassador to Berlin beginning in 1770, where he delved into German music with a passion, studying especially the intricate works of J. S. Bach and his sons, and theoretical texts about their style.

When he returned to Vienna in 1778, the Baron assumed the stature of an unassailable musical authority. "When he attends a concert," reported one music enthusiast, "our semi-connoisseurs never take their eyes off him, seeking to read in his features, not always intelligible to every one, what ought to be their opinion of the music." By 1782, Mozart's letters report that he was going to Baron van Swieten's "every Sunday at 12, and nothing is played there but Handel and Bach." The young composer couldn't get enough of it. Neither could his wife, Constanze, who, after hearing Bach's work, developed a love of intricate fugues. She wanted to hear nothing else. Mozart obliged with examples of his own.

Finally, there was the impact on Mozart's imagination of yet one more of J. S. Bach's sons: Carl Philipp Emanuel, whose dark, foreboding works mirror the psychological tone of Mozart's most turbulent music, like the D minor Concerto and the piano Fantasies (filled, like C. P. E.'s Fantasies, with sinister sounds and abrupt, unexpected mood shifts): music in which dramatic intensity and strangeness reign supreme. "He is the father," Mozart declared about Carl Philipp Emanuel, "we are the children."

Mozart's musical evolution was a process of forging these dis-

parate elements into an individual musical language, encompass-
ing the passion and creative abandon of one musical stream and the
clarity and charm of the other. He had mastered it all, and he knew
it. What he didn't see coming was the competition from across the
English Channel.

L ONDON'S PUBLIC CONCERT life had begun earlier than Vienna's, and its many venues—from Hickford's Room on Brewer
Street and the Great Room in Spring Gardens (both of which served
as platforms for the young, peripatetic Mozart in 1764) to other taverns all around town—flourished long before Mozart launched
his subscription concerts. These were the proving grounds for yet
another contender hoping for the title of world's greatest pianist:
Muzio Clementi, who had left Italy for England while still a student. By the end of his life, Clementi would actually surpass Mozart
in celebrity, earning the moniker "the father of pianoforte music."
But when he embarked on his very first musical tour of Europe
in 1781—a trip that unexpectedly brought him face to face with
Mozart in a contest of musical prowess—Clementi was still a new-
comer to the scene.

The tour took him first to Paris, where he performed for Marie
Antoinette. She didn't exactly lose her head over his artistry, but
found his playing charming enough (at least according to the later
historical writings of French pianist Antoine François Marmontel)
to recommend him to her brother Emperor Joseph in Vienna. Clementi traveled to Vienna in December of 1781 and accepted Joseph's
invitation to court—unaware of what the emperor secretly had in
mind.

He arrived to find that *two* pianists had been invited: Clementi
and Mozart. Both were put on the spot without warning. The men
were each asked to play solo and then, seated at the two pianos that
had been placed in the room, to take turns improvising variations
on a theme selected by the Grand Duchess. Mozart later recalled
that his piano was "out of tune and three of the keys were stuck."
But when he tried to point this out to Joseph, the imperial response

Muzio Clementi

was a wave of the hand. "Never mind," he said.

Clementi was all flash. His bag of technical tricks included playing scales in double notes (two at a time), single line passages with rapid repeated tones, phrases played in broken octaves (the hand quickly rotating back and forth between the thumb and little finger), and more. His printed compositions, like the Sonata op. 2, no. 2, which became known as "Clementi's celebrated octave lesson," give us a hint of what transpired. Pianist Amédée Méreaux, speaking with him in 1820, learned that in his adolescence Clementi had been "obliged to work twelve or fourteen successive hours to remain abreast of the daily regime he had imposed upon himself. It was the works of Sebastian and Emanuel Bach, of Handel and Scarlatti that he practiced and studied continually." In fact, much of his style emerged from the earlier music of Domenico Scarlatti: the tricky passagework, the changes in texture from sparse to thick, the dizzying runs across the breadth of the keyboard. Some of his effects, such as the use of rhythmic emphasis in unexpected places and the fragmentation of tunes created by breaking them up across octaves, anticipate Beethoven.

In the end, the contest was declared a draw. Mozart, of course, felt differently about the matter. In a letter to his father, he reported that Clementi had a good right hand, but "not a kreuzer's worth of taste or feeling." He was, claimed Mozart, a mere "mechanicus," a robot, and "a charlatan, like all Italians." The assessment was overly harsh. Mozart must have been secretly impressed; he even used one of Clementi's themes from the contest in the overture to his opera *The Magic Flute*.

Clementi was kinder to his adversary. "Until then I had never heard anyone play with so much spirit and grace," he conceded. The fact remains that Clementi's legacy rests mostly on a collection of technical exercises for students. In the next century, composer Claude Debussy would make fun of Clementi's famous piano collection *Gradus ad Parnassum* (1819–1825) in his own *Children's Corner Suite* (1906–08) with a piece called "Doctor Gradus ad Parnassum," made up of fast note patterns that travel up and down a simple major scale. Even today, we study Clementi for finger facility; for beauty and depth, we turn to Mozart.

M OZART'S ROLE as a concert producer carried risks. Indeed, a subscription series he launched in 1784 ran into trouble from the start. "My first concert in the theater was to have been tomorrow," he wrote. "But Prince Louis Liechtenstein is producing an opera in his own house, and has not only run off with the cream of the nobility, but has bribed and seduced the best players in the orchestra."

Nevertheless, by the following year, he was offering six concerts. The D minor Piano Concerto was premiered at the first of these, on the wintry eve of February 11. (The February date was no coincidence; during Lent and Advent, theaters were closed, making the public hunt for amusement even keener.) And the excitement he managed to generate led to two years of prosperity, culminating in the 1787 premiere of his fabulously successful opera *The Marriage of Figaro*.

Perhaps he decided to use Walter's special piano with one keyboard for the hands and a separate one for the feet as a kind of special attraction—an insurance policy for success. Mozart's father, Leopold, described the difficulty of moving this clunky instrument around. The lower keyboard, he wrote, "is about two feet longer, and is incredibly heavy. [The instrument] is taken every Friday to the Mehlgrube [for Mozart's subscription concerts], and also to Count Zichy's and Prince Kaunitz's." Apparently, the composer used it for extemporaneous musicmaking at Vienna's Burgtheater as well; and his student Thomas Atwood reported that at one lesson Mozart used it to demonstrate Bach.

PEDAL PIANOS

Although few composers write for the pedal piano today, the concept has a long and distinguished history. As early as 1460, a treatise written by the Czech physician Paulus Paulirinus cited a pedal clavichord (used mostly by organists to practice without making a lot of noise). J. S. Bach owned one. A little-known caricature published in Warsaw shows Chopin playing one with his bare feet. And pedal piano works have been written by such well-known composers as Franz Liszt, Robert Schumann (who convinced Felix Mendelssohn to inaugurate a class for the instrument at the Leipzig Conservatory), Charles-Valentin Alkan, Charles Gounod,

and Camille Saint-Saëns. Alkan even wrote a piece for four feet, called *Bombardo-Carillon,* in which the player's legs are likely to get entangled during performance. (When Swiss-American pianist Rudolph Ganz was asked to perform *Bombardo-Carillon* with a female pianist, he declined on the grounds that he didn't know her well enough.)

Contemporary composer Charlemagne Palestine has written for the handcrafted pedal piano still being produced by instrument maker Luigi Borgato in Vicenza, Italy. Borgato's *Doppio Borgato L 282–P 402* is made up of two superimposed concert grand pianos: the lower instrument is a pedalboard of thirty-seven notes—the range offered by many organs.

Was it worth the trouble? Though bulky, the new instrument had its advantages. Early pianos could not project sound very well. Extra bass notes played through a separate footboard could add volume, especially in passages where the orchestra was in full throttle. And there were other compelling incentives.

One was ego. Mozart himself confessed that he could be "as proud as a peacock." It was an apt description in more ways than one. At a rehearsal of *The Marriage of Figaro,* singer Michael Kelly was bemused to find Mozart on stage decked out "with his crimson pelisse and gold-laced cocked hat." Clementi was similarly taken aback at their first encounter: Mozart's adornments were so fancy, the Italian pianist mistook him for "one of the Emperor's chamberlains." (The red coat spotted by Kelly was likely one Mozart had finagled from Baroness Waldstätten. "I must have a coat like that," he wrote to her, "for it is one that will really do justice to certain buttons which I have long been hankering after . . . They are mother-of-pearl with a few white stones around the edge and a fine yellow stone in the center . . . Why is it, I wonder, that those who cannot afford it would like to spend a fortune on such articles, and those who can do not do so?")

It's really not surprising. Other than his mode of dress, there was nothing distinguishing about Mozart's looks. Contemporaries noted his small face, large nose, weak chin, and pale complexion. His hair was fair and thick, his hands small and beautiful, but his build was slight. His blue eyes "stared out on an alien world and suddenly flared up with a curious fire only when he was seated at the keyboard." His ears had no lobes. And "the line from the top of his brow to the tip of his nose formed an obtuse angle, with the bridge of the nose as its vertex."

He was, in a word, ordinary. So, in the end, neither his interest in costumes nor his attraction to the novel new instrument poses much of a mystery. They were simply part of a strategy to captivate his audience. Presentations at the Mehlgrube often included opportunities for gambling and refreshments, and attention spans were no better then than they are today. Concert promoters typically combatted the problem with a combination of star power and variety.

ABOVE
*Mozart in his
red coat*

OPPOSITE
*The Borgato
pedal piano*

It didn't hurt to offer a display of staggering virtuosity—a quality Mozart could demonstrate in abundance, especially on a piano built for both hands and feet.

So on February 11, 1785, Mozart had his newfangled, heavy double-keyboard instrument carried through the wintry, cobble-stoned streets of Vienna, past the stalls and booths that offered soft drinks, candy, and almond milk, up to the Mehlgrube in the Neuer Markt. The building stood next to the one that housed what would become Beethoven's favorite spot for drinking and smoking, the White Swan Inn.

At the appointed time, with his newly copied music placed in front of the orchestra, Mozart gave the signal to begin the D minor Piano Concerto. Then, playing with arms and legs flailing, a picture of consummate athletic and musical mastery, he created sounds that startled and entranced his small audience, and audiences for centuries to follow.

CHAPTER 4

Piano Fever

MOZART'S CONCERTOS CHANGED the piano's standing. Before long, the instrument's inviting tones became a perfect conductor for the erotic current that flowed through the arts as the age of Romance took hold, serving the music of dreamy poets like Jan Ladislav Dussek (1760–1812)—the first to sit with his side to the audience, the better to show his profile)—and thunderous fire-brands like Ludwig van Beethoven (1770–1827), who could reduce the delicate, early instrument to splinters. In sheer usefulness, it easily trumped everything that had come before. As time went on, the piano would also accommodate the rhythms and harmonies of jazz, the edginess of modernism, the spicy inflections of world music, and the intensity of rock.

But the utility of the piano explains only half the story of its success. Its ascendance at the end of the eighteenth century was also a matter of a shifting political and social climate. Revolutions

Franciolini harpsichord, ca. 1890

MIM/HOLLY METZ

engulfed America and France; dramatic changes occurred nearly everywhere else. Out of the turmoil, the era spawned a new, mushrooming middle class—unprecedented numbers of men and women now eager for the accoutrements of fine living—and a riotous demand for pianos signaled their arrival.

Of course, it started slowly. *The Beggar's Opera* performance in London's Covent Garden in 1767 was the first production to feature "a new instrument called Piano Forte"; the next year, a recital by Johann Christian Bach marked the instrument's London debut as a solo vehicle. The handful of leading craftsmen turning out pianos during that time produced only around thirty to fifty of them per annum. But by 1798, piano maker James Shudi Broadwood could barely keep up with demand, writing to a wholesaler, "Would to God we could make them like muffins!" Five decades later, England had become the center of the piano world, with some two hundred manufacturers; by 1871 the number of pianos in the British Isles was estimated at 400,000. By then, piano fever had become an epidemic.

Why the piano? Keyboards had long been considered a symbol of prosperity. In the sixteenth and seventeenth centuries, harpsichords adorned with beautiful paintings—of Orpheus charming the animals, or of battle scenes on horseback—were choice trophies of a charmed life, and essential accessories in any fine home.

As emblems of civilized living, they often sported pithy mottoes as well. "Listen, watch and be silent if you wish to live in peace," read one wise pronouncement on an instrument built by the famous Ruckers family of Antwerp. Another, more wistfully philosophic, proclaimed: "I was once an ordinary tree, although living I was silent; now, though dead, if I am well played I sound sweetly." Sometimes, the message was more pointed: "To take a wife," declared the decoration on one instrument, "is to sell one's freedom."

Despite that cynical message, most of these keyboards were intended for the women of the household. Indeed, one of the best sources of income for professional musicians was teaching, especially of aristocracy's daughters. These were fertile grounds—in more ways than one. Private music lessons were not only lucrative, they also offered certain opportunities against which the only defense was parental vigilance. In a satiric report that reveals the pervasiveness of concerns about this danger, a 1754 article in the *Connoisseur* announced the invention of a "female thermometer" for measuring "the exact temperature of a lady's passions." The device, created by a Mr. Ayscough of Ludgate Hill, consisted of a glass tube filled with a mixture of distilled extracts of lady's love, maidenhair, and "wax of virgin-bees." It could supposedly detect the full range of feminine response, from "inviolable modesty" to "abandoned impudence," and was remarkably accurate, claimed the author, when used at the theater and the opera.

The moral hazards of piano lessons. The Comforts of Bath: The Music Master, *by Thomas Rowlandson (1756–1827)*

Despite this wariness, all authorities agreed that musical training for young women was indispensable. Diderot's *Encyclopédie* described instrumental skill as "one of the primary ornaments in the education of women." As an anonymous pamphlet written around 1778 explained, such musical accomplishment was critical so that young ladies could "amuse their own family, and [foster] that domestic comfort they were by Providence designed to promote."

Portrait of Miss Margaret Casson at the piano, 1781, by George Romney (1734–1802)

Those on the prowl for a husband knew that honing their skills at riding, reading, and especially music making offered a sure pathway; publications like the influential periodical *Godey's Lady's Book* repeatedly told them so. Critic Henri Blanchard in France could report in 1847 that "Cultivating the piano is something that has become as essential, as necessary, to social harmony as the cultivation of the potato is to the existence of the people . . . The piano provokes meetings between people, hospitality, gentle contacts, associations of all kinds, even matrimonial ones . . . and if our young men so full of assurance tell their friends that they have married twelve or fifteen thousand francs of income, they at least add as a corrective: 'My dear, my wife plays piano like an angel.' "

When it came to cultivating musical skills, a keyboard was the medium of choice for good reason. Writer John Essex pointed out in *The young ladies' conduct: or, rules for education, under several heads; with instructions upon dress, both before and after marriage. And advice to young wives* (1722) that among the various musical instruments, some were "unbecoming the Fair Sex; as the *Flute, Violin and Hautboy* [oboe]; the last of which is too Manlike, and would look indecent in a Woman's Mouth; and the *Flute* is very improper, as taking away too much of the Juices, which are otherwise more necessarily employ'd to promote the Appetite, and assist Digestion." (Female "juices" seemed to be of special concern to such authorities. Dr. Edward Clarke, a Victorian-era Bostonian, cautioned the woman of his day against engaging in intellectual activity: too much thinking could place a strain on her energy, he claimed, which she otherwise needed for "the periodical tides of her organization.")

All the merits that social critics had attributed to the harpsichord were easily transferred to the piano. Indeed, for a while, the two often occupied the same dwelling. More than half the instruments confiscated from the homes of noblemen killed or run off in the French Revolution were pianos, and many shared their quarters with harpsichords. (The historical shift toward the newer instrument was evident in an inventory taken of the confiscated items: almost all of the harpsichords had been built before 1780; most of the pianos, after.)

Naturally, the instrument had a special place in fine Victorian homes, which featured a formal area for entertaining so that the inhabitants could demonstrate a flair for stylishness, and thereby denote—as Mrs. Jane Ellen Panton (the authoritative author of *From Kitchen to Garret,* which went through eleven editions in a decade) put it—"that they are worth cultivating, for no doubt they will turn out to be desirable friends." Drawing rooms typically contained sofas, chairs, a sewing table (though "the very best Sewing-Machine a man can have is a Wife," exclaimed *Punch* in 1859, with tongue firmly in cheek), a round table for the center of the room, and, most conspicuously, a piano. The instrument, wrote Mrs. Panton, was an absolute necessity (not the least because, as the Reverend H. R. Haweis reiterated, "the piano makes a girl sit upright and pay attention to details," and it was well suited to feminine mood swings: "A good play of the piano has not infrequently taken the place of a good cry upstairs").

Yet, admitted Mrs. Panton, the object itself was, after all, not very attractive. And so propriety demanded that certain measures be taken. The piano was best covered with serge, felt, or damask, "edged with an appropriate fringe . . . which thus makes [it] an excellent shelf for odds and ends of china and bowls of flowers." If the family could afford a grand piano, it was a good idea to fit a big palm in a brass pot into the bend of the instrument. "This gives a very finished look to the piano." An upright, however, had to be turned around so that the player would face her audience; then, the instrument's naked back could be covered with "a simple full curtain," topped with a piece of Japanese embroidery, a photograph frame, a cup for flowers, and

Sewing table piano

perhaps some ornaments. As Victorian-era prudishness set in, some upstanding citizens also took to putting coverlets over the instrument's legs out of an exaggerated sense of modesty.

Some piano builders began creating special models with the homeowner in mind. An "upright grand Piano-forte in the form of a bookcase" was patented by William Stodart in 1795 (there is evidence that Haydn visited Stodart's shop and approved of the device); the early nineteenth century also saw the introduction of a square piano in the form of a sewing table.

Highly decorated upright pianos featured giant lyres, arabesques, and flutings; one extant sample includes a medallion bust of Beethoven. The odd-shaped "giraffe" upright piano (its verticality highlighted with an outlandish case that rises high above the keyboard, tracing the increasing length of the instrument's strings as they grow in the bass end of the instrument before swooping down at the top like an animal on the prowl for fresh water) added an exotic ambience to a room. In 1866, American Charles Hess even applied for a patent for a convertible bedroom piano complete with foldout mattress and drawers.

For those concerned about lack of space, John Isaac Hawkins, an English engineer living in Philadelphia, patented a vertical "Portable Grand Piano," a mere fifty-four inches tall. (Thomas Jefferson purchased one for $264 in 1800, but promptly returned it because it would not stay in tune "a single hour.")

THE STRANGEST KEYBOARD OF ALL

Of the many designs for keyboard instruments that came along, perhaps the most bizarre was one that produced its tones by means of
live animals. In 1892, the Italian journal *Gazetta musicale di Milano* carried an announcement of an instrument called the Catano—a wooden
case with rows of compartments into which different-sized cats were
placed: big ones to meow the lowest notes, kittens for the treble. "The
heads are fastened in loopholes," read the description, "and their tails
are operated by a species of keyboard at the end of the case, like that
of a concert grand. When a key is put down, a cat's tail is pulled, and
he begins to caterwaul loudly or otherwise according to the force with
which the key is manipulated . . . Anyone who has studied music can
easily play the Catano," claimed the advertiser, "but for purposes of
accompaniment, especially in sacred music, the Catano is not considered particularly useful or appropriate."

According to the December 1869 issue of the periodical the *Folio,*
an American version of the device was introduced in Cincinnati by a
man named Curtis. He announced a "Grand Vocal and Instrumental
Concert" featuring no less than forty-eight cats in his Cat Harmonicon.
The first number on the program was to be "Auld Lang Syne." Unfortunately, according to the report, the cats became overly excited, "paid no
attention to time, tune, rhythm or reason, but squealed, mewed, yelled,
spat, and phizzed in the madness of pain and terror," drowning out the
accompanying organ in a welter of wails.

There must be something special about Cincinnati. Apparently that
same city was the first to introduce a Porco-Forte in 1839, which used
pigs instead of cats.

For those homes where no one was around to play, there
were "self-acting" instruments, a primitive version of the modern player piano, produced in 1825 by pianist Muzio Clementi
(who had founded his own piano business). A more sophisti-

A Hawkins portable piano

cated version was developed in 1863, when a French patent was granted to J. B. Napoléon Fourneaux for a pneumatic piano called the Pianista.

The distribution of sheet music and instructional books also increased greatly by the end of the nineteenth century, with sales of such pieces as "The Lost Chord" reaching 500,000 between 1877 and 1902, and "The Holy City" selling 50,000 copies a year by the 1890s. Do-it-yourself manuals such as *The Art of Playing at Sight, by One who has taught Himself* proliferated.

Not every family had the disposable cash to acquire the instrument of its dreams. To make their pianos affordably attractive, manufacturers began offering a three-year payment plan. One enterprising publisher went even further: London's *Pianoforte Magazine,* published from 1797 to 1802—one of many periodicals and collections that cropped up to supply sheet music to the swelling number of players—came with vouchers; a complete set could be redeemed for a free piano.

In England, the newly cultivated middle class explored other tantalizing artistic commodities for their homes, but with less success. Helped along by factory owners who arranged excursions to art fairs for their workers, mobs of day trippers often searched avidly for works of art to acquire. Author Nathaniel Hawthorne witnessed these consumers, greeted by brass bands, lavish refreshments, and rows of canvases, as they "sought to get instruction from what they beheld." For art dealers, it was like shooting fish in a barrel. The *Times* commented sourly that conducting these marketing events was "like feeding infants strong meat." These ordinary men and women of the Industrial Revolution, noted Charles Dickens, could not hope to discern the aesthetic value of a new painting: "The thing is too still after their lives of machinery; the art flows over their heads in consequence." Choosing a piano was a safer bet, though its narrow association with femininity became so fixed in the public's mind that when Charles Hallé (1819–1895), the first pianist to play all of the Beethoven Sonatas in London, asked some English gentlemen during a visit in the 1840s if any of them played an instrument, they regarded it as an insult. Nevertheless, women were generally unwelcome in the domain of the professional musician. Indeed, when Elizabeth Stirling passed the music-composition test at the University of Oxford in 1856, she was refused a degree.

There were notable exceptions, like the Linley sisters of Bath, who were immortalized in a portrait by Thomas Gainsborough in 1772. Elizabeth and Mary Linley became well-known performers while in their teens (under the tutelage of their father, Thomas), though both gave up the business at the first sign of a marriage proposal. Then there was Lady Hallé, who performed with her husband, Charles, until his death, and was anointed by Queen Alexandra "violinist to the queen."

Across the Channel, Clara Wieck, who married composer Robert Schumann, maintained a serious career for most of her life, though her touring caused her fragile husband more than a little heartache.

A giraffe piano

And even though Oxford refused to grant accreditation to Elizabeth Stirling, the Paris Conservatory appointed Hélène, Marquise de Montgeroult, one of the first piano professors at its founding in 1795. Almost fifty years later, in 1842, the school gave Louise Farrenc a similar position.

Women were never completely absent from show business, of course, and in 1868 Londoners were treated to the skills of a Batavian woman who played "two different arias with each hand at the same time and likewise sang a fifth." But on the concert stage, in taverns, or at the theater, instrumental performance was primarily a male occupation. (In some instances, only a very well built male would do: Eugen Sandow, the strongman, famously carried both a piano and its player off the stage as part of his act. Unfortunately, one day in 1899 he dropped both and was sued for damages.)

It was not, in any case, a career for the faint of heart. Just traveling from city to city was wearying. And then there was the challenge of facing an audience that often considered musical concerts a place in which to pursue more pressing activities. Charles Hallé was once congratulated, in fact, for playing at a volume soft enough to allow "the ladies to talk." For that reason, Franz Liszt claimed that the opening page of his *Fantasy on Bellini's La Sonnambula* was written specifically for the audience to "assemble and blow their noses" as they settled down in their seats.

There was always a danger that the audience might actually turn ugly. At one concert at Vienna's Mehlgrube in 1789, a customer complained that he disliked the music. "A virtuoso from the full orchestra who was firmly holding the beat gave him a sturdy box on the ears, almost like Achilles did to Thersites in Homer," says one report.

> Thereby the *point d'honneur* of the nobility present was attacked. One Herculean Youth, together with many young ladies, cried: Allons! Storm the Bastille! The uncouth Orpheus was pounced upon. He was encircled. He had to kneel down and beg pardon. The remaining chorus of the sons of Apollo found that ignominious for their noble art. They armed themselves to avenge the disgrace of their colleague. The waiters and busboys hurried to bring them reinforcements. Now the skirmish became universal. All sounding instruments were squashed and smashed. The silver spoons of the waiters and bottles, glasses, and chairs flew everywhere. Finally this comical barricade was overcome by the superior strength of the enemy. The conquered inhabitants tried to save themselves by fleeing, and the victors too parted laughing, after they had admired the wreckage their bravery had caused.

Decades later, even the celebrated Liszt continued to find audiences disruptive at times, though a good deal less violent; during some of his performances, fans impatiently interrupted the music making by shouting out requests for pieces they would rather hear.

At least they cared. Leopold Mozart complained in 1768 that in Vienna audiences at plays were "not curious to see serious and rational things, of which they have little or no concept. They like nothing but foolish tricks, dancing, devils, spirits, magical spells . . . But in serious scenes, or at touching and beautiful actions onstage, and the most sensible ways of speaking, [a gentleman] talks in a loud voice to his lady, so that honorable people cannot understand a word." It's awfully hard for a musician to win out over foolish tricks and magical spells. Keyboardist James Hook, who was music director at London's Vauxhall Gardens from 1774 to 1820, regretfully competed with fireworks, tightrope dancers, and parachuting balloonists for his audience's attention.

ON AUDIENCES *by Vladimir Horowitz*

There are three kinds of audience. One is social; they come because the artist is well known and they have to be seen. That's the worst. They're asleep from beginning to end and don't know what's going on. Then there are the professionals who listen only to the notes to see if there is a mistake. They don't listen to the music. My father-in-law, Maestro Toscanini, used to say that for a mistake you never go to jail. The third is the best audience. They come because they want to hear me, they believe in me, and they want to hear the best. Sometimes I don't give the best, but they will come again because they know it wasn't my night.

I can tell what kind of audience I have by how they listen. Applause doesn't mean anything. Silence is the success of the artist. If they listen to every note and don't cough too much or move or rustle their programs, they are attentive. The concentration of the artist is contagious to the public, and the public starts to be a little hypnotized. They're listening to the music, not just to the notes and whether you play too fast or too slow. That's secondary. That's for the critics to show that they know something. The artistry you cannot erase.

As the piano's popularity continued to grow, it gained a foothold in the New World as well. After George Washington was inaugurated in 1789, he and his wife, Martha, hired composer Alexander Reinagle (1756–1809) to give piano lessons to her granddaughter, Nelly Custis, who made it a regular practice to play for foreign dignitaries and members of Congress. One diplomat described Nelly as the kind of "celestial" being dreamed of "by poets and painters," and announced that she played the piano "better than the usual woman of America or even of Europe." (How she viewed her audience was another matter: she once confessed to playing for over an hour in an attempt to "attune the souls" of "two homely Spaniards," but in the end gave up and declared one of them just a "crazy count.")

The instrument even reached beyond the big cities into America's western territories. "'Tis wonderful," wrote Ralph Waldo Emerson in *Civilization* (1870), "how soon a piano gets into a log-hut on the frontier." Diaries of the homesteaders fill out the story. Living in the mining town of Aurora, Nevada, in the 1860s, a Mrs. Rachel Haskell recorded that in the evening, after dinner, her husband would come into the sitting room and place himself near the piano as their daughter, Ella, accompanied the entire family in song. Rachel's daytime regime included instructing Ella at the piano, along with practicing the multiplication tables with her sons, making dinner, and visiting friends.

The trend caught the attention of W. W. Kimball, who settled in Chicago in 1857 and announced that he wanted to sell pianos "within the reach of the farmer on his prairie, the miner in his cabin, the fisherman in his hut, the cultivated mechanic in his neat cottage in the thriving town." He based his new business on the installment plan—as did D. H. Baldwin, a Cincinnati dealer who hired an army of sewing-machine salesmen in 1872 to recruit new customers.

Naturally, the piano was an essential component in the homes of America's cultured class. In Mark Twain's Hartford, Connecticut, residence, the writer would bang out African-American spirituals on a Steinway baby grand (that is, when it wasn't being used for recitals organized by his wife, Livy). Louisa May Alcott played a

Chickering square piano in her parlor in between her boat rides with Henry David Thoreau at Walden Pond. Visitors to literary homes can still see the evidence: Emily Dickinson kept a Wilkinson in Amherst, Edna St. Vincent Millay owned two Steinways, Robinson Jeffers had a Steinway grand, Frederick Douglass a Kimball upright, and Kate Chopin took breaks from playing cards to enjoy her French Pleyel.

Eugene O'Neill adored his player piano, a coin-operated instrument with stained-glass panels, and named it "Rosie." (O'Neill's wife, Carlotta, described it as "the sort of piano that, in years past, was in salons and 'other places!' This particular one," she explained, "was in one of the 'other places' in New Orleans.") When architect Frank Lloyd Wright established his winter colony at Taliesin West in the desert of Scottsdale, Arizona, in 1937—a rugged architectural laboratory with a minimum of comforts—he quickly gathered eighteen pianos to provide a semblance of civilization.

And once again, the piano was promoted as a tool to regulate the emotional life of the tender sex. The critic of the *New York World*, A. C. Wheeler, laid out the argument in 1875:

[It] may be looked upon as furniture by dull observers or accepted as a fashion by shallow thinkers, but it is in reality the artificial nervous system, ingeniously made of steel and silver, which civilization in its poetic justice provides for our young women. Here it is, in this parlor with closed doors, that the daughter of our day comes stealthily and pours out the torrent of her emotions through her finger-ends, directs the forces of her youth and romanticism into the obedient metal and lets it say in its own mystic way what she dare not confess or hope in articulate language . . . A woman must put her woman impulses into action. So, not wishing her to become a lecturer or a telegraph-operator or to play *Lady Macbeth*, he gives her the piano . . .

Presently it becomes her companion, her confidant, her lover. It tells her what no one else dare utter. It responds to her passion, her playfulness, her vagaries, as nothing else can.

Little wonder the American home, like those in Europe, became a center of piano activity. It helped prepare the way for the invasion of the European virtuosos, who would soon find audiences from one side of America to the other eager to hear the instrument in the hands of the masters.

CHAPTER 5

Performers on the Road

T HEY CAME, they played, and they conquered. But first they had to travel, by road, sea, or rail—a tricky matter for any virtuoso musician in search of an audience. The diaries of English historian Charles Burney, who embarked on "the grand tour" of the European continent in the early 1770s, illustrate the problems.

Like many men of his social standing, Burney felt the wide world beckoning, with places to see, people to meet, and music to hear, and he dutifully answered the call. "If knowledge be medicine for the soul," he wrote, offering a moral argument for his excursions, it is as important "to obtain it genuine as to procure unadulterated medicine for the body." As he traveled, he recorded his concert experiences, encounters with great musicians (including C. P. E. Bach and Frederick the Great), and, not least, the hardships of the journey.

Trekking to Bohemia, he felt assaulted by excessive heat and cold, "together with bad horses, and diabolical wagons." As he journeyed, he met "half-starved people, just recovered from malignant fevers, little less contagious than the plague, occasioned by bad food." At a time when the English upper class routinely enjoyed up to twenty-five dishes at dinner, this was alarming.

Yet it could have been worse. In Burney's day, additional dangers lurked, like being snatched by pirates—from 1500 to 1800, Algerian and Moroccan corsairs regularly nabbed people at sea, as well as from towns along the English Channel—or attacked by bandits. (Mozart's contemporary composer Giuseppe Maria Cambini told of being abducted from a ship and released only after a Venetian patron paid his ransom.) Leopold Mozart, who hauled his little prodigies all around Europe in search of celebrity and riches, complained of "impassable roads, uncomfortable carriages, wretched accommodations, avaricious innkeepers, corrupt customs officials, and marauding highwaymen."

PLAYING IN EXOTIC CLIMES

Even in the late twentieth century, travel to distant regions could present all sorts of challenges. Touring the world in 1960, pianist Joseph Bloch, a fixture at the Juilliard School as professor of piano literature, arrived in Borneo and unexpectedly ended up performing in a leper colony; in Sendai, Japan, the temperature in the concert hall was below freezing, and he had to soak his hands in a bowl of hot water between each piece. And in Iran, he found his piano mysteriously draped in cloth: it turned out to be an upright pretending to be a grand. He thought the performance had gone well nevertheless until an audience member approached him afterward. "Next time," he asked, "would you play something we like?" "What would that be?" Bloch wondered. "The theme from *Dr. Zhivago*," came the reply.

Indeed, young Wolfgang Mozart once had to join a convoy of coaches to avoid Italian outlaws. And there were other hazards as well: he was so lonely on the road that he fantasized an alternate mythical world; hopping from city to city, he was stricken by serious illnesses (as was his sister, who nearly died); and he barely survived a major carriage accident. Conditions for travelers were so dangerous that many Europeans never ventured beyond their borders: in 1784, isolated Venetians, curious about life on the distant shore, eagerly paid to view an imported stuffed horse.

Nevertheless, for professional musicians, there was little choice. Some actually fared well: Giuseppe Sarti (1729–1802), whose music Mozart quoted admiringly in his opera *Don Giovanni*, traveled to Russia at the request of Empress Catherine II and was rewarded with his own village in the Ukraine. But that was unusual. Throughout the eighteenth century, keyboardists were so poorly paid that they were often forced to earn extra income by selling lottery tickets or painting portraits.

A century earlier, the social status of itinerant musicians had been even worse. Dishonorable burials were the norm—reapers had a saying, "There lies a musician," when they came across large anthills, and musicians were routinely suspected of the worst kind of behavior, including witchcraft. (In 1615, a fiddler seen wading across the Rhine as he played was accused by Dominican monks of sorcery. The local magistrate found that it was possible to wade across the Rhine even without the devil's help, but nevertheless sentenced the man for mischievous wantonness.)

Mozart was not the only tender soul who found touring psychologically torturous. In the nineteenth century, Clara Wieck (later Clara Schumann), arriving alone in Berlin just short of her twentieth birthday, expressed a litany of worries: about hostile critics, playing the wrong pieces, choosing the right piano, and more. She even developed physical symptoms: "I strained my lungs so much playing yesterday that I still can not catch my breath today," she wrote to her beloved Robert Schumann. "It is so strange that after playing a difficult piece I always become hoarse and get a sore throat. It makes me really scared." (Her diaries recount one "unplayable" piano after another at performance venues, which certainly didn't buoy her confidence.)

Clara Wieck

Louis Moreau Gottschalk (1829–1869), America's first international touring virtuoso, summed up the "torments" of a musician's life with this list: "The horrible monotony of concerts, the invariable repetition of the same pieces, the daily round of railroad cars, isolation in the midst of the crowd (the saddest thing of all) . . ." Things seemed little changed over a century later, when rock songwriter Billy Joel and rhythm and blues artist Ray Charles recorded a gripping duo performance of Joel's lament for the pianist whose only solace was his "Baby Grand."

ANXIETIES OF A PERFORMING MUSICIAN *by Yefim Bronfman*

I sometimes find hotels and airports irritants, like everyone else. But for me, that doesn't outweigh the fun of being on the road. It's often harder to be home, in a way. My greatest concerns involve finding good pianos, adjusting to different altitudes and concert halls, and dealing with repertory. The worst pressures come from having to meet deadlines when you are really busy, making sure that when you get to a place you are ready to perform the promised program. You have to practice months ahead of time, of course, and then face the music, whether you feel ready or not.

Stress is bad enough even when you are well prepared, and I often have sleepless nights and suffer from bad dreams. One is that I am playing the Brahms Second Piano Concerto in Carnegie Hall, and I don't know the music. Cellist and conductor Mstislav Rostropovich once told me he also had a nightmare—that he was playing the Dvořák Cello Concerto unprepared. "And when I woke up," he said, "it was true."

We musicians are involved in a kind of endless self-examination: Why didn't I do better at my last concert? When should I prepare for the one that is coming up? There are endless questions, and the answers aren't always forthcoming. Unfortunately, sometimes you have to fail in order to learn.

It was Rostropovich who helped me deal with this anxiety. One night, I was about to play the Tchaikovsky First Piano Concerto with him and the Vienna Philharmonic. I went to his room and said, "Maestro, I'm so nervous I don't know what to do." He had the perfect answer. "Remember," he told me, "no matter what happens tonight, we'll go out after the concert and have a nice dinner. It's not like being a pilot, when if you make a mistake everyone dies!"

Still they traveled, searching out fresh horizons. In Europe, the most practical destinations were big cities and lofty courts, but even faraway regions held temptations.

Franz Liszt visited Russia several times and left an indelible

John Field

imprint on the course of pianism there (as well as on the heart of Princess Carolyne zu Sayn-Wittgenstein, who left her husband and followed him to Weimar). Clementi made two separate Russian trips, principally to stir up interest in the instruments he was manufacturing. (Clementi's piano battle with Mozart in Vienna took place while Emperor Joseph II was entertaining the Grand Duke—the future Tsar Paul I—and Duchess of Russia. No doubt it helped open doors. Although Paul was assassinated in 1801, his son Alexander took over, keeping power in the family.) Clementi brought his student and employee John Field along on the visit. And when Clementi left, Field decided to stay and establish his career there.

At first, Field worked simply as a piano "plugger," showing off Clementi's instruments (one thinks of George Gershwin, who got his start a century later by demonstrating songs for a Tin Pan Alley publisher). In both London and on the road, he played for hours as potential customers listened in. "I have still in recollection," wrote composer Louis Spohr after witnessing one such evening, "the figure of the pale overgrown youth whom I have never seen since. When Field, who had outgrown his clothes, placed himself at the piano, stretched out his arms over the keyboard so that the sleeves shrunk up nearly to his elbows, his whole figure appeared awkward and stiff to the highest degree; but as soon as his touching instrumentation began, everything else was forgotten, and one became all ear."

Once out from under Clementi's thumb, however, Field made a fortune performing and teaching in St. Petersburg and Moscow (while developing a reputation for extravagant living and degenerate behavior). As might be expected of the originator of the piano

"Nocturne," music that depicts the night in all its quiet mystery, his playing was dreamy and melancholic rather than blistering. In fact, startled by the intensity of a Liszt recital, he turned to a companion and asked, "Does he bite?"

Yet of the various distant prospects for commercial success, none seemed more inviting than the New World, although views of what awaited musicians there were divided. *La France musicale* outlined one popular notion in 1845: "The European artist imagines that America is a country of gold, where he will acquire a fortune in two or three months, where the president of the union will have him honored by congress; where the inhabitants of each city will give him serenades and carry him in triumph, for the great satisfaction of his enormous self-esteem."

However, a contrasting outlook was expressed by the director of the Paris Opéra, who claimed that the young nation across the Atlantic was "excellent for electric telegraphs and railroads but not for art." He received a swift rebuttal from American composer William Henry Fry, who admitted that his countrymen "excelled in making electric telegraphs to carry ideas without persons," but also insisted that "it was not a necessary consequence that we built railroads to carry persons without ideas." Moravian-born opera impresario Max Maretzek, an American transplant, nevertheless dismissed the idea that his new countrymen had any understanding of art. "Instead of having been provided with a delicately palpitating heart like other races of mankind," he declared, they had in its place "a silver dollar coined in their own mint."

That perspective was so prevalent that Gottschalk was actually turned down for an audition at the Paris Conservatory with the explanation that "America was only a country of steam engines." (He was in good company: twelve-year-old Liszt had also been denied admission to that institution, simply because he was a foreigner.) Perhaps this belief is what discouraged Berlioz, Schumann, Liszt, and Wagner from embarking on the voyage to America, despite the financial incentives. But by the 1840s, ocean steamers had shortened the trip to just two or three weeks. For many, it seemed well worth the risk.

Leopold de Meyer

VISITORS SOON DISCOVERED that Americans were not so culturally deprived after all. One writer in 1830 found the country as piano-mad as England: "In cities and villages, from one extremity of the union to the other, wherever there is a good house . . . the ringing of the piano wires is almost as universal a sound as the domestic hum of life within." But, as P. T. Barnum found, it helped to have a gimmick, and touring pianists quickly learned the value of a little showmanship.

This was already the modus operandi of Austrian pianist Leopold de Meyer (1816–1883), who began his American adventure in 1845. During his travels in Russia and Eastern Europe, he had developed a reputation as "the Lion Pianist." Caricatures typically depicted him as a crouched figure playing the keyboard with hands, elbows, and a knee, as if he had just sprung from a hiding place in the jungle foliage.

He billed himself as "the Paganini of the Piano" (after Niccolò Paganini, the fire-breathing Romantic violinist who was said to be in league with the devil) or, simply, as "the Greatest Pianist of Modern Times." Critics noted the great mass of sound he produced. His virtuoso compositions "are to other musical works," said the *New York Daily Tribune*, "what the Niagara at the Falls is to other rivers." He attributed his overwhelming power to one simple fact: he was, he said, "the only one of the great pianists who is fat." "Indeed," reported the influential *Dwight's Journal of Music*, "his physique is extraordinary; he is himself a Grand Piano, and can stand any amount of violent vibrations without any symptom of exhaustion."

He had some very odd quirks, like gawking at the audience while he played, with what the *Brooklyn Star* called "a kind of insane stare." But his theatrical instincts were impeccable. He invited "Ladies and

Gentlemen who have a desire to become acquainted" with his technique to take seats on stage next to him. And he designed programs especially suited to his newfound public. Variations on "Hail, Columbia" and "Yankee Doodle" caused such a furor that in Philadelphia one critic worried for his safety. In a Pittsburgh church, wrote a correspondent, "men, women and children would be standing up in the pews, or leaning forward with breathless attention to catch each succeeding note—and then, falling back as if in utter exhaustion from the intensity of the feeling, excited by the performance, [they would] listen with silent astonishment! They were literally music mad."

"The Lion" had other tricks up his sleeve. He imported grand pianos—still a rarity in the United States, where uprights and squares were the norm—and called them "Monster pianos," to attract attention. The ploy backfired in St. Louis when city authorities charged him the exorbitant fee of seventy-five dollars for a license to perform. "Mein Gott!—shust for play mein piano two-tree night?" he exclaimed. "I know it's more than usual," was the reply. "But then, Mr. de Meyer, your piano is such a *large* one!"

By 1846, the publicity schemes hatched by de Meyer and his business partner, G. C. Reitheimer, who happened to be his brother-in-law, were starting to generate bad press. Reports appeared that they were paying for good reviews (not an uncommon practice), and that Reitheimer was handing out free tickets to fill halls—something then called "deadheading," and now known as "papering the house." The *Morning Telegraph* christened him "the Lyin' Pianist." His career was never quite the same.

Up came another European visitor, the Viennese-born, Parisian-educated Henri Herz (1803–1888), who began to give de Meyer some competition. Herz's concert tours had taken him to Belgium, England, Germany, Spain, Poland, and Russia, and he was now ready to vanquish the American audience. "My idea," he wrote his brother, Charles, "is to take music everywhere money is to be made." Arriving in America in 1846, he found the response a bit tepid at first. So he hired manager Bernard Ullman and developed a strategy.

HOW THE PIANO HAD CHANGED

The great virtuosos who visited America had the advantage of playing an instrument that had grown in heft and volume over early models. In fact, during the early nineteenth century the piano changed from a delicately constructed and lightly strung five-octave instrument, like that made by Johann Andreas Stein (1728–1792), to a six-and-a-half-octave instrument, like those produced by Stein's son-in-law, Johann Andreas Streicher (1761–1833), and by another maker, Conrad Graf (1782–1851). By the end of Beethoven's life (in 1827), seven-octave instruments were available.

They were increasingly brighter. The early Stein pianos had string tensions of several thousand pounds, but by 1830 pianos made by Streicher and Graf were capable of supporting fourteen thousand pounds of tension. This still pales in comparison with the modern piano, of course, which sustains forty thousand pounds of tension by means of a three-hundred-pound cast-iron plate.

In England, piano maker Joseph Smith began experimenting with iron braces as early as 1799; by the 1820s, some English and French firms were using iron bars screwed to the wood framework, and the full cast-iron frame was patented in 1825 by the American Alpheus Babcock (1785–1842). It was not adopted in Europe until the middle of the nineteenth century.

There were other substantial changes as well. In 1821, the London branch of the French piano firm Érard developed and patented the double-escapement mechanism, the kind used in the modern grand piano, which facilitated greater speed in musical performance (because the hammers were made ready to repeat their movements more quickly after striking). In 1826, the French piano maker Jean-Henri Pape (1789–1875) obtained a patent for felt-covered hammers (layered atop leather), which produced a much sweeter sound than earlier models. Then Alfred Dolge (1848–1922) had the bright idea of using a single, thick layer of felt, and it quickly became the norm.

The invention of cross-stringing in the 1820s, a method of arranging piano strings inside the case so that they overlapped each other diagonally, produced a more efficient use of space, and allowed the bass strings to resonate across the center of the instrument rather than to one side; though credited to Alpheus Babcock and Jean-Henri Pape, its first patented use in grand pianos in the United States was by Henry Steinway Jr. in 1859.

Herz was far more refined than his rival—"de Meyer may break a piano," purred one critic, "but Herz can break a heart"—yet, realizing that "the Lion" had discovered a winning formula, he set about composing his own arrangements of American patriotic tunes. Then he launched a series of "monster concerts" with multiple instruments played by a gaggle of performers. It had been done before, even in the best European cities: writing from Vienna about Carl Czerny (1791–1857), the former Beethoven protégé, Frédéric Chopin noted with some condescension that Czerny had "arranged another overture for eight pianos and sixteen pianists, and seems quite happy about it." But Herz had few cares about potential snobs: one of his events, with eight pianos and sixteen players, featured his arrangement of the Overture to Rossini's opera *Semiramide,* and it was a rousing success. The *Evening Mirror* estimated the audience at 2,600 to 2,800. (In the twentieth century, pianist Eugene List resurrected the monster-concert idea, with even larger numbers of pianos and performers, often employing students and amateurs.)

Henri Herz

Apparently the production values were not very high. One reviewer noted that the pianos were out of tune with each other, and expressed the hope that the pianists would "mind the conductor's arm and baton a little better on the next occasion." Another thought that Herz had "buried" the music, and that the pianos, scattered all around the stage, looked like a "coffin-maker's exhibition at a National fair." The very concept itself sometimes caused head scratching. In San Francisco, Herz announced a "Monstre Concert" in which a *Marche Nationale* would be performed on four pianos; but some music lovers showed up in the mistaken belief that the pianist was going to singlehandedly play all four instruments at once, and a local paper criticized him for raising false expectations.

Nevertheless, he regarded his concert programs as a success. Bernard Ullman's definition of music, revealed Herz, was "the art of attracting to a given auditorium, by secondary devices which often become the principal ones, the greatest possible number of curious people so that when expenses are tallied against receipts the latter exceed the former by the widest possible margin." And Ullman's mind continued to percolate with plans for musical spectacles, like a "thousand candles concert," in which the hall was illuminated entirely by candlelight (though, according to Herz, one customer shouted out that he had counted only 998 flames). But a proposed "political concert" in Philadelphia, with a *Constitution Concerto*, was, in Herz's view, over the line. (He also refused a concert offer made by freed slaves in New Orleans; apparently, the possibility of offending important patrons put the idea off limits.) This pianist's greatest opportunity came not in the big Eastern cities, though, but in the fledgling towns of California, where in 1849 forty thousand people raced to find their fortunes in gold.

Herz went, hoping to garner a piece of the action. He learned that miners could be a rough audience—the publication *Alta California* complained of "uproar and confusion, and disorderly and disgraceful behavior" at one concert. (Context is everything: rock pianist Bruce Hornsby once grumbled when an audience *didn't* engage in that mode of conduct.) And conditions were often primitive: Sacramento had no concert hall to play in, and one had to be cobbled together. In Benicia, Herz arrived to find that there wasn't even a piano on hand. When one was located at the other side of town, he rallied the audience to go fetch it and carry it back.

Yet he certainly knew how to deliver what the people wanted. He entertained with fanciful versions of familiar melodies, including

his own published variations on "Oh Susannah." At his final concert, in San Francisco, he shared the stage with one Signor Rossi, a
magician and ventriloquist who also offered imitations of animals
and insects. It was hardly the kind of performance found in the
salons of Paris, but no one in the audience complained.

They kept coming. Sigismond Thalberg (1812–1871) had challenged Liszt to a piano duel, and survived. Arriving in America
in 1856 ready to display his brilliant technique, he turned to (who
else?) Ullman, who set up a grueling schedule of performances
every night (except Sunday) for eight months, sometimes engaging
the pianist for two or three recitals a day (including special presentations for schoolchildren).

In the view of the critics, his note-perfect renditions were too
"dry and monotonous." (In New York, one writer claimed that
an Englishman who had followed Thalberg for three years in
the hope of hearing a wrong note finally "blew out his brains in
despair.") But his skill was impressive, especially for giving the
impression of having three hands going at once. In *Dwight's Journal of Music,* a correspondent described the approach: "This man
plays a few notes of the melody in the middle of the piano with
his right hand; at the same time his left, full of 'muttering wrath,'
crawls up and attacks the melody, and then the right steals way
up to high C, sees what's to be seen, and then softly tumbles back
just in time to carry on the melody, while the left hand leaves for
the lower regions." His matinee performances attracted ladies of
leisure in large numbers, especially once Ullman provided them
the added incentive of being served chocolate, cake, and ice cream
during the intermissions by black waiters dressed in livery uniforms.

Thalberg's American tour also signaled another new wrinkle
in the concert business. The piano maker Chickering, based in
Boston, began supplying him with pianos in different cities while
advertising his endorsement of their product. It was the start of
what would soon become an all-out manufacturing war in the
piano world.

These and other European musicians all made their mark on the

American scene. But the United States also offered musical exports, beginning with Louis Moreau Gottschalk. This son of New Orleans, trained in Paris and having played throughout Europe, then swept through the Caribbean and South America like a force of nature. "You wonder that you never knew before that the piano was capable of such power," glowed the *New York Herald*.

Caricature of Gottschalk conducting his monster concert in Rio de Janeiro, October 5, 1869 (A Vida Fluminense, October 2, 1869)

His success was due in part to a willingness to tap into the national pride of each host country along the way. He "flattered the Swiss with his arrangement of excerpts from Rossini's *William Tell*," wrote Jeanne Behrend, who edited Gottschalk's diaries. He drove "the Spanish populace wild with his *Siege of Saragossa*, a 'symphony' for ten pianos based on Spanish tunes and national airs. It had all the effects dear to the battle pieces that had raged in parlors and concert halls since Franz Kotzwara's popular *Battle of Prague* (1789)—trumpet calls, military marches, drum rolls, cannon fire, etc.—effects later used stunningly by Tchaikovsky in his *1812 Overture*." He composed similar works geared to audiences in Chile, Uruguay, Cuba, and Brazil—where he presented the world's largest monster concert, featuring eight hundred musicians.

Back home, Gottschalk took portions of his *Siege*, substituted American anthems for the Spanish ones, and called his piece *Grand National Symphony for Ten Pianos: Bunker Hill*. He fashioned a solo piano piece out of it as well, *National Glory*, by adding to the conglomeration "Oh! Susanna" and another Stephen Foster song, "Old Folks at Home." As the Civil War raged, he produced a similar composition, *The Union*, with references to "The Star-Spangled Banner," "Yankee Doodle," and "Hail, Columbia." President Abraham Lincoln attended a Gottschalk concert and became a fan.

("Tall, thin, his back bent, his chest hollow, his arms excessively long, his crane-like legs, his enormous feet, that long frame whose disproportionate joints give him the appearance of a grapevine covered with clothes," is how the pianist described the president.)

TWOSOMES, THREESOMES, AND MORE

As monster concerts waned, the idea of smaller piano ensembles still flourished: two-piano teams like those of Robert (1899–1972) and Gaby (1901–1999) Casadesus of France, Vitya Vronsky (1909–1992) and Victor Babin (1908–1972) of Russia, and America's Arthur Ferrante (1921–2009) and Louis Teicher (1924–2008) continued to find large, enthusiastic audiences.

Today, the tradition is carried on by piano duos like the French sisters Katia and Marielle Labèque and by slightly larger assemblages like the American Piano Quartet, which features four players on two pianos, and the British-based Piano

The hands of piano team Vronsky and Babin

Circus, a six-piano ensemble created in 1989 that specializes in new music. But these acts bear little resemblance to the massive piano gatherings staged by Gottschalk and his ilk.

The piano duo was, in a way, just an extension of the duet for two people at a keyboard that had flourished from the pens of Mozart, Schubert, and many others. Those tended to have a certain domestic quality because of the close physical proximity of the players. (The famous Mozart family portrait of about 1780 by Johann Nepomuk della Croce shows Wolfgang and his sister, Nannerl, performing together at a single instrument.) Nevertheless, some composers continuously pushed the boundaries, increasing the population on the piano bench even to the point of danger: W. F. E. Bach wrote *Das Dreyblatt* for three performers at one keyboard—as

Piano circus

pianist Joseph Smith has written, "It provides a male pianist with a fine pretext for embracing two female colleagues" (or, he adds, a woman pianist with the opportunity to enjoy the intimate company of two males). Rachmaninoff and Percy Grainger also published works for three players at a piano. Cécile Chaminade (better known for her solo piano piece *Scarf Dance*) wrote a work for four players squeezed together on one bench. But of course, she was Parisian.

At the time, keyboard cannon fire and patriotic marches were a specialty of another unusual pianist named Blind Tom (1849–1908), a black, autistic savant celebrated for his ability to duplicate at the keyboard anything he heard. Born into slavery and sold to a Georgia lawyer, General James Neil Bethune, who presented him as a carnival attraction throughout the South, Tom was strangely gifted with an extraordinary memory. People were invited to play *or* recite anything and have him re-create it on the spot.

His original musical compositions included piano tone poems like *The Battle of Manassas*, in which the Union and Confederate armies are heard to draw closer to each other, with patriotic themes clashing amid the fist-pounding bombast of explosions in the instrument's bass.

As his fame spread, he performed at the White House for President James Buchanan and, while on a European tour, played for pianists Ignaz Moscheles and Charles Hallé, who both attested to his talent. A musician named Joseph Poznanski was hired to tutor

Tom and transcribe his musical creations for publication; he told the *Washington Post* in 1866 how the collaboration between them worked: "I would play for him and he would get up, walk around, stand on one foot, pull his hair, knock his head against the wall, then sit down and play a very good imitation of what I had played with additions to it."

Gottschalk became aware of Blind Tom when he read an article about him in the *Atlantic Monthly*, but he dismissed the legitimacy of the report. Musically uneducated audiences who were so impressed, he said, reminded him of an assembly he once saw that was called to witness a mathematical prodigy solve "the most complicated problems instantaneously from memory." Who could judge the performance? asked Gottschalk. "He might have answered what he wished. The honest people did not know a word of algebra, and ingenuously thought that what they heard was really marvelous."

Gottschalk's own music offered a great deal of Americana. Much of it can still thrill: *The Banjo*, with its strums and patterns reminiscent of American folk traditions; *Bamboula*, an exciting, rhythmically charged homage to New Orleans; and the sweetly melancholic *The Last Hope*, which became so popular that he couldn't escape performing it at every stop. The pianist came to call it his "terrible necessity."

His diaries reveal all the highs and lows of an adventurous musical career on the road. "Unfortunately, yellow fever rages cruelly at St. Thomas," he recorded while traveling through the Caribbean. "Two days after our arrival our steamer had already lost seven men belonging to it; three servants on board who were attacked with the same plague succumbed in a few hours." On another occasion, he noted that "the latest political events at Barcelona [Venezuela] are of a nature to cure radically all artists who have the insane idea of making a tour there." After an arduous trip across the North American continent, he felt despondent: "The devil take the poets who sing the joys of an artist's life."

On the other hand, after returning to New York in 1862, he

paused to remember the pleasures he had experienced during years of roaming "at random under the blue skies of the tropics, indolently permitting myself to be carried away by chance, giving a concert wherever I found a piano, sleeping wherever the night overtook me—on the grass of the savanna, or under the palm-leaf roof of a *veguero* [tobacco grower] with whom I partook of a tortilla, coffee, and banana . . ." He saw "the seasons succeed each other in perpetual summer" and found, in the evenings, under palm trees, "beautiful, dreamlike girls" who would whisper words of love in his ear. "The moralists, I well know, condemn all this; and they are right," he admitted. "But poetry is often in antagonism with virtue."

Its ways are also unpredictable. In December of 1869, at the age of forty, the pianist collapsed while giving a piano recital in Rio de Janeiro. He died soon after. In a poetic twist of fate, the original piece he had been playing was entitled *La Morte* (Death). Writing from Berlin, Liszt's American piano student Amy Fay described her shock. "But what a romantic way to die!—to fall senseless at this instrument, while he was playing *La Morte*. . . . The infatuation that I and 999,999 other American girls once felt for him still lingers in my breast!" He would have been pleased to hear it.

DEATH BY KEYBOARD

Gottschalk wasn't the only artist to either die in the midst of a performance, or soon after. Organist Anton Cajetan Adlgasser (1729–1777), an acquaintance of Mozart's, fell over and died of a stroke while performing at the Salzburg Cathedral. Mozart succeeded him as court cathedral organist in 1779. (Once, when Wolfgang and his father heard an organist who was so drunk he could barely play, Mozart suggested that they walk over to him, lean in to his ear, and whisper, "Adlgasser!")

Like Gottschalk, Charles-Valentin Alkan (1813–1888) also wrote piano pieces about the end of life. He was plagued by constant worries about his health, though they seem to have been entirely unfounded. Early pieces included *Morte* (*Death*) and *Le Mourant* (*The Dying*), a portrait of a man at the moment of his demise. The composer lived another fifty years after writing it, finally succumbing to an accident at home.

Spanish composer Enrique Granados (1867–1916) was killed when his ship was torpedoed in World War I. But he wouldn't have been on the ship if his trip home from New York had not been delayed because of an invitation to perform at the White House. Indirectly, it was the music that led to his demise.

Virtuoso Simon Barere (1896–1951) holds the distinction of being the only pianist to drop dead (literally) on the stage of New York's Carnegie Hall. This Russian-American pianist was known for a blazing technique, and he gave annual recitals at the hall. On April 2, 1951, he was just beginning the Grieg Piano Concerto with Eugene Ormandy and the Philadelphia Orchestra when he suffered a cerebral hemorrhage.

Some well-known musicians took their own lives (or attempted to). Robert Schumann jumped into the Rhine, only to be rescued by a fisherman. Hungarian composer and pianist Rezsö Seress (1889–1968) composed a 1933 song called "Gloomy Sunday" that was banned by the BBC after it set off a spate of suicides (many by people clutching the sheet music as they died). The composer himself jumped out a window, years after surviving the Holocaust.

Perhaps the saddest example of death by keyboard, however, is the case of Alexander Kelberine (1903–1940). He programmed his very last concert to include only works dealing with death. (In a mixed review, a critic observed that the pianist demonstrated "not lack of musicianship so much as a psychic turmoil.") With a pending divorce instigated by his wife, the despondent pianist took an overdose of sleeping pills and expired at the age of thirty-six.

As the twentieth century approached, legendary pianists continued to travel the world, sharing the unique musical traits that had been fostered in Russia, Germany, France, Italy, America, and elsewhere—creating musical history, establishing schools and competitions, and fostering new audiences. Strategically positioned to promote the piano, some formed alliances with the instrument's makers, often with tumultuous and even disastrous consequences. The golden age was really just beginning.

Meanwhile, composers of every sort continued to supply pianists with music to perform. Despite the large swath they cut across time and geography, many of these creators fell naturally into a handful of stylistic categories: there were the Combustibles, the Alchemists, the Rhythmitizers, and the Melodists. Their stories will be revealed in the pages that follow.

CHAPTER 6

The Four Sounds

ALL OF THESE PIANISTS—amateur and professional—drew on the music available in their time, a repertoire that mushroomed decade by decade. That creative storehouse is still expanding, as composers explore the instrument's endless possibilities, drawing from its strings, hammers, and soundboard suggestions of the gentle resonance of an orchestra's winds, the boisterousness of its brass, the feather-light strums of its harp, and more. The piano's design makes it all possible.

Across the keyboard, different locations, or registers, provide their own individual sonic imprints. On the far left side, the lowest, deep bass notes are capable of sinister mutterings and thunderous growls. In the middle of the instrument, where the singing ranges of men and women meet, the sound is solid, clear, and warm. The highest treble notes, on the far right, tinkle, glitter, and ring like chimes.

ON SHAPING THE PIANO'S SOUNDS *by Murray Perahia*

Ideally, what you hear in your head should be translated directly to the tips of your fingers. But one has to work on techniques to produce sounds—not just to play fast but to bring out a bass note, for instance, or a contrapuntal melodic line. When I play a phrase on the piano I will try to hear the horn, say, or the oboe, and try to create the same effect on the piano. You have to listen very carefully to orchestras and try to re-create those sounds at home. The more I hear nuances of sound, the more I realize the wealth of colors a pianist must understand and produce. It can be frustrating.

Playing the piano is so much the art of illusion. It's not even so much producing a color as the illusion of a color. The more beautiful your instrument, the more possibilities you have.

These vibrations are all picked up and amplified by the piano's soundboard. In modern pianos, it's a thin sheet of spruce—fine-grained and elastic—maintained in an arch shape and kept under a constant level of tension. As the strings cause this diaphragm to vibrate, it transmits its waves to the surrounding air, which then move the elastic membranes of our ears. We experience these vibrations as sound when the varying pressure on our eardrums induces oscillations in small bones, which in turn cause a spiral-shaped structure called the cochlea to generate an electrical signal to the brain.

A player can further shape the outcome through foot pedals hanging below the keyboard's center. On modern instruments, there are usually three: on the far right, the sustain, or damper, pedal, moves the dampers (which muffle the vibrations after a depressed key has returned to its original position) away from the strings, allowing them to continue resonating; on the left, the una corda, or soft, pedal, shifts the playing mechanism over so that the hammers will strike only two strings (in Beethoven's day it was only one string, hence the "una") rather than the three assigned to most notes; and in the middle, the sostenuto pedal sustains only certain selected notes (those that are struck and held just before the pedal is depressed). Using these, pianists can add bloom to the sound, dull it, or suspend a choir of tones in the air while allowing others to bubble up and disappear without a trace.

PEDAL TECHNIQUE

Using these devices effectively is a delicate science. Pianist Anton Rubinstein described the sustain pedal as "the soul of the piano." It makes a singing line possible, imbues a work with atmosphere and vibrancy, and even conveys a sense of musical respiration. In the early eighteenth century, however, some regarded it as a scourge. When the sustain pedal is held down, the vibrations of all the strings that have been struck continue to ring out; the commingling of these sounds can easily turn to mud. "Our piano performers must have lost their sense of hearing!" exclaimed Friedrich Wieck, father of Clara Schumann. "What is all this growling and buzzing? Alas, it is only the groaning of the wretched piano-forte . . . with the pedal incessantly raised." Charles Hallé reported in 1840 with some amusement that when he performed Beethoven in Paris on a piano with a broken pedal mechanism, "all the critics praised me for my judicious and sparing use of the loud [sustain] pedal."

During Mozart's life and the early career of Beethoven, the pedals were operated by a pianist's knees, rather than by his feet. After 1805 it was the norm to have four or five of them, including the "moderator," by which a strip of cloth was moved over the strings to muffle the sound. Around 1820, Clementi's grand pianos featured another pedal, allowing some strings to vibrate "sympathetically," thus enhancing the tone of the instrument. (People eventually tire of such novelties, but there always seems to be a new one just around the corner. In America in 1815, a report appeared of a piano with a pedal that lifted a section of the top of the lid and allowed it to fall, simulating the sound of cannon fire. It was said to be especially effective for battle pieces.)

In Beethoven's era, composers began to use "pedal markings" in their printed music: one symbol for pressing the pedal down, another for releasing it.

As the nineteenth century wore on, more sophisticated techniques for the sustain pedal emerged, including the "half pedal," in which the mechanism was depressed only partially, and the "flutter pedal," in which the pedal was depressed and then released in a rapid series of motions, adding resonance while constantly clearing the air. The "sostenuto pedal" (the one that allows a pianist to sustain selected notes while others remain unaffected) was introduced by the piano maker Xavier Boisselot at the Paris Exhibition of 1844. A blind French technician named Claude Montal is often credited with its invention (Alexandre-François Debain also built such a mechanism), though Albert Steinway perfected and patented it in 1876.

Beethoven's pedal marks in his Sonata op. 53. At Ped. *the dampers are raised, and at the burst, they are lowered again.*

The great pianists often used these pedals in combination, the way a painter mixes tinctures to find just the right color. Some, including Beethoven, used the sustain pedal along with the una corda pedal to create a special sonority for highlighting themes that recurred within a piece. According to one observer, Chopin also "often coupled them to obtain a soft and veiled sonority . . . [and] he would use the soft pedal alone for those light murmurings which seem to create a transparent vapor round the arabesques that embellish the melody and envelop it like a fine case." As Chopin biographer Frederick Niecks remarked, "Every pianist of note has, of course, his own style of pedaling." For example, the difference between the playing of Sigismond Thalberg and Franz Liszt, who met on the piano field of battle, was described by one witness as that between "an atmosphere charged with electricity and quivering with lightning" (Liszt) and one "floating in a sea of purest light" (Thalberg). Their pedal techniques had much to do with it.

Even the shape of the piano's individual tones provides a foundation for myriad styles and musical approaches. The very name *piano* actually suggests what we hear when its keys are struck.

Uttered out loud—"p-ia-n-o"—the word begins with a small burst of air, as the *p* escapes abruptly from pursed lips; linguists call this an unvoiced plosive. It's the first thing we detect as the instrument's soft hammers are flung against taut strings; there is a subtle but percussive pop on impact, a barely discernable *p*.

In its wake, a soaring diphthong arises: *ia*—two vowels strung together and held out just long enough to suggest the birth of a song. But this new sound soon becomes pinched—only briefly—by the nasal *n*, before sailing outward, with rounded lips, into a final *o*, in an intimate gesture of openness.

Listen to the tones emanating from the instrument and you'll discover a similar sonic profile. Play any simple chord and after the initial percussive hammer strikes (*p*), as the strings begin to vibrate, the sound stirs and blossoms like the singing of vowels. But pay close attention and you'll notice a slight wavering—as if the strings are ever so softly repeating that *n*—while the music fades slowly into the openness of the surrounding air. (Those wavering sounds are known as "beating," and they result from a slight out-of-tuneness that occurs between the strings.) The sound is in constant flux, brimming with life.

Musicians may exploit any part of that tonal configuration, along with the instrument's dynamic flexibility, to achieve their musical goals: emphasizing its percussive beginning, for instance, for rhythmic vitality; its long, leisurely diphthong for languid melodies; the loud roar of hammered keys and the whispers from those gently pressed for music filled with emotional turbulence; the magical resonances that occur when tones interact in particular combinations, creating a unique atmospheric chemistry. That's why the piano can perfectly render the lyrical simplicity of a Mozart melody or the rhythmic snap of an Oscar Peterson run, the explosive din of Beethoven's fury or the shimmering mists of a Bill Evans ballad.

THE MYSTERY OF THE STRINGS

The piano's strings are tuned, raised or lowered in pitch, either through length (the longer the string, the lower the vibration) or tension (the higher the tension, the higher the pitch). However, getting them to work in harmony is no simple matter.

The most beautiful, pure, "natural" harmonic relationships—that of octaves, (say, from C to C), or fifths (from C to G)—cannot coexist in an instrument with fixed pitches. The tones that lie a fifth and a tenth above a fundamental pitch actually occur naturally in all vibrating bodies as soft "overtones," ghost sounds that result from the physics of vibration. But the mathematical proportions that create these harmonies (in the case of octaves, two pitches vibrating in the relationship 2:1, and for fifths, two pitches vibrating in the relationship 3:2) create scales that diverge from each other as the tones are multiplied across the keyboard. For that reason, it is not possible to tune a piano so that it can produce both pure octaves and perfect fifths.

The modern solution to this dilemma is a tuning known as equal temperament, in which the natural proportions are adjusted so that the tones can blend. Partly as a result of this compromised tuning, and partly because inherent stiffness in the strings creates a condition known as "inharmonicity," or out-of-tuneness, there is a roughness to the piano sound in the form of "beating," a sort of "wah, wah, wah" that intrudes on the beauty of a harmony.

There is a gain and a loss from this system: the serene, glowing sound of natural thirds, for example, becomes duller and rougher in modern "equal temperament" tuning. On the positive side, however, it makes the instrument more versatile by eliminating the harsh clashes, known as "wolves," that occur when pure octaves, fifths, and thirds are left to battle it out in a nontempered tuning. (The rate of the "wah, wah" sound is actually used by technicians to find a proper tuning as they tighten or loosen the piano's strings.) In some cases, the slight "beating" in the piano's harmonies actually brings more life to some of the repertoire (particularly in the works of Romantics like Chopin).

In order to maximize the acoustical beauty of the piano's sound, the thicknesses of the strings are also adjusted: stiffness in the bass end of the instrument is combated by employing "wound" strings, a steel core wrapped in a copper wire. In addition, tuners often adjust the pitch of bass notes downward and that of high treble notes upward.

The science of the piano's strings also plays a role in the instrument's ability to express a variety of tone "colors." That's because if you strike the strings with force, the higher overtones (the soft pitches that ring out above the "fundamental" tone of any vibrating object) are amplified. Strike them softly, and these added vibrations are subdued. We hear the differences as changes in "timbre."

An ancient cosmologist might note a relationship between the four components of the piano's sound (the percussive pop, singing diphthong, shimmering wave, and gradations of volume) and the primary building blocks of the world described by Empedocles in the fifth century BCE: earth, water, air, and fire. They are, it turns out, also convenient metaphors for describing the nature of the musical universe.

The element of fire, for example, suits the Combustibles, figures like the turbulent Ludwig van Beethoven, rock 'n' roll's Jerry Lee Lewis, and jazz avant-gardist Cecil Taylor, who bring edge-of-your-seat volatility to the keyboard, exploiting the piano's vast dynamic range to give birth to music that can smolder and explode.

The supple nature of water suggests the quality of the Melodists, such as Romantic composer Franz Schubert, classicist J. C. Bach, and jazz pianist George Shearing, whose streams of tones suggest sinuous waves, rising and falling and curling back on themselves in soft arabesques. Jean-Jacques Rousseau, who declared that melody was the basis of all musical expression, claimed it was born of our most primitive impulses crying for release. But others have compared melody to nature's gentle geometry: the soaring arcs of birds in flight, the spirals that build nautilus shells, the graceful undulations found in desert sands.

Air befits the world of the Alchemists, musicians such as jazz pianist Bill Evans, impressionist Claude Debussy, and bebop eccentric Thelonious Monk, who are masters of atmosphere. Combining tones (and silence) in mysterious ways, they transform the mundane ingredients of musical composition into haunting, resonant worlds, like alchemists changing ordinary lead into gold. While melody seduces, alchemy entrances.

WHERE DO THEY BELONG?

Any system of classification is certain to be artificial, and in some ways indefensible. The pitfalls are obvious: jazz pianist and composer Dick Hyman, whose knowledge is encyclopedic, kindly agreed to nominate certain pianists for these four categories, and he initially labeled Dave Brubeck a Combustible. When questioned why Brubeck would belong in that category rather than with the Rhythmitizers, Hyman mulled it over, changed his mind, and sent this response: "My thinking right now is that because of his lengthy and inventive career, despite his being both rhythmic and combustible, he should be considered a melodist." In a separate letter, he admitted that the task was proving difficult. "Let me think some more about this," he pled, "because I believe you have a poetic idea that would be an improvement on the usual chronological classification."

Classical pianist Alfred Brendel weighed in by offering this comment in a personal note: "I have written about the different characteristics of Haydn next to Mozart, about Beethoven as well as Schubert. What I try to avoid are oversimplifications like: Mozart is predominantly this, Schubert that. Great music operates on too many levels to be reduced to a few lines. If I say that Mozart's and Schubert's *Cantabile* [an interpretive style that replicates singing] are vocal while Haydn's and Beethoven's are instrumental, this has to be understood in context, and in the right way."

These warnings are well considered. Nonetheless, the following chapters will make use of the characterizations outlined here, in the belief that such schemes can be useful as a platform for presenting ideas about music—as well as for sparking discourse.

Finally, the solidity of the earth is the fundamental quality of the Rhythmitizers, like rock performer Fats Domino, Latin jazz pianist Arturo O'Farrill, and classical composer Sergei Prokofiev: musicians who take the percussive "pop" that brings every piano tone to life and place it center stage. Rhythmitizers bring the swing to jazz, the spice to salsa, and the trance to minimalism. If melody tugs at the heart, rhythm's symphony of pulses ignites the rest of the body's musculature with music that twitches, lurches, taps its feet, and wriggles its hips.

No musician can be forced into just one of these types. Beethoven might unleash fireworks in one moment and conjure angelic reveries in the next. Most great artists find the boundaries permeable. Indeed, these essential musical elements are usually intertwined; almost all melodies are infused with a rhythmic contour. Still, composers, improvisers, and interpreters, no matter how chameleon-like, tend to display particular traits in their pieces, and history often remembers them in that light. For that reason, it's often possible to place diverse artists who worked continents and centuries apart, and in vastly different genres, within these four basic rubrics.

CHAPTER 7

The Combustibles

PART 1 *The New Testament*

M OZART'S ASSESSMENT of Clementi as a musical robot was at least partly a result of their conflicting agendas. The Italian-by-way-of-England Clementi had fostered an approach designed to dazzle an audience with technical prowess. (He said as much as he reflected on the competition with Mozart during an interview in 1806, adding that later in his life he managed to develop a more "melodic and noble style.") Some of his keyboard fireworks, like the precarious leaps and difficult double-note passages, were culled from Domenico Scarlatti's harpsichord music, a medium little concerned with pianistic nuance (though even Chopin saw the underlying value of Scarlatti's music, and assigned it to his students). Mozart certainly had technical command, but his art was centered on the ability of the piano's tones to embody a living narrative, to express the human condition through the language of music, rather than merely to generate momentary excitement.

Pianists today still reflect those opposing sensibilities. Some amaze through athletic prowess, others probe the human heart in its many guises. Both of these traits find vital expression in the tradition of the Combustibles: musicians whose volatile, unpredictable music echoes life's erratic tides. C. P. E. Bach was the movement's godfather. Mozart inherited its power. But perhaps no one better exemplified the Combustibles than the piano's second great superstar, Ludwig van Beethoven (1770–1827).

Romantic-era pianist Hans von Bülow perfectly captured Beethoven's significance when he described J. S. Bach's *Well-Tempered Clavier* as music's "Old Testament," and Beethoven's Piano Sonatas as its "New Testament." Less than a century separates these two monumental collections, yet the analogy seems apt. Bach summarized all that had come before; Beethoven pointed toward the future. Bach's music rings with heavenly certitude; Beethoven's radiates human struggle.

His life was as complex and outsized as his art—a roller-coaster ride of willful strife, earthy humor, crushing loneliness, explosive rage, and spiritual triumph. Beethoven's music similarly "takes at times the majestic flight of an eagle, and then creeps in rocky pathways," as an 1810 review in the Parisian *Tablettes de Polymnie* reported. "He first fills the soul with sweet melancholy, and then shatters it by a mass of barbarous chords. He seems to harbor together doves and crocodiles."

This description especially befits Beethoven's most intimate creations, the string quartets and piano sonatas—vehicles that served as his testing ground for new ideas. Many of his thirty-two piano sonatas, though experimental, are nonetheless beloved—especially the ones that have acquired nicknames: the dreamy "Moonlight" (Beethoven never called it that, and found its overblown eminence annoying); the tragic "Pathétique"; the blustery "Tempest"; the wistful "Les Adieux"; the monumental "Hammerklavier"; the rhythmically driven "Waldstein"; the tempestuous "Appassionata." None have the soaring melodies of a Chopin or Rachmaninoff. Yet a haunting beauty inhabits them all.

WHAT'S A SONATA? WHAT DOES ITS NUMBER MEAN?

The term "sonata" has been used in a variety of ways. It may simply indicate a piece (often in three or four movements) that is performed on an instrument rather than sung. Some of the first piano sonatas, like those of Scarlatti, are in simple binary form (an "A" section is played and repeated, followed by a "B" section that is played and repeated). But the phrase "sonata form" generally refers to a compositional design that came to prominence in the classical era in which a theme is sent on a metaphorical journey. After its initial statement, the theme moves away from its home key, explores new territory, meets other themes, develops, and finally returns once again to the key in which it began. There was no single way of constructing a sonata, however: in the hands of various composers, the scheme appeared in endless subtle variations. Some composers, like Beethoven, pushed the boundaries of the form until it was barely recognizable.

The numbers attached to the titles of these works are simply methods of cataloging. An opus number usually reflects that chronological place a work has in the career of a composer; but, as in the case of some of Beethoven's piano sonatas (op. 31, no. 1; op. 31, no. 2; and op. 31, no. 3), several pieces may share the same opus. The works of some composers have been organized by individual catalogers: J. S. Bach's "BWV" numbers indicate the Bach-Werke-Verzeichnis (Bach Works Catalog) system, created by German musicologist Wolfgang Schmieder in 1950, which groups the music thematically; Scarlatti's music (Domenico's, as opposed to his father, Alessandro's) has been labeled in three different systems—"K." numbers (set by Ralph Kirkpatrick), "L." numbers (by Alessandro Longo), and "P." numbers (by Giorgio Pestelli); Mozart's music carries "K." numbers as well, but these were assigned by Ludwig Ritter von Köchel, a composer, writer, and botanist; Haydn's "Hob." numbers refer to Anthony van Hoboken; and Schubert's "D." numbers are chronologically ordered according to Otto Erich Deutsch. Many other composers have been cataloged through special classification systems created by their devotees.

They each contain wonderfully memorable moments, like the hilarious opening of op. 31, no. 1, which seems to poke fun at pianists who can't manage to strike the keys with their left and right hands at precisely the same time; or the poignant juxtaposition of the sacred and the earthy in his penultimate sonata, op. 110, which uses a quote from the lament sung at Christ's death in J. S. Bach's *St. John Passion*, along with two folk songs, "Our Cat Had Kittens" and "I Am Down and Out"—a divine dove cohabiting with a pair of crocodiles. There is the stunning suspension of time in his last sonata, op. 111, where delicate trills grow into a shimmering, pervasive cosmic harmony, like the Big Bang in slow motion.

His was an art of severe contrasts. In his day, the Viennese were noted for the clarity and precision of their playing, the Londoners for their "singing" tone. As a pianist, Beethoven, the pounder, fit neither model. He was even accused of being abusive toward the instrument. Evidence of his piano style can be found in the printed music, where (as in the first movement of the "Moonlight" Sonata) the sustain pedal might be held down for long stretches, creating a pileup of irreconcilable tones. Some critics blamed his diminishing hearing. One essayist in Paris stated flatly that because of this loss, "accumulations of notes of the most monstrous kind sounded in his head as acceptable and well-balanced combinations." Of course, on Beethoven's piano the colliding sounds would have faded more rapidly than on a modern instrument, and such effects were not entirely without precedent.

But accounts of his performances bolster the image of a player who simply went to extremes. His pupil Carl Czerny reported that "the weak and imperfect pianofortes of his time could not withstand his gigantic style"; when composer Anton Reicha turned pages for Beethoven during the performance of a Mozart concerto, he found himself "mostly occupied in wrenching the strings of the pianoforte which snapped, while the hammers stuck among the broken strings. Beethoven insisted on finishing the concerto, and so back and forth I leaped, jerking out a string, disentangling a hammer, turning a page, and I worked harder than Beethoven."

BEETHOVEN CLEANS THE KEYBOARD *by Ferdinand Ries*

One evening at Count Browne's I was to play a Beethoven sonata (A minor, op. 23), a work not often heard. . . . As usual, Beethoven turned pages for me. At a leap in the left hand, where one particular note must be brought out, I missed the note completely, and Beethoven tapped me on the head with one finger. Princess L. who sat leaning against the piano facing me, noticed this with a smile. . . .

Later that evening Beethoven was also obliged to play and chose the D minor Sonata (op. 31 no. 2), which had just been published. The Princess, who probably expected that Beethoven too would make a mistake somewhere, now stood behind his chair while I turned pages. In bars 53 and 54 Beethoven missed the entry . . . It sounded as if the piano was being cleaned. The Princess rapped him several times on the head, not at all delicately, saying: "If the pupil receives one tap of the finger for one missed note, then the Master must be punished with a full hand for worse mistakes." Everyone laughed, Beethoven most of all. He started again and performed marvelously.

Pianos weren't the only objects endangered in his presence. Ferdinand Ries recalled that Beethoven "rarely picked up anything without dropping or breaking it. Thus he frequently knocked his inkwell into the piano, which stood beside his writing desk. No piece of furniture was safe from him, least of all anything valuable. Everything was knocked over, soiled, or destroyed. How he ever managed to shave himself at all remains difficult to understand, even considering the frequent cuts on his cheeks." Little wonder his apartment was a calamitous mess.

He had a notoriously short fuse, and could throw a plate of food at the head of his waiter while lunching at the Swan Inn; but his targets ranged all the way up and down the social ladder. Once, as he and literary luminary Johann Wolfgang von Goethe were on a walk and came face to face with members of the nobility, the poet stepped aside, and Beethoven refused to budge. "When two persons like

Goethe and I meet these grand folk," he wrote in August of 1812, "they must be made to see what our sort consider great."

This brute of a man was nevertheless capable of extraordinary tenderness. When Baroness Dorothea Ertmann, a fine pianist to whom Beethoven dedicated his A Major Piano Sonata, op. 101, lost a three-year-old son in 1804, she was inconsolable, yet found it impossible to weep. Beethoven summoned her to his home. Years later she told Felix Mendelssohn that when she arrived, Beethoven sat at the piano and stated, "We will now talk to each other in tones." He played for more than an hour, until Ertmann began to sob. "I felt as if I were listening to choirs of angels celebrating the entrance of my poor child into the world of light," she reported to her niece.

Beethoven and the Blind Maiden, *by Friedrich Bodenmüller (1845–1913). An artist's rendering of Beethoven conjuring the healing angels*

Beneath the roiling surface, Beethoven was a fragile poet. He was perpetually falling in love, and nearly always found it unrequited. He suffered from a host of infirmities, not the least of which was the progressive deafness that descended on him like a dark cloud while he was still in his twenties. In 1810, after a decade of suffering from that loss, he wrote, "If I had not read somewhere that man must not voluntarily part with his life as long as he can still perform a good deed, I would long ago have ceased to be—and, indeed, by my own hand." The affliction, he said, had left his life "poisoned forever." The "good deed" he pledged to continue was his gifting of great music to the world.

L IKE ALL COMBUSTIBLES, Beethoven's musical lineage began with Carl Philipp Emanuel Bach. While still a twelve-year-old living in Bonn, Beethoven studied with Christian Gottlob Neefe, a self-taught composer and organist who had used C. P. E.'s book *Essay on the True Art of Playing Keyboard Instruments* as a principal guide for his own education. He turned to it again for instructing young Beethoven, and the influence is easy to hear. Carl Philipp Emanuel's approach to music was often explosive, shifting moods on a moment's whim, the musical lines scampering and stalling, simmering and exploding like a teapot being moved on and off a burner.

In Bach's generation, similar tendencies were budding through-out the arts. Late-eighteenth-century garden designs, for example, highlighted nature's unruly freedom by intentionally pitting the wild against the cultivated—an approach that became known as "picturesque." "The Father of the Picturesque," William Gilpin, described it as a kind of artistic vandalism. "A piece of Palladian architecture may be elegant in the last degree," he claimed, but "should we wish to give it picturesque beauty, we must use the mallet instead of the chisel; we must beat down one half of it, deface the other, and throw the mutilated members around in heaps; in short, from a *smooth* building we must turn it into a *rough* ruin."

The *Maga₇in der Musik* saw C. P. E. Bach's music in just that light. "The greatest virtuosos who have been here in Hamburg, and stood beside him when, in just the right mood, he improvised," wrote editor Carl Friedrich Cramer, "have been astounded at his bold ideas and transitions, his daring," and his unprecedented shifts from one key to another—the way, that is, that he took a mallet to earlier rules of style. Charles Burney visited C. P. E. and left an account of the experience. "After dinner, which was elegantly served, and cheerfully eaten," he wrote, "I prevailed upon him to sit down again to a clavichord, and he played, with little intermission, till near eleven o'clock at night. During this time, he grew so animated and *possessed*, that he not only played, but looked like one inspired. His eyes were fixed, his under lip fell, and drops of effervescence distilled from his countenance. He said, if he were to be set to work frequently in this manner, he should grow young again."

In literary circles, that same volcanic quality became associated with an artistic movement known as Sturm und Drang (storm and stress) that swept through Europe on a wave of hysteria. Glorifying inner psychological struggle and hopeless love, it left a pile of youthful suicides in its wake following Goethe's *Sorrows of Young Werther* (first published in 1774), an epistolary novel in which the heartbroken protagonist ended his own life. *Werther* sparked imitators everywhere: hordes of young men adopted the character's style of dress (a blue coat and yellow breeches), and some also copied his actions.

Meanwhile, in the world of painting, artists like Henry Fuseli added to the general atmosphere of melodrama and dread with works like *The Nightmare* and *Horseman Attacked by a Giant Snake.* C. P. E. Bach was the composer who brought this disquieting quality to music, suddenly registering emotions in high definition—as something fluid, intense, uncontrollably alive. He even insisted that musicians experience these affects themselves, in order to communicate them fully to listeners.

Joseph Haydn

Composer Franz Joseph Haydn (1732–1809), Mozart's friend and Beethoven's teacher, took note, and developed his own version of the picturesque in works filled with quirkiness, novelty, and whim; it was a celebration of the unexpected. Mozart said that Haydn could shock like no one else. That was before Beethoven came along.

D ESPITE THEIR DEARTH of hummable tunes, Beethoven's sonatas grip us and refuse to let go. This is often due to his brilliant treatment of the simplest materials—there is genius hidden in the architectural scaffolding. His use of small musical cells as building blocks that reappear throughout a work in myriad permutations is a prominent feature even in his very first piano sonata, op. 2, no. 1. It opens with a rising figure (known in his day as a "Mannheim Rocket") that is methodically shortened and fragmented as it is repeated. With every contraction the theme gains in coiled energy, until it is whittled down to a single, explosive chord that triggers a dramatic release, like a sharp quill freeing the air from an inflated balloon.

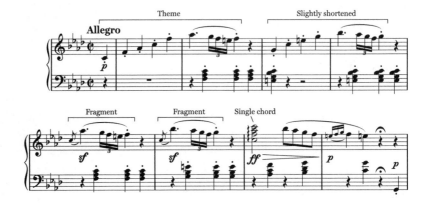

Opening of Beethoven Sonata op. 2, no. 1. The theme is increasingly shortened until it becomes a single chord.

The idea of manipulating tiny themes in this way is something he picked up from his teacher Haydn. (Beethoven once claimed you couldn't learn anything from Haydn, but his music says otherwise.) He never lost interest in it, or in the aesthetic principle expressed by the poet Friedrich Schiller—whose "Ode to Joy" Beethoven adapted for the finale of his Ninth Symphony—in which contrary forces clash in mutual destruction, leading to the creation of a new, joyful unity. Beethoven's musical constructions frequently mirrored this philosophical narrative. (When a biographer of his, Anton Schindler, a man whose personality, remarked one prominent conductor, was "as spare as his figure and as dry as his facial features," asked Beethoven about two of his piano works, the composer described them as "a contest between two principles, or a dialogue between two persons.") And so he wrote works of impeccable logic, seeding them, as in his first piano sonata, with a kind of musical DNA. Yet, he also shattered the old forms by setting in motion strange convergences and outlandish collisions, even blurring distinctions between endings and beginnings. In the end, he always managed to arrive at a moment of transcendent beauty.

As a result, Beethoven's works manage to be both solidly organic and unsettled at the same time: it is music that bristles with violence, but also entrances with tenderness; it is obstinate, and also accepting.

Beethoven's ability to transform the most ordinary materials into something utterly awe-inspiring was perhaps his greatest gift. Publisher Anton Diabelli famously sent an undistinguished waltz theme in 1819 to every important composer he could think of, including Franz Schubert and a pre-teen Franz Liszt, along with a request to each for a variation on it. He received fifty affirmative replies. Beethoven at first refused to join the pack, but then created his own set of variations on Diabelli's mundane piece, which he regarded as a mere "cobbler's patch." The result was his magnificent group of thirty-three *Diabelli Variations*. In the words of pianist Alfred Brendel, Beethoven took Diabelli's rather prosaic theme and left it "improved, parodied, ridiculed, disclaimed, transfigured, mourned, stamped out and finally uplifted." It is, like much of Beethoven's art, a bridge from the silly to the sublime.

Aldous Huxley mused in his novel *Point Counter Point* about how writers could emulate the techniques of this towering figure: "Meditate on Beethoven. The changes of moods, the abrupt transitions . . . More interesting still, the modulations, not merely from one key to another, but from mood to mood. A theme is stated, then developed, pushed out of shape, imperceptibly deformed, until, though still recognizably the same, it has become quite different." In a novel, the "transitions are easy enough," Huxley said. "All you need is a sufficiency of characters and parallel, contrapuntal plots. While Jones is murdering a wife, Smith is wheeling the perambulator in the park. You alternate the themes."

If only it were that simple. Beethoven's imagination produced works so daunting that scholar and pianist Charles Rosen believes they led to the great shift in music making from the home parlor back to the concert hall. He cited the time that Beethoven's student Carl Czerny informed him of a lady in Vienna "who has been practicing your B-flat Sonata for a month, and she still can't play the beginning." It was no surprise that she couldn't: even his trendily popular works, like the "Moonlight" Sonata, required tremendous technical skill. His true masterpieces, such as the last piano sonatas (of which that one in B-flat, op. 106, known as the "Hammerklavier," is a trial by fire even for professionals), brought the art of piano playing to the very pinnacle of difficulty, and splendor.

His works, representing a lifetime of searching, were embraced by the next generations of musicians with a nearly sacred sense of adoration. "Beethoven's music," wrote his contemporary the writer, critic, and composer E. T. A. Hoffmann, "sets in motion the lever of fear, of awe, of horror, of suffering, and awakens just that infinite longing which is the essence of romanticism." On an evening in 1837, a decade after his passing, a small group of musical friends gathered in the salon of writer Ernest Legouvé. Franz Liszt seated himself at the piano when the room, which had been lit by a single candle, was suddenly plunged into darkness. "Whether by chance or by some unconscious influence," remembered Legouvé, Liszt "began the funereal and heart-rending adagio of [Beethoven's] Sonata in C-sharp minor [the 'Moonlight']. The rest of us remained rooted to the spot where we happened to be, no one attempting to move . . . I had dropped into an armchair, and above my head heard stifled sobs and moans. It was Berlioz."

I F THE common image of Beethoven is of a man shaking his fists at the heavens, that of another icon among the Combustibles, Franz Liszt (1811–1886), is of a Greek god descended to earth. He certainly looked the part. Danish writer Hans Christian Andersen called him "the modern Orpheus . . . When Liszt entered the salon," he reported, "it was as if an electric shock passed through it. Most of the ladies rose . . . a ray of sunlight passed over every face."

All accounts describe him as tall, thin, and pale. One of his loves, Marie d'Agoult, was struck by his "great sea-green eyes in which glistened swift flashes of light like waves catching the sunlight." He wore his "perfectly lank hair so long that it spreads over his shoulders," wrote Charles Hallé, which created an odd appearance at times, "for when he gets a bit excited and gesticulates, it falls right

over his face and one sees nothing but his nose." It must have been a common occurrence because, as Hallé noted, "this curious figure is in perpetual motion: now he stamps with his feet, now waves his arms in the air, now he does this, now that."

His audiences couldn't get enough of it, or of the music he produced. Caroline Boissier, the mother of Liszt's young Swiss student Valérie, witnessed her daughter's lessons. "To tell you that his fingers have the speed of lightning, and sometimes the vehemence and might of thunder, to tell you that he accelerates certain *agitati* to the point of breathlessness," she wrote breathlessly, "and that these stormy moments are followed by a soft abandonment, a melancholy full of grace and feeling, and then by magnificent audacity and noble enthusiasm, would be to speak to you in an unknown language, since, not having heard him, you can have no idea of what he is like . . . One no longer hears the piano—but storms, prayers, songs of triumph, transports of joy, heart-rending despair." Hyperbolic as that sounds, the best musicians of his time agreed.

ABOVE LEFT
Franz Liszt as a young man

ABOVE RIGHT
Liszt in his later years

Liszt's exciting style, which masterfully combined the musical and the theatrical, owed much to two important models. The first was his piano teacher Carl Czerny. When this former student of Beethoven's first allowed Liszt to audition, the prodigy was a mere eight years old: "a pale, delicate-looking child," remembered Czerny, "and while playing he swayed about on the seat as though drunk, so that I often thought he would fall to the floor . . . I was amazed at the talent with which Nature had endowed him." The older pianist took him in hand.

Liszt's only teacher before Czerny had been his father, who rewarded his precocious son with "a couple of good slaps" for daring to attempt Beethoven's great "Hammerklavier" Sonata (the one that poor lady in Vienna couldn't even begin). It "hardly reformed me," he reported, and the piece remained close to his heart throughout his life. But by the age of twelve, the time for any such restraints was long gone. After Liszt performed in a small Viennese hall, the London journal *The Harmonicon* announced, "He is already placed by the side of the greatest pianoforte players of the present day." Thanks to Czerny, Beethoven attended this event; at the end of the concert, he embraced the young pianist and kissed him on the forehead. Some took it as an anointing.

The other great influence on Liszt was violinist Niccolò Paganini, a musician who threw off such sparks when he played that nearly everyone believed there was sorcery at work. In 1831, when he was nineteen, Liszt attended Paganini's Paris debut and resolved on the spot to do by means of the piano what Paganini had accomplished with his violin.

Composer Hector Berlioz described Paganini as "a man with

Liszt in concert, from a Hungarian magazine, April 6, 1873. Drawings by János Jánko

long hair, piercing eyes and a strange, ravaged countenance." His personal doctor, Francesco Bennati, supplied more details: Paganini, he reported, was of average height and "his thinness and his lack of teeth, which gives him a sunken mouth and more prominent chin, make his physiognomy appear to be of a more advanced age. His large head, held up by a long, thin neck, appears at first glance to be rather strongly out of proportion to his delicate limbs . . . The left shoulder is an inch higher than the right . . ."

The critic of the *Leipziger Musikalische Zeitung* explained the effect this unattractive man had on his audience: there is "something so demonic in his appearance that at one moment we seek the 'hidden cloven hoof,' at the next, the 'wings of an angel,' " he wrote. "He threw me into hysterics," confessed Mary Shelley. The great Goethe was actually rendered speechless: "I heard something simply meteoric and was unable to understand it."

The writer Stendhal encouraged the buzz, claiming that Paganini's abilities were not due to conservatory training, but were "a consequence of an error in love, which, it is said, caused him to be thrown into prison for many years. Alone and abandoned . . . nothing remained to him but his violin. He learned to translate his soul into sounds." And the violinist took every advantage of this folk-legend status. Commenting on two pieces he wrote in 1828 that contained an impressive effect known as "double stops" (harmonies played on two strings at a time), he revealed himself as a showman in complete control of his resources—he knew just how his public would respond. "One made listeners cry," he stated with satisfaction. "The other, entitled 'Religious,' made the audience feel contrite."

ON-STAGE CHARISMA *by André Watts*

What does it mean to have the kind of stage charisma that Liszt enjoyed? One big aspect is simply the ability to communicate with an audience. Some pianists seem to be playing just for themselves. They like to peer inside the music, but don't hold the picture up for the public.

Establishing a connection with the audience involves a bit of magic. As Josef Hofmann said, we are all playing a percussion instrument, pretending to make it sing. But the unreasoning interior belief that you have accomplished this can be very powerful. It is the real core of being an exciting performer.

Unfortunately, performers with a lot of charisma are sometimes accused of superficiality. It seems to me that this has less to do with the music than it does with human limitations. There are pianists with absolutely nothing to communicate who are considered profound simply because of the boredom they engender. Curiously, many people are afraid to connect profundity with fun. Herbert von Karajan was considered a more profound conductor than Leonard Bernstein because he kept his eyes closed, while Bernstein liked to dance around on the podium. But that's nonsense. Does the fact that Beethoven displays a good sense of humor in his music make him less deep?

Similarly, although we applaud an athlete for his or her skillful ease of execution, a pianist who looks like he is struggling to produce what is inside the music is assumed to be a deep thinker when, actually, it just means he is struggling. Frankly, when I pay my money to attend a performance, I don't want to hear struggle—you were supposed to have struggled last month, in your practice room!

And that brings up another aspect of this dynamic: we often resent a pianist who makes it look effortless. Sometimes this stirs up feelings of envy—it just doesn't seem fair! And this same way of thinking can extend to an artist who is prolific—imagine the criticism Schubert would receive were he writing today!—or multifaceted.

Chefs often say that people eat with their eyes. But something that looks light might be heavy, and vice versa. The same is true of musicians.

Liszt could be equally calculating. Friedrich Wieck, Clara's father and piano teacher (and Schumann's teacher as well), witnessed a Liszt performance in 1838. "He played the Fantasy on a C. Graf [a piano made by Conrad Graf], burst two bass strings, personally fetched a second C. Graf in walnut wood from the corner and played his Etude. After breaking yet another two strings he loudly informed the public that since it didn't satisfy him, he would play it again [on a third piano]. As he began, he vehemently threw his gloves and handkerchief on the floor."

Those gloves often came in handy. At one concert in 1846, he dropped a pair and started a near riot as a group of women rushed to seize them. They cut the material into fragments and shared the pieces. The gesture was typical of Liszt, though he probably got the idea from Czerny, who expressed definite notions about how to make an entrance. Begin, he said, with bows toward the principal boxes, then toward the sides, and lastly toward the middle. After this, the performer can take his seat—but not without "depositing his dress hat and drawing out his white handkerchief." Dropping gloves was simply Liszt's additional flourish. (No teacher could bestow the innate talent it took to pull it off, of course. Liszt had no choice but to tell his American student William Mason: "You lack my personality!")

In the twentieth century, jazz celebrity Jelly Roll Morton would carry on this stylish tradition, making it a point, after a dramatic arrival, to remove his overcoat, fold it, and place it in plain view of his audience so that its fancy silk lining would be clearly visible, before carefully wiping off the piano bench or stool with a large silk handkerchief.

Liszt's recitals—he called them *monologues pianistiques*—were unusual in featuring a lone performer instead of a variety show. Thus he announced, with self-described impudence, "Le concert, c'est moi" (I am the concert) in imitation of Louis XIV, who famously declared that *he* was the state. (Another pianist, Ignaz Moscheles [1794–1870], had actually established the solo recital a few years earlier with a series he called Classical Piano Soirées.) Despite the absence of collaborators at a Liszt event, there was no lack of entertainment. He used every trick in the book. At a concert in 1835, he actually fainted in the arms of the page turner. "We bore him out in a strong fit of hysterics," reported Henry Reeve, who later became editor of the *Edinburgh Review*. "As I handed Mme de Circourt to her carriage, we both trembled like poplar leaves, and I tremble scarcely less as I write."

CREATIVE FAINTING *by Wanda Landowska*

A certain pianist . . . hired women for twenty francs a concert to simulate fainting in the midst of his playing of a fantasia [that he] attacked so fast that it would have been humanly impossible to carry on at that speed to the end. Once, in Paris, the hired woman, having fallen soundly asleep, missed her cue; the pianist was playing Weber's Concerto. Counting on the fainting of this woman to interrupt the finale, he had started it at an impossible tempo. What to do? Flounder like a vulgar pianist or simulate a lapse of memory? No, he simply played the role of the hired woman and fainted himself. The audience rushed to the help of the pianist, who was all the more phenomenal, since he added to his lightning performance a fragile and sensitive nature. He was carried backstage; men applauded frantically, women waved their handkerchiefs, and the fainting woman, waking up, really fainted, perhaps in despair at having missed her cue.

FROM *Landowska on Music*

Liszt's improvisational skill was also a big draw. In Milan, a silver chalice was placed at the entrance of the hall, into which people slipped little pieces of paper on which they had written themes for him to use as a springboard. Liszt was taken aback by some of the notes. One said, "Milan Cathedral." Another, written by a man "struck by the advantage there would be in having oneself transported from Milan to Venice in six hours, gave me for a theme: the railway," the pianist wrote to violinist Lambert Massart. "I hastened to open the final note. What do you think I found this time? One of the most important questions of human life to be decided by arpeggios . . . *Is it better to marry or remain a bachelor?*" Liszt's wise reply: "Whatever the decision that you reach, whether to marry or remain single, it is certain that you will always regret it."

But the main attraction was his spellbinding artistry. Liszt's playing was often bombastic, searing, and jaw-dropping—qualities that can be found in his Piano Concertos and in many solo piano works, like his demonic set of *Mephisto Waltzes*. Philosopher Friedrich Nietzsche wrote to Liszt that in his search to find someone who grasped the true essence of what he called the "Dionysian"—reflecting the character of Dionysus, god of ecstasy and intoxication—"it is to you above all that my eyes turn again and again."

The pianist's technical wizardry was helped along by new developments in the instrument that allowed for greater speed across the keyboard. He also had a secret weapon: a practice piano with keys that only moved when tremendous exertion was applied. "I had it made specially, so that when I have played *one* scale on it I have played ten; it is a thoroughly impossible piano," he explained to Wilhelm von Lenz, after mischievously allowing the amateur pianist to struggle with it during an audition.

PLAYING LISZT IS NOT EASY *by Alfred Brendel*

Often, it is only one step from the sublime to the ridiculous.

The [Liszt] pianist should be careful not to take that step. It is up to him whether pathos turns into bathos, whether Liszt's heroic fire freezes into a heroic pose, whether his rapt lyricism is smothered under perfumed affectation. He should give the passages of religious meditation simplicity, bring out the devilry behind the capriciousness, and convey the profound resignation behind the strangely bleak experience of his late works.

—EXCERPTED FROM "LISZT MISUNDERSTOOD," IN *Brendel on Music*

Liszt's style was in complete contrast to that of his biggest competitor, Sigismond Thalberg, with whom he "dueled" at a concert in 1827. According to one witness, Liszt was "constantly tossing back his long hair, his lips quivering, his nostrils palpitating," while Thalberg "entered noiselessly" almost "without displacing the air. After a dignified greeting that seemed a trifle cold in manner, he seated himself at the piano as though upon an ordinary chair." Liszt, the man Heine called "the Attila, the scourge of God," was anything but cold, on stage or off.

His numerous affairs included several with notorious women like Marie d'Agoult, who described herself as "six inches of snow covering twenty feet of lava"; Countess Marie von Mouchanoff, a powerful socialite, described by Heine as "a Pantheon in which so many great men lie buried"; Carolyne zu Sayn-Wittgenstein, the cigar-smoking princess; and Countess Olga Janina, who, in a jealous rage, threatened Liszt's life with a poisoned dagger and a revolver, and ultimately sent scandalous articles about him to his most powerful acquaintances, including the Grand Duke of Weimar and the Pope. There were consequences to his reckless behavior: he managed to alienate his good friend Frédéric Chopin—who once announced, "I wish I could steal his manner of rendering my own Etudes"—by having a tryst with Marie Pleyel, wife of the piano manufacturer, in Chopin's apartment.

But Liszt was also an intellectual explorer and a spiritual seeker. His musical experiments influenced nearly every important composer who followed. Liszt's ambiguous, radical harmonies in his late piano piece *Nuages Gris* (*Grey Clouds*), for example, anticipated the impressionists, as did the watery cascades in works like his *Les jeux d'eaux à la Villa d'Este* (*The Fountains of the Villa d'Este*). Meanwhile, his ferocity captivated other Romantic pianist-composers, like Charles-Valentin Alkan and Anton Rubinstein. And his melodic reveries wound their way into the music of countless leading composers, including Richard Wagner (his son-in-law).

He had expressed interest in religious matters from an early age, even attending meetings of the Saint-Simonians, a sect deeply concerned with social equality, the emancipation of women, and the fair distribution of wealth. He took minor Holy Orders in 1865, and though the historian Ferdinand Gregorovius, who saw him in Rome, suggested he was "Mephistopheles disguised as an Abbé," Liszt was well known for his many kindnesses. (Chief among these was his impressive ability to forgive wrongdoing. Typical was his instruction to Princess Carolyne on how to treat the irascible and erratic Richard Wagner. "He is sick and incurable," wrote the pianist. "That is why we must simply love him and try to serve him as best we can.") He created piano arrangements of Beethoven symphonies, Wagner operas, Schubert songs, and music by Saint-Saëns, Berlioz, Chopin, and others, specifically to speed the dissemination of works by those composers he admired. His tender side was expressed musically as well. It can be heard in many of his lyrical piano pieces, like the *Liebesträume*, and the *Six Consolations*, where sumptuous phrases glisten like pearls against a plush background of undulating harmonies. When he wasn't setting a hall ablaze, this was the quality he brought to his piano playing. It could break your heart.

PART 2 *Still Setting Blazes*

THE COMBUSTIBLES tradition lived on after Liszt in the works of musicians like the Eastern Europeans Béla Bartók (1881–1945) and Zoltán Kodály (1882–1967). Both men were attracted to vital folk traditions that grew in the wild, far from civilization's meddling ways. Collecting Hungarian, Romanian, Bulgarian, and Slovak peasant tunes and dances, they used them as models, and created music filled with pounding, irregular rhythms and prickly harmonies. More than one observer found the results hard to take. Frederick Corder, in the *Musical Quarterly* of July 1915, decided Bartók's pieces represented "the composer promenading the keyboard in his boots." The eminent Percy A. Scholes, writing in London's *The Observer* in May of 1923, announced that in the

Béla Bartók with pianist György Sandor

presence of Bartók's music he "suffered more than upon any occasion . . . apart from an incident or two connected with 'painless dentistry.'" Yet, by mid-century (especially after Bartók's death), this music was widely accepted and even celebrated as essential to the Western canon.

In Russia, Igor Stravinsky (1882–1971), the grand master of twentieth-century music, also turned to irregular accents and provocative, explosive sounds to rouse his listeners. Stravinsky underwent stylistic changes throughout his life, crafting tone paintings of Russian peasant culture (in ballets like *The Firebird* and *The Rite of Spring*), mischievous caricatures of popular styles (such as his *Ragtime* of 1918, an odd, cubist version of early jazz), and even uncompromising abstract works. But rhythmic drive and an anarchist's sensibility were always at its core.

Conductor Pierre Monteux responded with shock as Stravinsky played a piano reduction of his revolutionary *Rite of Spring* in 1912: "Before he got very far I was convinced he was raving mad . . . The very walls resounded as Stravinsky pounded away, occasionally stamping his feet and jumping up and down." (Stravinsky's foot stamping was apparently a regular practice. At a rehearsal of the ballet before its premiere, remembered dancer Marie Rambert, Stravinsky "pushed aside the fat German pianist, nicknamed Kolossal by Diaghilev, and proceeded to play twice as fast as we had been doing and twice as fast as we could possibly dance. He stamped his feet on the floor and banged his fist on the piano and sang and shouted.")

Stravinsky aimed in *The Rite of Spring* to grab the listener by the collar rather than the heartstrings. He conveyed the primeval essence of the ballet's story, the ritualistic sacrifice of a young virgin, by sabotaging the notion of normality at every moment. (In one famous passage, the changes in groups of accented pulses—from 9 to 2 to 6 to 3 to 4 to 5 to 3—come so swiftly, and with so much force, that they seem like an artillery barrage.)

His unruly rhythms could be unnerving, even to professional musicians. Stravinsky wrote his *Piano Rag Music* for Arthur Rubinstein, but the pianist declined to play it. "I'm more than proud to own your manuscript," he explained, "but I'm still the pianist of the old era. Your piece is written for percussion rather than for my kind of piano."

"He did not like my answer," reported Rubinstein. " 'I see that

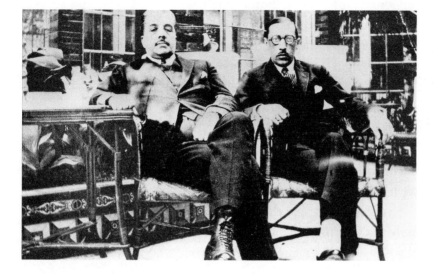

ABOVE
Stravinsky playing The Rite of Spring *by Jean Cocteau*

LEFT
Ballet impresario Sergei Diaghilev, who commissioned The Rite of Spring, *and Igor Stravinsky*

you don't understand this music,' he said a little impatiently. 'I shall play it and make it clear to you.' He then banged it out about ten times, making me more and more antagonistic to the piece. Now he became angry. A disagreeable quarrelsome exchange followed. 'You still think you can sing on the piano, but that is an illusion. The piano is nothing but a utility instrument and it sounds right only as percussion.' "

Arthur Rubinstein

The two were operating in different worlds. "You pianists become millionaires by playing the music left to you by the starving Mozart and Schubert and the poor mad Schumann, the tubercular Chopin, and the sick Beethoven," Stravinsky told Rubinstein, resentfully. "He was right," wrote Rubinstein in his autobiography *My Many Years*. "I always felt that we were vampires living off the blood of these great geniuses."

Stravinsky's own piano playing, reported American composer Elliott Carter, was "remarkable . . . filled with electricity . . . incisive but not brutal, rhythmically highly controlled yet filled with intensity so that each note was made to seem weighty and important."

His conducting had the same quality: at rehearsals in the 1920s and '30s, a typical eyewitness report pictured "a little man who bends his legs like a fencer taking guard, who splays his thighs like a horseman, who snaps his elbows back like a boxer on the attack, who looks alternately, or all at once, like a bird, an engineer, a Kobold [spirit in human form], and a surgeon."

Stravinsky's music, driven by a powerful rhythmic engine—no matter how disruptive its incessant gear shifts—was often laced with caustic collisions and biting wit. For a time, it also embodied conservative, "neoclassical" principles (as, for example, in his elegant, tightly constructed *Concerto for Two Solo Pianos,* one of the most beautiful duo-piano pieces ever written). At the end of his life, it lurched headlong into atonality, the musical language that rejects the very idea of a traditionally ordered musical universe with a tonal center. It wasn't for everyone. Yet, like the works of all of the Combustibles, it was never less than exhilarating.

The irrepressible energy of the Combustibles also erupts in more recent works by contemporary classical composers like the aforementioned Elliott Carter (b. 1908), whose 1961 Double Concerto for Harpsichord and Piano with Two Chamber Orchestras—declared by Igor Stravinsky the first true American masterpiece—produces a swirl of sounds so dense and furious that the music might be likened to an orchestral traffic jam. Like C. P. E. Bach, Carter creates music populated by human characters. Indeed, much of his chamber music, like the 1997 Quintet for Piano and String Quartet, is like a raucous family gathering. The music unfolds like a scene at a holiday table: the father carves the turkey while an annoying uncle, slightly tipsy and out of tune, demands attention; at the same time, conspiratorial kids unleash some practical jokes, just as a neighbor barges in with breathless news.

Carter's restless and ever-changing musical textures arise through that sort of emotional counterpoint, with each instrument (or, in a solo work, each theme) representing a particular psychological state. As his personalities move through a range of rhythms and sonorities—sometimes at different speeds and at cross purposes—the result is explosive and unpredictable. He is considered by many to be the greatest composer of his era. Well past the age of one hundred he continues to produce music prolifically, with increasing attention to the piano.

THE CLASSICAL WORLD was not alone in pursuing these tumultuous qualities. In the mid-twentieth century a new audience ripe for "storm and stress" emerged: modern American teenagers, who found in the brash, unruly world of rock 'n' roll a perfect outlet for their sense of alienation (and hormonal frenzy). Like the social fabric of C. P. E. Bach's Germany, America in the 1950s offered a facade of cheerful orderliness beneath which simmered a current of pent-up, wayward emotions. Eventually, a firestorm was inevitable. And renegade pianist Jerry Lee Lewis (b. 1935) happily applied the accelerant.

One of his biographers, Nick Tosches, described a television appearance by the rocker hosted by Steve Allen. "He sat at the big piano and he looked sideways at the camera, eyeballed it the way he had looked at those girls in the Arkansas beer joint, and then he began to play the piano and howl about the shaking that was going on. He rose, still pounding, and he kicked the piano stool back. It shot across the stage, tumbling, skidding . . . Steve Allen laughed and threw the stool back, then threw other furniture, and Jerry Lee played some high notes with the heel of his shoe. Then he stopped and looked at the camera sideways again. Neither he nor Steve Allen had ever heard louder applause."

Lewis had migrated from Ferriday, Louisiana, to Memphis, Tennessee, to join Sam Phillips and his Sun Records label where rhythm-and-blues stars Howlin' Wolf, B. B. King, and Ike Turner got their start. His uninhibited style borrowed elements from each of them, including western swing, boogie-woogie, rhythm and blues, and country, a mix to which he added the feral impulses of a Louisiana puma. Many of the sounds he used were already on record: Ike Turner, playing piano for Jackie Brenston on Phillips's first produced hit, "Rocket 88" (which was released by Chess Records), employed the techniques that characterized Jerry Lee's approach, including his pounding rhythms and wild glissandos—fast, continuous streams of notes performed by sliding one's fingers or fists across the keys. But in his adoption of these standard piano "tricks," Lewis reached new levels of volatility.

On Dick Clark's television show *American Bandstand*, in 1957, reported critic Richard Corliss, "he tore through the number and, toward the end, shook his long, slicked-back blond hair until it fell forward, like a toupee attached at the brow line, virtually covering his face." It was the same effect that Liszt had achieved with his long, flowing locks and wild gyrations. "Hair wasn't supposed to do that, not in the '50s," claimed Corliss. "Jerry Lee's hair was a creature from a horror film, a

LAST MAN STANDING *Jerry Lee Lewis*

redneck monster that arose, erupted and smothered its host." Other singer-pianists were sharing the spotlight at the time—Little Richard, Ray Charles, and Jerry Lee's fellow Louisianans Fats Domino, Allen Toussaint, and Huey "Piano" Smith—but none conveyed quite that level of danger and unpredictability. The public responded by buying millions of copies of his records.

Lewis managed to match Liszt as a destroyer of pianos, too. In 1958, at a live rock extravaganza in Brooklyn's Paramount Theater, he argued forcefully with guitarist Chuck Berry over who would close the show. Berry had the final say; his contract guaranteed him the honor. So, according to Nick Tosches,

Jerry Lee Lewis

> Jerry Lee did as he was bid that night; he went on before Chuck Berry. He had the crowd screaming and rushing the stage, and when it seemed that the screams had grown loudest and the rushing most chaotic, he stood, kicked the piano stool away with violence, and broke into "Great Balls of Fire." As the screaming chaos grew suddenly and sublimely greater, he drew from his jacket a Coke bottle full of gasoline, and he doused the piano with one hand as the other hand banged out the song; and

he struck a wooden match and he set the piano aflame, and his hands, like the hands of a madman, did not quit the blazing keys, but kept pounding, until all became unknown tongues and holiness and fire, and the kids went utterly, magically berserk with the frenzy of it all; and Jerry Lee stalked backstage, stinking of gasoline and wrath.

He dared Berry to follow *that*.

Some pianists are still trying. They include conceptual artist and "environmental music" composer Annea Lockwood, who created a work entitled *Piano Burning*. Debuted in London in 1968, it requires the performer to select an upright piano in disrepair, put it in an open space with the lid closed, and set it on fire with a twist of paper doused in lighter fluid. (Optional balloons may be stapled to the piano.) "Play whatever pleases you for as long as you can," she suggests. To which any responsible writer would add, please do not try this at home.

THE JAZZ WORLD embraced the Combustible spirit too, through ferocious improvisations by pianists such as Earl "Fatha" Hines (1903–1983)—"one of those jazz artists," said composer Gunther Schuller, "for whom slowing down [was] next to impossible"—as well as perhaps the wildest pianist of all, Cecil Taylor.

Born in a small Pennsylvania town, Hines studied first with a German teacher named Von Holz, who took him through "Czerny and big books of composers like Chopin." But it wasn't long before he came into contact with a different kind of sound, and it changed his life. One day it floated down from a club above a restaurant in Pittsburgh—where he was enjoying a meal with some companions—and just grabbed him. "It had a beat and a rhythm to it that I'd never heard before," he remembered. An older cousin helped him to slip into the club unnoticed, and there at the piano was Toodle-oo Johnson, playing "Squeeze Me." Hines never looked back.

He found several pianistic models. First came pianist Jim Fellman, who "had a wonderful left hand. He didn't use his fifth finger, but stretched his fourth finger to [make harmonies] . . . When he showed me this," remembered Hines, "my hands were too small and I couldn't do it . . . but he showed me how to stretch my fingers so that in time I could." In payment for the lessons, Fellman asked for "some Mail Pouch chewing tobacco and a few bottles of beer, and some afternoon we'll go up and sit down and I'll show you a few things." It was a deal Hines could afford.

Next, "a fellow came to town from Detroit, named Johnny Watters." He was the mirror image of Fellman—he kept stretching his *right* hand. "His hand was so large he was applying the melody with his middle fingers and using his thumb and last finger for [harmonies] . . . Johnny was a guy who loved Camel cigarettes, and his beverage was gin. Between the two of them [Fellman and Watters] on different afternoons, I spent what little money I had; but by putting their two styles together I think I came up with a style of my own."

Once his eyes and ears had been opened, he learned from everyone he could. "We had met [Charles Luckeyeth] Luckey Roberts at my auntie's place . . . He had three rooms in his apartment with nothing but pianos sitting in them. One reason for this was that he had very strong hands and could break anybody's piano down. He had fingers as big as my thumbs, and I remember him playing for us on a torn-out piano, and the keys were flying out as he played!"

Then ragtime star Eubie Blake and his songwriting partner Noble Sissle came through Pittsburgh, recognized Hines's talent, and encouraged him to branch out: "If I catch you here again I'm going to take this cane and wrap it around your head," warned Blake. "You've got to get away from here." He took the advice, landing in Chicago in 1925; the town was then home to Jelly Roll Morton, King Oliver, and Louis Armstrong.

"There was an awful lot of racketeering in Chicago," recalled Hines, "and as they went on the gangsters got into bigger clubs and theatres like the Grand Theatre . . . Erskine Tate was across the street at the Vendome Theatre, where they showed movies—no sound—and had live musicians." Hines eventually played with

Tate. "Louis Armstrong and I were there together, and from the Vendome we went to our regular work." The two stuck together, performing at clubs like the Sunset, where Hines met premier dancers including Buck and Bubbles and Sammy Vanderhurst. In some ways, dancers played as large a role in the development of jazz as the instrumentalists. "They did things with their feet that looked impossible," he said.

One of those dance acts was Brown and McGraw. "She was very cute and he was a handsome little fellow, and later on they got married. They were both short, but he had sharp uniforms and she was well developed and always wore a pretty dress. They had a riff they used that later became very popular with big bands. It used to go *bomp-bomp-bomp-bu-bomp*, *bomp-bomp-bomp-bu-bomp*, and Louis used to take his trumpet and do it right with them."

Hines performed at bigger and better venues, like the Grand Terrace, owned by Al Capone, who began to think of the pianist as his personal property and sent along bodyguards to protect him when he was on the road. Over the course of a long career, he toured the world (on a U.S. State Department–sponsored tour of the Soviet

Union, he sold out the ten-thousand-seat Kiev Sports Palace, after which the Kremlin cancelled concerts in Moscow and Leningrad as being too dangerous); performed for the Pope and at the White House; and influenced countless pianists through his recordings. He almost gave up the piano in the early 1960s, ready to retire to his tobacconist's shop, anxious, he claimed, to take up bowling. But critic Stanley Dance talked him into re-emerging in 1964, at which point the pianist garnered a host of awards and captured an entirely new generation of fans.

Earl Hines
© VERYL OAKLAND

His playing was Lisztian in its showmanship and fire. "It unfolds," wrote critic Whitney Balliett,

in orchestral layers . . . He will play the first two choruses softly and out of tempo, unreeling placid chords that safely hold the kernel of the melody. By the third chorus, he will have slid into a steady but implied beat and raised his volume. Then, using steady tenths [harmonies he learned from Jim Fellman] in his left hand, he will stamp out a whole chorus of right-hand chords in between beats. He will vault into the upper register in the next chorus and wind through irregularly placed notes, while his left hand plays descending, on-the-beat chords that pass through a forest of harmonic changes. (There are so many push-me, pull-you contrasts going on in such a chorus that it is impossible to grasp it one time through.) In the next chorus—bang!—up

Cecil Taylor

goes the volume again and Hines breaks into a crazy-legged double-time-and-a-half run that may make several sweeps up and down the keyboard and that are punctuated by off-beat single notes in the left hand. Then he will throw in several fast descending two-fingered glissandos, go abruptly into an arrhythmic swirl of chords and short, broken runs and, as abruptly as he began it all, ease into an interlude of relaxed chords and poling single notes.

That maze of turbulence in a Hines solo suggests the essence of unconventional pianist Cecil Taylor (b. 1929), whose performances typically unleash an unrelenting blizzard of notes fueled by a ferocious spirit. At New York's Kool Jazz Festival in Carnegie Hall in 1984, Taylor began backstage, with wails that resonated throughout the bowels of the hall, before suddenly springing into view, dressed in white and sporting his usual array of wiry dreadlocks. Everything about the pianist, including those aggressive strands of hair that point in all directions like accusatory fingers, seems designed to project an aura of calibrated mayhem.

Once he was situated on the piano bench, Taylor swiftly struck the keyboard with his entire forearm. Within seconds, an explosion of sounds lurched and skittered from one end of the instrument to the other—gathering into prickly clumps or darting off into beads of melody. The tones swirled and crunched and thumped, pausing intermittently for just the length of a breath before rippling along again in another torrent of energy. The music began to resemble an unstable weather system. The piano rocked and shivered and moaned. And many members of the audience began pouring out through the exit doors.

Recognized for his individuality with a Guggenheim Fellowship and a MacArthur "genius" grant, the pianist nevertheless views himself as part of something larger. He has compared his improvisations to the startling, lifelike constructions of Spanish architect and sculptor Santiago Calatrava. Calatrava's curvaceous bridges and buildings—like the fifty-four-story twisting tower in Malmö, Sweden, named "Turning Torso," and Chicago's winding Spire (known by locals as "the Twizzler")—seem like forces of nature. Yet Taylor's natural world is filled, not with gentle spirals, but with randomness and fury.

He is, in fact, simply a recent link in that tradition that began with C. P. E. Bach's blazing fantasies, a celebration of the unpredictable, the impetuous, and the human spirit unbounded.

CHAPTER 8

The Alchemists

PART 1 *Chemistry*

C LAUDE DEBUSSY (1862–1918) offered audiences the antithesis of Beethoven's thunderous hammerings. Like the Zen
master who contemplates the sound of one hand clapping, Debussy
imagined a piano played entirely "without hammers," an instrument born of an ethereal world where, in Charles Baudelaire's poetic
vision, in place of percussive strikes softly intoxicating "sounds and
scents swirl together in the evening air."

Transporting us to such realms beyond the ordinary is the goal of
the Alchemists. Debussy used the term himself when, as a young
student at the Paris Conservatory, he was criticized for his breaches
of convention. "Monsieur Debussy . . . has a pronounced tendency—
too pronounced—towards an exploration of the strange," reported
the Académie des Beaux-Arts. "One has the feeling of musical color
exaggerated to the point where it causes the composer to forget the

importance of precise construction and form." In response, Debussy declared that he was not interested in "the science of the beaver"—rejecting the notion that composers should behave like nature's dutiful little construction workers—but rather "in the alchemy of sound."

His secret elixir was *harmony*: the intermingling of several pitches all sounding at once. His harmonies did not behave according to the traditional formulas, however, which had evolved from simple beginnings in the medieval church into a complex system known as "tonality." Debussy tossed aside these long-established rules of musical syntax, and set out on a new path.

Debussy found the inspiration for his new musical approach in the hothouse of the French avant-garde, where, on the cusp of the twentieth century, poets, painters, and musicians all fervently sought hidden "correspondences" between various sensory impressions. (The idea was not entirely new. The German Romantic writer Novalis had proclaimed, nearly a century before, that words themselves think, paint, and sing.) Their gathering place was a bookshop named L'Art Indépendant, where patrons included symbolist poet Stéphane Mallarmé and Debussy's favorite painter, Gustave Moreau, along with such remarkable artists as Edgar Degas and Henri de Toulouse-Lautrec. All worked toward a new artistic language: "liberated from convention," said Baudelaire, and "intensely aware of mystery." Their ideal was the dream world described by an opium-intoxicated Edgar Allan Poe, "where the sky of a more transparent blue recedes in depth like a more infinite abyss, where sounds ring out as in music, where colors speak, where perfumes tell us of the worlds of ideas."

Claude Debussy

THE TONAL UNIVERSE

Mozart's sonatas, Chopin's preludes, and thousands of other musical works from the seventeenth through the nineteenth century are held together by the principles of the "tonal system," in which musical tones behave like celestial bodies, with a center of gravity (like our sun), around which other tones (like the planets) revolve. The relationships between these tones are governed by varying degrees of attraction.

For example, the harmonies, or *chords* (stacked tones), built on the first degree of a scale (the tonic) may serve as a "home" from which the musical narrative departs (creating a sense of tension) and returns (bringing a sense of release). Certain chords, like that built on the fifth scale member (called the dominant) pull toward the tonic so strongly that they facilitate that sense of conclusion.

The key of a piece determines the tonic. In C, the tonic chord is a form of C. In the key of D, it is a form of D—every key has its own tonic, just as every small town has a road its residents call Main Street: they share the same name, even though we wouldn't confuse one for another.

This tonal process is not just allegorical, but has a basis in nature: the chords that best convey a feeling of stability naturally arise from the physics of vibrating objects. When strings are set in motion, they produce not only a single "fundamental" tone, but also additional, weaker "overtones," in ghostlike whispers, the strongest of which comprise what musicians call a major chord.

As musical techniques evolved over the centuries, composers increasingly devised ways to get around tonality's most basic, restrictive formulas. By the Romantic Era (the nineteenth century), musicians became so good at this that the music often seemed to drift endlessly, no longer anchored to a particular center—a perfect musical metaphor for the age of endless yearning. Nevertheless, an underlying recognition of tonal principles continued loosely to govern the art of composition through the early twentieth century.

Musicology's most famous guru of analysis, Heinrich Schenker

(1868–1935), developed a way of charting even the most complex music within a system of simple hierarchies—as they drove musical motion inevitably toward a center—and his theories have been an important influence on many pianists, including Murray Perahia. "We should get accustomed to seeing tones as creatures," he wrote in his *Harmonielehre,* because music obeys natural urges, just like those found in living organisms.

The art of perfumery, as practiced by scientists like biophysicist Luca Turin, is actually a perfect metaphor for Debussy's harmonic world. Turin plots the arrangement of molecules in a fragrance the way a chess player manipulates pieces on a board. When these microscopic structures are blended in the right combinations in his laboratory, they fill the air with startling and inexplicable effects.

A substance called oxane gives the impression of sweat on ripe mango. Another, gardamide, is strangely redolent of grapefruit *and* hot horses. When Turin releases a cloud of tuberose—composed, he says, of "several hundred molecules flying in tight formation"— an evolving aromatic narrative begins: first, with a suggestion of rubber dusted with talcum, which is then replaced by something "meaty and carnation-like," before it finally settles into the bloom of a "white flower." Or so he told writer Chandler Burr, who dubbed him "the Emperor of Scent."

The mysteries of sensation conjured by these vapors—as their chemical structures mingle with memory and desire—also thrive in Debussy's complex bundles of sound. Unfailingly sumptuous, and built with as much intricate detail as Turin's formulations, these sonorities become more than mere vibrations: they stir our imaginations with suggestions of a glint of moonlight, or the color of the ocean, or fragments of tuberose and oxane. (In a letter to his publisher, Debussy referred to his piece *Reflets dans l'eau* [*Reflections in the Water*] as representing his most "recent discoveries in harmonic chemistry.") And they changed music forever.

Marie d'Agoult

THE IMPRESSIONIST milieu of turn-of-the-century Paris bears surprising similarities to the one engendered in America in the 1960s, when an entire generation—fueled by youthful rebellion, mystical yearning, and chemical intoxication—found itself captivated by a mad sensory swirl of music, painting, and theater. Liszt was perhaps the invisible godfather of it all. He once even enjoyed a hallucinogenic experience at a party. Marie d'Agoult, Liszt's mistress, recounted the incident during which Liszt and others smoked cigars prepared with the leaf of the *Datura fastuosa*: "You, Franz, were singing at the top of your voice, and, armed with a pair of snuffers, were going around the room striking the chairs which, you said, were singing out of time and tune." (This all took place in 1836, exactly a century before the film *Reefer Madness* was released in a futile attempt to discourage American youth from similar wayward behavior.)

Debussy met Liszt and recalled the way he had "used the pedal as a kind of breathing." Indeed, he found that Liszt's poetic spirit, his harmonic innovations, and his musical depictions of flowing fountains (in pieces like *Les Jeux d'eaux à la Villa d'Este*) all suggested a music supple enough "to adapt itself to the lyrical impulses of the soul and to the whims of reverie."

Debussy was also impressed by Liszt's son-in-law composer Richard Wagner, whose rich harmonies, in hyper-Romantic operas such as *Tristan und Isolde,* he called "the most beautiful thing that I know." (Clara Schumann found *Tristan*'s over-the-top emotionalism "repulsive"; it's not music at all, she said, but a "disease." Yet there was no escaping its impact.) Debussy studiously absorbed *Tristan*'s colorful techniques, but ultimately rejected Wagner as "a beautiful sunset who has been mistaken for a sunrise." He even poked fun at *Tristan* by quoting its opening bars in a light-hearted ragtime piece entitled *Golliwogg's Cakewalk*. (Debussy had little love for things that were not French. On a tour in 1910, he described Vienna as "an old city covered in makeup, overstuffed with the music of Brahms and Puccini, the officers with chests like women and the women with chests like officers." In Budapest, he found that "the Danube refuses to be as blue as a famous waltz would have us believe.")

After all, the French attraction to elegant, polished surface textures had little in common with a German inclination toward heavy sonorities and melodramatic intensity—the difference between a light soufflé and bratwurst with potatoes. Debussy's music was never a vehicle for raw, heart-throbbing, Wagnerian passion. It was an abstract picture in sound, constructed of shimmering cascades and swirling arabesques. And that's why the idea of alchemy was important. Melody alone, explained Debussy, no matter how lovely, "cannot express the varying states of the soul, and of life." To reach those ideals, he blended individual tones into dazzling, resonant combinations and set them adrift on the sea of his imagination, untethered from the old rules of musical order.

WHAT ELEMENTS went into Debussy's new musical language? First, he drew on a French tradition of using exotic harmonies—in musician's parlance, "extended chords" with "higher" scale members, such as sevenths, ninths, and elevenths—that extended all the way back to Baroque composer François Couperin. (Begin any major scale by counting the first note as number 1 and notes 7, 9, and 11 will be easily found. Add them to a basic major or minor chord and the sound takes on a bouquet of color.) Indeed, French composers of the early twentieth century relied a great deal on their Baroque brethren as models.

Next, he imbued his work with that sense of mystical beauty tinged with terror philosopher Immanuel Kant labeled the "sublime." Kant found it in tall oaks, and lonely shadows in a sacred grove. Debussy drew instead on Edgar Allan Poe's dark tales and haunting poems, such as *The Fall of the House of Usher* and "The Raven." Poe was held in contempt by many of his own American countrymen, but Europeans, especially the French, found him an ideal muse. "I spend my existence in the House of Usher," stated

Debussy. His compatriot composer Maurice Ravel told *The New York Times* that Poe was his "greatest teacher in composition." (For his part, Poe proclaimed that "the soul most nearly attains that great end for which . . . it struggles—the creation of supernal beauty"—through music. "We are often made to feel, with a shivering delight," he wrote, "that from an earthly harp are stricken notes which cannot have been unfamiliar to the angels.") Poe's sad and sinister narratives—what D. H. Lawrence called his "horrible underground passages of the human soul"—shared the feeling tone of the Alchemist's art.

Debussy also borrowed the techniques and textures of the "Impressionist" painters and transferred them to music (though neither the painters nor the musicians cared for the term "Impressionist," which was derisive, suggesting work that was overly vague or lacking in content). Thus, the pointillist effects found in Georges-Pierre Seurat's *A Sunday Afternoon on the Island of La Grande Jatte* (1886)—a scene rendered entirely through small dots of paint—made their way into Debussy's 1903 piano piece *Jardins sous la pluie* (*Gardens in the Rain*), where an incessant patter of tiny rhythmic strokes forms a larger tone painting over time. (The "golden section," an ancient aesthetic proportion commonly found in nature—introduced to Debussy by mathematician Charles Henry—also shows up in the structure of *Jardins sous la pluie* and in other of his major works.)

But one of the most striking influences on Debussy and his colleagues was the World's Fair (known as the Exposition Universelle) of 1889. Paris was electrified by this gathering (indeed, electric lights were one of the sensational novelties of the event). The city's just-completed Eiffel Tower served as an entryway, and exhibits from around the world included a *village nègre* with four hundred indigenous people, an American Wild West show with Buffalo Bill and Annie Oakley, and gamelan music performed by an ensemble from Java. French composers were quickly swept up in this Far Eastern sound, with its unusual tunings and repetitive cycles. The effects were well suited to their longed-for atmosphere of beguilement, and they soon began incorporating various aspects of the Eastern aesthetic into their works.

WORLD MUSIC COMES TO PARIS

Music from around the world had a special allure for the French composers, and traces of many influences can be found throughout their repertoire. Intimations of gamelan are heard in Debussy's use of the whole-tone scale, which divides the musical octave into six equal parts, and the pentatonic (five-note) scale (which can be played using only the black keys of the piano). In his piano piece *Pagodes* (*Pagodas*), he even emulated the rhythmic cycle of the gamelan "great gong." Maurice Ravel (1875–1937) was similarly enchanted, even making use of an Indonesian poetic form (*pantun*) in his gorgeous Trio in A minor for piano, violin, and cello.

Both composers frequently incorporated the exotic sounds of other lands as well—especially Spain, in pieces such as Debussy's *Soirée dans Grenade* and Ravel's *Alborada del gracioso*. These suggestions of foreign places worked as powerfully in their own way as the gentle mists, natural landscapes, and distant tolling bells that permeated works like Debussy's *Des Pas sur la neige* (*Footprints in the Snow*) and Ravel's *La Vallée des cloches* (*Valley of the Bells*).

Out of all these ingredients, Debussy made of the piano an instrument of heightened nuance by controlling incremental tonal shadings and dynamics; using an endless variety of hammer strokes and pedal movements; finding sensuousness in lingering resonances; and breathing life into harmonies, which expanded and condensed as they traveled along the keyboard. His languorous First Prelude, *Danseuses de Delphes* (*Dancers of Delphi*), is a useful illustration.

Debussy told an admirer that this piece grew from his impressions of an ancient Greek column he saw in the Louvre, carved in the form of a female figure. As pianist Paul Roberts has noted, it is a sculpture in tones, through which the composer conveyed the paradox of "immobility suggesting movement, and weight suggesting weightlessness." The printed music demonstrates these contradictions in myriad ways.

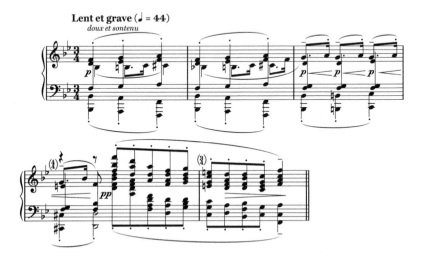

First line of Debussy's First Prelude

Right from the beginning, Debussy presents a riddle. Curvaceous lines above and below the notes suggest that each phrase should be taken in a single breath, creating a unified flow. At the same time, little dots by the individual harmonies command that they be played with a short articulation, ensuring that each one sounds independent and alive. A pianist must figure a way to accomplish both goals at once.

The volume of sound gently undulates like an ocean at low tide, with the music diminishing at times into a distant echo, even when hefty chords are being played in both hands. It's another paradox: at the softest possible volume, the sonorities remain full-bodied. They are often bell-like and clear, though sometimes pungent and occasionally jazzy. The hands begin by moving in opposite directions—with plangent bass tones descending as treble harmonies reach toward the sun—then become coupled, moving en masse like weighty blocks of stone. Everything works according to

Debussy's untraditional sensibility, but the result is always perfectly cohesive, as well as haunting.

Naturally, Debussy's approach was not to everyone's taste. Writing in the *New York Sun* on July 19, 1903, critic James Huneker made no bones about his dislike of this composer and what he represented. "I met Debussy at the Café Riche the other night and was struck by the unique ugliness of the man," he reported.

> His face is flat, the top of his head is flat, his eyes are prominent—the expression veiled, and somber—and, altogether, with his long hair, unkempt beard, uncouth clothing and soft hat, he looked more like a Bohemian, a Croat, a Hun, than a Gaul . . . Rémy de Gourmont has written of the "disassociation of ideas." Debussy puts the theory into practice, for in his peculiar idiom there seems to be no normal sequence . . . The form itself is decomposed. Tonalities are vague, even violently unnatural to unaccustomed ears.

History, of course, has been kinder to Mr. Debussy.

OTHER ARTISTS BUILT on Debussy's lead with innovations of their own. French composer Olivier Messiaen (1908–1992) expanded Debussy's language, inspired, he explained, by the mysteries of limitation, or rather, as he put it, by "the charm of impossibilities." He created exotic scales by formulating several that could be transposed (shifted to another key) only a limited number of times before they repeated themselves. (As an example, the six-note whole-tone scale, in which each member is exactly a whole step away from its neighbor, can be played beginning on the note C or by beginning on the next-higher note, C-sharp—the black key just to the right of C. But when it is played again beginning on the very next available note on the keyboard, D, the tones that are sounded turn out to be the same as when the scale was begun on C. Therefore, the whole-tone scale is limited to only two distinct versions.) Messiaen's music was constructed out of a myriad of such strange symmetries.

He also applied this limiting approach to rhythms that sound the same whether played forward or backward (and are therefore impossible to reverse) and then added Hindu rhythms and the melodies of natural birdcalls to the mix (he meticulously catalogued the songs of hundreds of varieties of birds). This may all seem heady stuff, but the effect was profoundly gorgeous. "It is a glistening music we seek, giving to the aural sense voluptuously refined pleasures," he wrote.

Messiaen's music was a ritual offering, a catalyst provoking what W. H. Auden called the "abstract insight" that "wakes/Among the glaciers and the rocks/The hermit's sensual ecstasy." In works like *Quartet for the End of Time* (written while in a prison camp in World War II) and *Twenty Visions of the Infant Jesus* (a vast masterpiece for piano), Messiaen's lavish sounds can leave a listener dizzy with sensation.

A USTRIAN ARNOLD SCHOENBERG (1874–1951) is often regarded as a composer of methodical, even mathematical, instincts rather than a weaver of spells. But his formative years were as deeply linked as Debussy's to the world of poets, philosophers, and painters. (He was drawn especially to poets Rainer Maria Rilke and Stefan George. George, who thought of himself as a disciple of French symbolist Stéphane Mallarmé, shared the Impressionist interest in colors, forms, and moods rather than traditional narrative.) Schoenberg's hunt for the principles that would lead music into the future led him to invent a system of composing in which all twelve tones are treated as equals—eliminating the basic distinction between dissonances (unstable sounds) and consonances (harmonious ones) on which Western music had rested. But this plan, an attempt to rescue music from a situation in which all the old rules already seemed to have collapsed, came to fruition late, in 1923.

Early on, his friendship with painters Wassily Kandinsky and Franz Marc placed him in the circle of Der Blaue Reiter (The Blue Rider), the name given to an exhibition and published *Almanac* (in 1911) that together aimed at rekindling the spiritual in art. Schoenberg, who was a painter as well as a composer, contributed an essay to the *Almanac*, in which he quoted philosopher Arthur Schopenhauer on finding the essence of art in the unconscious: "The composer reveals the innermost essence of the world and pronounces the most profound wisdom in a language that his reason cannot understand; he is like a mesmerized somnambulist who reveals secrets about things that he knows nothing about when he is awake."

Kandinsky, who introduced himself to Schoenberg by letter after first hearing his music in 1911, came to believe that the goal of painting should be a kind of eye music: "Color is the keyboard, the eye is the hammer," he wrote. "The soul is the piano with its many strings." The moods evoked by Schoenberg's short, dark-hued piano works, like those of his op. 11 (1909) and op. 19 (1911) pieces, resonate, like Kandinsky's paintings, with that inner, murky world that lies beyond normal awareness. His musical efforts transcend logic to become something a biographer of his, Allen Shawn, called "permanently strange," for reasons that can't fully be explained.

Schoenberg's students Anton Webern (1883–1945) and Alban Berg (1885–1935), who formed, with their teacher, what is known as the "Second Viennese School" of composition, took very different roads. Berg's "freedom" from traditional tonality retained connections to Romantic music. Webern, on the other hand, distilled Schoenberg's method down to its essence, often arranging the series of twelve tones into delicately astringent melodies too difficult for the average listener to comprehend, as if the dots in a pointillist painting had become its subject matter, so magnified that the whole, organic picture could no longer be perceived. The allure of this music is felt mostly by those thrilled to know the secret order that governs it all.

THE PARISIANS AND the Viennese were not alone in their quest for music that transports. Russia experienced a similar artistic revolution. At its forefront was a bizarre composer named Alexander Nikolayevich Scriabin (1872–1915), who announced to the world that he was God.

Indeed, at the time of his death he was at work on a project called *The Mysterium*, intended to usher in the Messianic Age. In its first stage, *The Prefatory Action*, he planned to suspend bells from clouds in order to summon people from around the world to a temple in India. There, Scriabin planned to sit at the piano, surrounded by instrumentalists, singers, and dancers in constant motion. Pillars of incense and streams of colored light would enhance the effect. The libretto, describing the birth of the cosmos and the union of its feminine and masculine principles, and the music, expressing the dissolution of the ego and the cessation of time, would together awaken the audience to a higher spiritual plane. Unfortunately, he never got the chance to try it out.

What had inspired this mystical fervor? In part, it was a spiritual practice known as theosophy, founded by a Madame Helena Petrovna Blavatsky in 1875. But Scriabin had long entertained an interest in altered states of mind, such as synesthesia—the condition in which sounds, colors, numbers, or other sensory qualities are inextricably linked. In his view, musical tones corresponded to specific colors (C is intense red; E, sky blue; D-sharp, flesh with a glint of steel). Indeed, he actually included a part for a "color keyboard" that projected lights of different hues in the score of his *Prometheus: Poem of Fire*.

Like Debussy, Scriabin also fell under the sway of his country's symbolist poets, with whom he often gathered at the Journalists Café on Stoleshnikov Lane in Moscow, or at his own apartment. Among them were Vyacheslav Ivanov (described by poet Alexander Blok as having "bear-like eyes that look out from the side of his head," and by Scriabin as "magnificent . . . we are alike") and

Pianist Josef Hofmann and Alexander Scriabin, Moscow, ca. 1892

Konstantin Balmont, who, after hearing Scriabin's music, wrote: "Scriabin is the singing of a falling moon. Starlight in music. A flame's movement. A burst of sunlight. The cry of soul to soul."

CONFESSIONS OF A SCRIABIN PLAYER *by Garrick Ohlsson*

Though I haven't revealed this to many people, there are two composers who seem to exert a mysterious power when I play. They seem to take over, as if *they* are playing *me*. I become the instrument. In a larger sense, we are all instruments, or vessels for great art, and some composers will filter through our personalities better than others. But there are differences. When I play Liszt's towering pieces, I lose myself more than in other music. Suddenly *he* is in the driver's seat. I feel an incredibly large presence.

It's slightly different with Scriabin, but he also possesses me, taking me into his strange, alchemical world. At the end of a Scriabin performance, my heart is beating faster, beyond what the physical effort required. I have become intoxicated.

In lots of other music I can get into a "zone," and feel hyper-aware of things. But with these particular composers, I actually feel less in charge, as if I'm being controlled by something very powerful outside of myself.

Scriabin's piano playing was often bombastic, compulsive, and feverishly erratic. But it could also be transcendental. Writer and architect Alexander Pasternak recorded his impressions of Scriabin the pianist: "As soon as I heard the first sounds on the piano, I immediately had the impression that his fingers were producing the sound without touching the keys. His enemies used to say it was not real piano playing, but a twittering of birds or a mewing of kittens. His spiritual lightness was reflected in his playing: in his gait, his movements, his gesticulations, the way he jerked his head up when he spoke."

Interestingly, Debussy had dipped into the very same musical waters that had shaped young Scriabin when, as a student, he traveled to Russia with Mme Nadezhda Filaretovna von Meck, Tchai-kovsky's secret benefactress. He was only eighteen in the summer of 1880 when she hired him to give piano lessons to her children and serve as a chamber pianist for her gatherings. Their travels included stops in Florence, Vienna (where the young composer heard Wagner's *Tristan* for the first time), and Moscow, where he could fully satisfy his curiosity about contemporary music by such Russian masters as Modest Mussorgsky. But Debussy remained utterly French, and Scriabin, Russian to the core.

RUSSIA'S MUSSORGSKY *by Claude Debussy*

Mussorgsky is little known in France and for this we can excuse ourselves, it is true, by remarking that he is no better known in Russia. . . . Nobody has spoken to that which is best in us with such tenderness and depth; he is quite unique, and will be renowned for an art that suffers from

no stultifying rules or artificialities. Never before has such a refined sensibility expressed itself with such simple means: it is almost as if he were an inquisitive savage discovering music for the first time, guided in each step forward by his own emotions . . . He composes in a series of bold strokes, but his incredible gift of foresight means that each stroke is bound to the next by a mysterious thread. Sometimes he can conjure up a disquieting impression of darkness so powerful that it wrings tears from one's heart.

La Revue Blanche, APRIL 15, 1901,
TRANSLATED BY RICHARD LANGHAM SMITH

Scriabin's earliest writings gave no hint of what was to come. His justly famous piano Etude in C-sharp minor, op. 2, no. 1, of 1887, a dusky, lyrical piece that exquisitely captures the Russian heart, suggests a composer of deep nationalistic and Romantic inclinations. The piano pieces that soon followed owed much to the delicate, introspective side of Frédéric Chopin. Yet by 1897, with the creation of a piano concerto (harshly rejected by the venerable Nikolai Rimsky-Korsakov), Scriabin was exhibiting signs of a search for radical new musical paths.

Scriabin's evolving musical language used melody and chords built from unusual scales (like some used by Messiaen), resulting at times in a sound world similar to that of many late-twentieth-century jazz musicians. Indeed, the vibrant, strangely ambiguous harmony on which he based *Prometheus,* a combination of tones sometimes referred to as the "mystic chord," has become standard fare in that genre. Scriabin himself referred to it more perplexingly as the "chord of the plemora," a harmony that would unveil a hidden world beyond man's normal comprehension.

According to one of his biographers, Faubion Bowers, the composer used to amuse his guests by playing the first three measures of his last Sonata (the Tenth), followed by the scale of G Major. "You hear," he would say, "my music lies between the tones." How many others perceived things in exactly the same way is an open question.

Many critics remained unimpressed with this wild, holy man of music. "As a kind of drug, no doubt Scriabin's music has a certain significance, but it is wholly superfluous," wrote Cecil Gray in *A Survey of Contemporary Music,* published in London in 1924. "We already have cocaine, morphine, hashish, heroin, anhalonium, and innumerable similar productions, to say nothing of alcohol. Surely that is enough. On the other hand, we have only one music. Why must we degrade an art into a spiritual narcotic?"

OPPOSITE
Modest
Mussorgsky

NEVERTHELESS, SCRIABIN'S "MYSTIC chord," as well as the iridescent harmonies of Debussy and Ravel, became attrac-

tive fodder for jazz artists in the late 1950s who had grown tired of the brashness and showy virtuosity of the bebop style and sought a new direction. Pianist Bill Evans (1929–1980) and trumpeter Miles Davis (1926–1991) adopted these rich, colorful musical structures for their 1959 jazz ensemble recording, *Kind of Blue*—and sparked a revolution.

Bill Evans

What they created perfectly reflected French poet Paul Verlaine's ideal of something "vague in the air and soluble, with nothing heavy and nothing at rest." But the atmospherics of Debussy, Scriabin, and Baudelaire had now been transformed into a uniquely American art form. *Kind of Blue* became, in the words of pianist Herbie Hancock, "a doorway." (Hancock would eventually expand that portal with his own piano wizardry on later Miles Davis recordings, such as *Sorcerer* and the stunningly beautiful *Nefertiti*. In the hands of this supremely intelligent pianist, Debussy's "chemical" discoveries entered the jazz mainstream with a new level of range and sophistication. The mysterious, evocative chords that he used came about, Hancock once revealed, through special formulations

Herbie Hancock
FRANCIS WOLFF

in which some tones were placed in close proximity while others were separated by a wide expanse.)

Both Davis and Evans had been inching toward the new aesthetic for years. For Miles, it began with a fascination with the dreamy, impressionistic Claude Thornhill band, whose sound "hung like a cloud," according to Thornhill's arranger, Gil Evans (no relation to pianist Bill). Collaborations between Davis and Gil Evans, such as the breezy *Birth of the Cool* (recorded in 1949 and 1950, but released in 1957), were also landmarks in jazz history.

Davis was influenced by several musicians who seemed to share this sensibility. One was pianist Ahmad Jamal, admired by Davis for his "concept of space, his lightness of touch, his understatement." Another was Bill Evans, whose playing was described by the trumpet great as "quiet fire." "The sound he got," said Miles of Bill Evans, "was like crystal or sparkling water cascading down from some clear waterfall." Not surprisingly, Bill Evans had long been immersed in the music of Debussy and Ravel. ("He used to bring me pieces by Ravel, like the *Piano Concerto for the Left Hand*," said Miles.) Pastel-like harmonies and an introspective lyricism became hallmarks of his style; and his contributions to *Kind of Blue* clinched his place in jazz history.

As usual, critics remained of two minds. Some, like John S. Wilson, found Evans's perfumed, French-inflected approach too emotionally detached; it was, he said, not really jazz at all, but "more like superior background music." Pianist Cecil Taylor less kindly called Evans "merely a cocktail pianist." Yet venerable jazz writer Nat Hentoff viewed the pianist differently:

> His narrow back hunched over the piano, Evans, after a few minutes, gives the impression of having entered the instrument. The body we see is simply a husk waiting to be filled again when the set is over. It is the distilled quality of Evans' intensity that I am trying to convey . . . Those who complain that Evans is too removed from his audience, that he makes no overt signs to draw them into his music, are simply not willing to give that music at least a little of the concentration Evans does. Communication is there, and don't shoot the piano player if you're blocked.

There is no question that he exerted a tremendous influence on the next generations of jazz artists, as exemplified by the elegant pianism of contemporary players like Andy LaVerne (b. 1947) and Bill Charlap (b. 1966).

THE GENIUS OF BILL EVANS *by Bill Charlap*

Bill Evans's music was spiritual and transporting, but very much the expression of a private world. There is a video on which he talks to his brother Harry about the collective unconscious and the creative spirit, and he was clearly interested in breaking down barriers to consciousness through music. That's part of the alchemy he created. Of course he was also meticulous, disciplined, and intense. But one of the first things people respond to in his music is that spiritual depth.

Part of it comes from his sense of harmony and touch—which derives from Nat Cole, Teddy Wilson, Bud Powell, and Art Tatum, but also from Brahms, Chopin, and Debussy. He is a "rhythmitizer" as well—every great artist is. Yet, there is less of a raw feeling to his playing than you often find in jazz, more of a European sense, and that makes it different from the hard-driving sound of Powell or Cedar Walton.

One of the important facets of Bill's art was the way in which he developed material—in the manner of a completely literate and technically accomplished composer. This aspect informs his interpretations of other people's songs too. For him, it was not just a matter of adding new, pretty harmonies to a standard; it had everything to do with structure and formal design, along with intuition. He said himself that it didn't come easily to him. And that was a good thing: he had to put together every little piece of the puzzle, and this helped him form a unique musical language. But as Bernstein said of Beethoven, though he may have toiled mightily to get it right, he knew when he got it.

Bill Charlap with singer Tony Bennett

Musical patterns that lent Debussy's music a sense of opaqueness, like the symmetrically built whole-tone scale, which seems to have no real beginning or end, had shown up in earlier jazz piano works, like Bix Beiderbecke's impressionistic *In a Mist* (1927), as well as in quirky European takeoffs on early jazz styles, like Paul Hindemith's *Foxtrot* (1919), not to mention the slightly jazzy and harmonically ambiguous *Grey Clouds* of Franz Liszt (1881). (Beiderbecke was also a trumpeter, whose sensuous, sultry sound was

described perfectly by musician Eddie Condon as "like a girl saying yes.") But the sophistication and harmonic intricacy of Bill Evans's elegant renderings were matched by perhaps only one other musician in the jazz pantheon: Edward Kennedy "Duke" Ellington (1899–1974), a great bandleader and one of America's best modern composers in any genre.

Duke Ellington in a rare informal pose

Ellington reinvented himself throughout a long, distinguished career, which began with a pampered childhood, piano lessons with a Mrs. Marietta Clinkscales (!) and performances at high-school parties—where he learned that tickling the ivories can impress the girls mightily. "I ain't been no athlete since," he declared after discovering how effective his piano playing could be on the opposite sex.

The piano was an important influence on his compositional style, which combined blocks of harmonies moving as they would under the fingers of a jazz keyboardist with the painterly sensitivities of an Impressionist. He had a gift for blending the colors of instruments, and, most importantly, a talent for exploiting the particular sounds and personalities of his ensembles' individual members. The result was unique.

After arriving in New York, he and his band The Washingtonians worked their way through Harlem's top nightspots, from the Orient Café and Club Barron to the Club Kentucky, where they would run into such celebrities as George Gershwin, Al Jolson, Fanny Brice, and Irving Berlin. One night at the Club Kentucky, remembered Ellington sideman Sonny Greer, "movie star Tom Mix, in full cowboy outfit, sat in on drums." Before long, Duke was turning out landmark works like *East St. Louis Toodle-Oo,* where the growls and wah-wahs of the trumpets conjured a musical atmosphere that became known as "jungle music." Later, his increasingly sophisticated writing in large pieces such as *Black, Brown and Beige* (at its premiere, Ellington was presented with a plaque of appreciation signed by thirty-two eminent musicians, including Aaron Copland, Walter Damrosch, Benny Goodman, Fritz Reiner, Leopold Stokowski, and Paul Whiteman) and a string of sacred works earned him a Pulitzer Prize nomination. The Pulitzer commission turned him down (causing the entire music committee to resign), but Duke

Billy Strayhorn

remained stoic: "Fate is being kind to me," he said. "Fate doesn't want me to be famous too young."

Fame did not remain elusive, however. Duke's highly collaborative process with band members, and especially with pianist/arranger Billy Strayhorn, a student of the French Impressionist tradition who became his musical alter ego, resulted in ingenious compositions and recordings hailed by musicians and critics around the world. In March of 1971 he was inducted into the Swedish Academy of Music, the first writer of nonclassical music to be made a member of the two-hundred-year-old institution. At his seventieth birthday party, hosted at the White House by President Richard Nixon, he was awarded the Presidential Medal of Freedom. At that event he summed up his life's philosophy. "I am reminded," he said, "of the four freedoms Billy Strayhorn created for our sacred concerts . . . I use those four moral freedoms by which Strayhorn lived as a mea-

sure of what we ourselves should live up to. Freedom from hate. Unconditionally. Freedom from self-pity. Freedom from the fear of possibly doing something that would benefit someone else. And freedom from the fear of being better than one's brother."

Perhaps that explains why, when he told audiences, "I love you madly," they believed him—and loved him madly, right back.

Yet another compelling style in the Alchemist tradition emerged in the hands of pianist McCoy Tyner (b. 1938), who absorbed the floating sounds, exotic scales, and static ambience of the French school and reframed them into a hard-edged, rhythmically gripping style. Tyner, especially in his work with another

Kind of Blue sideman, saxophonist John Coltrane, added rawness and fervor to the chemistry, generating music of primal intensity.

Finally, there was the stunningly original musical alchemist Thelonious Sphere Monk (1917–1982). His sound world bore little resemblance to Debussy's; nevertheless it entranced, mostly through a sense of utter strangeness. Monk undermined listeners' expectations with quirky dissonances, craggy rhythms, and a highly unusual way of handling silence, which became as tangible in his musical world as "negative space" is in an abstract painting. (Monk's wife, Nellie, described the combination of disruptive rhythms and highly percussive attacks as "Melodious Thunk.")

DUKE ELLINGTON *by Oscar Peterson*

He thrived on spontaneity. He recognized not one single thing in life, musically speaking, as an insurmountable challenge. He was a great one for always saying, "Oh, don't worry about it. You can do it. You'll get the gist of it as we play it . . ."

Strangely enough, there was a very unique phenomenon that took place when you played with Ellington. Regardless of the apprehension you may have had starting in, somewhere along the line, almost in a subliminal manner, you would be swept up and engulfed in this musical tidal wave. And, before you knew it, you, too, were a contributing factor to that tidal wave . . .

OPPOSITE
Thelonious Monk

Edward Kennedy Ellington was able to do this because he was a man of great tenderness, kindness, and affection. I've heard him go to the microphone hundreds of times and give the speech about how much he loved the audience and how much the band loved the audience. And I found myself believing it because I know that, in the times that I spent with Duke personally, I never heard him utter one derogatory word about anyone. That's a very strange thing in this world today—for anyone, not just people in the music field.

I think if I had to pick out two of the most outstanding qualities of his playing, the first would be the harmonic sense that he had in playing behind someone, playing with the band and filling in maybe only two beats. The voicing or the choice of chords that he decided to use in just that short space would add so much to the composition that it was just unbelievable. It was marvelous to hear.

The second aspect of his playing in which I reveled was the type of runs that he would play. These runs were so spontaneous and unorthodox that if as a pianist I was to take them apart and start practicing them, they would be very difficult to play . . . But Duke played them with complete abandon, because he felt them at the particular time that he played them; he just believed that they could be played and he'd run them. If you mentioned them to him afterwards, he wouldn't even remember what he'd played.

FROM *"In Memoriam—Duke Ellington, 'The Man': Reflections by Oscar Peterson,"*
IN *Sound Magazine,* NOVEMBER 1974

Despite his musical idiosyncrasies and notoriously bizarre behavior (which sometimes included falling asleep at the piano or dancing in circles in the midst of a performance), Monk was embraced by the greatest musicians of his era. He appeared on the cover of *Time* magazine and received a posthumous Pulitzer Prize Special Citation. The music, like the man, was a study in odd, erratic behavior. But it easily swept listeners up into its own, compelling realm.

PART 2 *Shock and Awe*

THE IMPRESSIONISTS and their descendants could hold us spellbound with harmonic beauty. But the Alchemist's toolkit also included other ways of sparking a state of wonder. While Debussy dreamed of a piano *without* hammers, American composer John Cage's (1912–1992) "prepared piano" seemed to contain an army of them. In place of the usual warm, round tones, Cage's instrument offered percussive thumps, wild twangs, and clanging bells, as if aliens had invaded its mechanism and added their own otherworldly noisemakers.

These effects were achieved by inserting objects such as screws, bolts, or pieces of rubber between the piano's strings. The result was reminiscent of Indonesian gamelan—the sound that had intrigued Debussy at the 1889 World's Fair. But Cage arrived at his alchemy in exactly the opposite manner of Debussy, who extended the world of harmony through intricate new formulas. In Cage's world, the sonorities, with their ambiguous pitches, made the very idea of harmony irrelevant.

John Cage preparing a piano, ca. 1960
ROSS WELSER

John Cage first used his "prepared piano" technique in 1938, when dancer Syvilla Fort asked him to supply music for a choreographed work. It has since been adopted by many others, from classical composer George Crumb to rock stars like the Velvet Underground (1967), the Grateful Dead (1968), and David Bowie (1979).

How does one prepare a piano? On the inside cover of his *Sonatas and Interludes*, John Cage offers a map of the piano strings and instructions for where to insert various objects. But the descriptions of the materials are fairly vague. Cage prefers it that way, as his recollection of his first attempts makes clear. In a foreword for Richard Bunger's *The Well-Prepared Piano* in 1972, he relates the story:

Having decided to change the sound of the piano in order to make a music suitable for Syvilla Fort's *Bacchanale*, I went to the kitchen, got a pie plate, brought it into the living room, and placed it on the piano strings. I played a few keys. The sound changed, but the pie plate bounced around due to the vibrations, and, after a while, some of the sounds that had been changed no longer were. I tried something smaller, nails between the strings. They slipped down between and lengthwise along the strings. It dawned on me that screws or bolts would stay in position. They did. And I was delighted to notice that by means of a single preparation two different sounds could be produced. One was resonant, the other was quite muted. The quiet one was heard whenever the soft pedal was used . . . When I first placed objects between piano strings, it was with the desire to possess sounds (to be able to repeat them). But, as the music left my home and went from piano to piano and from pianist to pianist, it became clear that not only are two pianists essentially different from one another, but two pianos are not the same either. Instead of the possibility of repetition, we are faced in life with the unique qualities and characteristics of each occasion.

This approach to musical sound was a natural development for Cage. He realized early on, he confessed, that during his student days, while studying with Arnold Schoenberg, "I had never . . . had any feeling for harmony. For this reason, Schoenberg told me I would always come to a wall." He leaped over that wall by putting aside traditional elements like harmony and re-evaluating the very nature of musical experience. It began with a spiritual journey.

Around 1950, Cage remembered, he was "very confused and disturbed. I couldn't take the concept of art as communication from one person to another as being true." He searched for clarity through Eastern philosophy and studied the works of Aldous Huxley, Sri Ramakrishna, and Zen master D. T. Suzuki. Through them he developed a new goal: the cultivation of a "sober and quiet mind, like Daniel in the lion's den or Jonah in the whale. We're in the same situation—acoustically at least—every day," he claimed. That is, we are inundated with noises that disturb. The way to escape this situation, he decided, was to make an internal adjustment. "It became clear that a sober mind would be free of likes and dislikes," he concluded, "and open to the rest of the world which is, so to speak, divine influence." The key was to stop resisting the uncontrollable.

It was a radical break with past notions of the nature of music. Igor Stravinsky once wrote that "the murmur of a breeze, the rippling of a brook, the song of a bird" were merely "promises of music; it takes a human being to keep them: a human being who is sensitive to nature's many voices, of course, but who in addition feels the need of putting them in order." John Cage felt no such need. He embraced all sounds—from the ambient noise of a room full of people to the fire engines housed across the street from his Manhattan loft, which often wailed in the middle of the night. He stood the musical world on its ear with a piano work entitled *4'33"*, during which a pianist sits silently for that length of time, enabling an audience to become aware of the "music" of everyday sounds around them (from the coughs and sniffles of listeners in the hall to the rush of traffic outside). In its first performance in 1952 in Woodstock, New York, pianist David Tudor simply raised and lowered the piano's lid to signal the work's beginning and end.

The transportive quality of his music came about through its intensification of the moment, whatever that moment might bring, without concern about aspects of musical craft like form, rhythm, or harmony, which now became secondary considerations. Cage tossed coins, for example, to select the musical parameters of a piece through random passages in the *I Ching* (the Chinese *Book of Changes*). He composed a work for twelve radios in which the sounds are dependent on what programs happen to be airing at the time of the performance. He shocked listeners into a concentrated state of attention, and the possibility of awe, without ever losing the element of mystery that was, for him, all-important. Like his friend and colleague composer Morton Feldman (1926–1987), Cage believed in a music beyond intellect. "What was great about the fifties," explained Feldman, "is that for one brief moment—maybe, say, six weeks—nobody understood art."

Aside from that first prepared piano piece for Syvilla Fort, his best-known works in the genre are the playful, ear-opening *Sonatas and Interludes* (1946–1948). There were precedents, of course, like the Janissary effects on instruments of Mozart's time. Closer to his day, turn-of-the-twentieth-century composer Erik Satie, idolized by Cage, wrote *Le Piège de Méduse,* a piece that called for sheets of paper to be placed on the piano strings. Indeed, many composers, including Brazil's Heitor Villa-Lobos, Maurice Ravel, and American maverick Henry Cowell, similarly tampered with the piano's sound in various compositions throughout the 1920s. Cowell (1897–1965) was the most adventurous of the group; Cage was his student for a time, and called him "the open sesame for new music in America."

Among Cowell's innovations was the "tone cluster," produced by hitting the keyboard with a full fist or an arm. In *The Aeolian Harp,* he played the piano by stroking its strings, evoking, as in the Samuel Taylor Coleridge poem of the same name, "such a soft floating witchery of sound/As twilight Elfins make, when they at eve/Voyage on gentle gales from Faery-Land." In *The Banshee,* he scraped the strings to emulate screeches and howls; these approaches together became known as the art of "string piano."

CAGE AND COWELL both exerted a huge influence on composers interested in writing the kind of music that opened a window on the "now," the ephemeral moment. These included musicians like Terry Riley (b. 1935), whose rhythmically insistent 1964 work *In C* (for an ensemble of about thirty-five musicians, though fewer or more are acceptable) is often considered the first composition of the minimalist school; Steve Reich (b. 1936); Philip Glass (b. 1937); and John Adams (b. 1947). They all transfixed their listeners' attention with short, repeated patterns that change gradually over time.

In Reich's work *Piano Phase*

of 1967, for example, interlocking musical patterns drift out of "phase" with each other like a chain of railroad cars that became disengaged while rounding a curve. No longer slavishly yoked, they separate and form new, ever-changing spatial relationships.

To Reich, the slowness of these unfolding changes was crucial. "To facilitate closely detailed listening, a musical process should happen extremely gradually," he wrote. The experience, he explained, should resemble "placing your feet in the sand by the ocean's edge and watching, feeling, and listening to the waves gradually bury them." Glass was greatly influenced by Indian raga, and Reich by African drumming (as well as by his admitted difficulty in mastering some of the traditional Western musical techniques; in that sense, both Cage and Reich built strengths from their perceived weaknesses).

MINIMALISM'S FOREFATHER

Erik Satie instigated some of the concepts that have become trendy today, such as "ambient music" and "minimalism." He proudly created a kind of furniture music, sounds that simply hung in the air without demanding attention, and also wrote pieces intended to go on forever (or nearly forever), such as a *Perpetual Tango* that looped without end, and a piece called *Vexations* (c. 1893) which is intended to be repeated 840 times in succession.

OPPOSITE
Terry Riley

There is no record of *Vexations* being performed during Satie's lifetime, but it was played in full on September 9, 1963, at the Pocket Theatre in New York by a tag team of pianists that included John Cage, David Tudor, Christian Wolff, Philip Corner, Viola Farber, Robert Wood, Mac-Rae Cook, John Cale, David Del Tredici, James Tenney, Joshua Rifkin, and Howard Klein, the *New York Times* reviewer who had been sent to cover the event. According to Cage, however, Klein's exuberance unfortunately outweighed his ability to hit the right notes. The performance lasted from 6 p.m. to 12:40 p.m. the following day. John Cale reported that admission to the event had been five dollars, but those attending received a refund of five cents for every twenty minutes they remained, and anyone staying to the end was entitled to a twenty-cent bonus. Only one person sat through the whole thing, an actor named Karl Schenzer. (That feat garnered him an appearance on the television game show *I've Got a Secret*.) Pop artist Andy Warhol told writer George Plimpton that he attended the performance of *Vexations* at the time he was editing his film *Sleep*, which became famous for its repetitive structure.

However, the minimalist idea actually appears throughout musical literature in various ways. Seventeenth-century composer Henry Purcell wrote a *Fantasia Upon One Note*, in which a tone is sustained throughout the entire work. Maurice Ravel's *Boléro* consists of a melody and rhythmic tattoo that repeat and build over the work's entire length before reaching a final, blazing climax. The composer was shocked by how popular this work became. "I've written only one masterpiece—*Boléro*," Ravel told composer Arthur Honegger. "Unfortunately, there's no music in it." Ravel's *La Valse*, in which a lilting ballroom waltz gathers energy and eventually assumes gargantuan proportions, has similarly minimalist qualities. The composer called it "a fantastic and fatefully inescapable whirlpool."

Even the skillful Hungarian composer György Ligeti (1923–2006), who declared himself "the extreme antithesis to John Cage and his school," inevitably acknowledged Cage's importance. Ligeti's complex, gorgeously crafted sound world made him a favorite in the repertoires of many late-twentieth-century artists. Yet his *Symphonic Poem for 100 Metronomes* simply set the mechanical timekeepers in motion and, in a Cage-ian tip of the hat to nature, allowed each to wind down at its own rate.

Ligeti's objection to Cage and his followers, he explained, was that "they believe that life is art and art is life . . . my artistic *credo* is that art—every art—is *not* life. It is something artificial." The minimalists would be hard-pressed to disagree. Their trancelike effects arise not from embracing the randomness of the moment, like Cage, but by carefully manipulating a listener's focus, inducing what psychologists call "entrainment," so that he or she surrenders to the power of rhythmic repetition and a fascination with forms that linger and mutate like slowly drifting clouds. (One motivation for the emergence of the minimalist style was no doubt a perception that abstract contemporary music, in turning away from the dance roots of more accessible styles, lacked the visceral impact that can be achieved through rhythm.)

John Cage pointedly marked the difference between his approach and that of Steve Reich. "He made his 'process' music so that anyone listening to it could follow it—could understand what is going on," explained Cage. "He wants people to understand what's happening, whereas I want people to be mystified by what's happening—as I am mystified by the moon or by the change of weather. The reality of our life is a mystery."

A DIFFERENT ASPECT of music's eternal mystery—the ancient idea of a harmony of the spheres—occupied musicians like La Monte Young, who abandoned the piano's modern tuning in favor of pure resonances that occur in nature. (On a modern piano, these natural harmonies must be "tempered," or adjusted so that they will blend well, in order to avoid harsh collisions which would occur when playing much of the standard repertoire.) Young's *The Well-Tuned Piano* (begun in 1964), his seminal work, can exceed six hours in length, its long drones enveloping a listener as the music journeys from softly meditative moments to maelstroms of sound, often with stunning, unearthly effects.

Abandoning the modern system of "equal temperament" makes possible a wider sound world, leading some composers, like the irascible renegade Harry Partch (who built his own assortment of instruments with unique tunings), to declare the ordinary piano "twelve black and white bars in front of musical freedom." Experiments in tuning have always occupied a place in musical history, from the ancient Greeks onward, often in the hope of uncovering the secrets of music's magical powers. Many musicians regard these issues with deep seriousness. However, for some, like American pioneer Charles Ives, who wrote a work for two pianos tuned a quarter-tone apart, thus creating a scale with twenty-four rather than twelve notes in an octave, tuning was simply another playful element in the composer's toy box. (Similarly, even George Gershwin found the possibilities delightfully fascinating. He collaborated with microtonal composer Hans Barth on a quarter-tone version of the second of his *Three Preludes* for a Carnegie Hall concert in 1930.)

ONE OTHER APPROACH to transcending the ordinary was familiar to fans of Liszt and Paganini: mind-boggling virtuosity. Displays of superior musical technique were central to the concept of musical alchemy in the eighteenth century, when counterpoint—the art of combining melodies together in a musical texture of intricate juxtapositions, with parts often fitting together like pieces in a vexing puzzle—was likened to the philosopher's stone. In the right hands, it seemed a dark science touched by the divine, a skill beyond the ability of mere mortals. Some believed that its practitioners cultivated this art in "secret laboratories." (The Dresden Kapellmeister Johann David Heinichen, in a 1728 treatise, reflected the general sense of fear generated by imitative counterpoint—like that found in a fugue—when he compared it to irrational superstition, and called its enthusiasts fanatics.)

That fascination with musical virtuosity as something touched by the otherworldly, as many believed of the music making of Paganini and Liszt, continues to this day. Audiences can regard it with the astonishment of desert wanderers confronted with the parting of the Red Sea. American composer Conlon Nancarrow (1912–1997) stirred such jaw-dropping reactions beginning in the 1940s, with his *Studies for Player Piano*. These pieces transformed a quaint parlor instrument, whose rolls filled with punched holes allowed families to hear great piano performances in their own homes, into a medium for music technically beyond the ability of mere mortals to execute. In Nancarrow's works, musical lines shoot by like lightning; phrases run, skip, dance, and collide at different speeds; bursts of energy seem to threaten to tear the instrument apart.

"We had a player piano in the house when I was a child," he said of his upbringing in Texarkana, Arkansas, "and I was fascinated by this thing that would play all of these fantastic things by itself. And so from then on I had this way in the back of my mind." In late 1939, he read in Henry Cowell's *New Musical Resources* a proposal to use the player piano for the performance of difficult rhythms. It gave him just the push he needed.

PIANOS THAT PLAY THEMSELVES

Before it became the plaything of avant-garde composers, the player piano, with a built-in mechanism for reproducing performances that had been prerecorded, was a valued home-entertainment center. It enabled families, even those lacking musical skills, to enjoy "live" performances of their favorite pieces on demand.

The origins of the instrument date back at least to the eighteenth century, when Haydn and Mozart composed pieces for mechanical organ. The mechanism was adapted to pianos, and Muzio Clementi (in his role as piano maker) offered a "self-acting pianoforte" in London around 1825. A French patent was granted to J. B.

An early player piano

Napoléon Fourneaux for a pneumatic piano in 1863; another patent was granted in the United States in 1881 to John McTammany, a Cambridge, Massachusetts, inventor. The German company Welte produced an improved model in 1887. Before long, the Pianola, a version created by American Edwin Scott Votey in 1895, became all the rage.

Word spread. There was even a player piano on Captain Robert Falcon Scott's 1910 expedition to the Antarctic. Igor Stravinsky composed an *Etude for Pianola* in 1917, and Paul Hindemith offered up a *Toccata for Mechanical Piano* in 1926. Such artists as Claude Debussy, Alfred Cortot, Sergei Rachmaninoff, Arthur Rubinstein, and George Gershwin all made piano-roll recordings.

By the end of the twentieth century, many piano manufacturers were offering electronic, digital versions of the player piano that eliminated the need for clunky paper rolls. Nevertheless, QRS Music Technologies, a firm founded in 1900 in Chicago, continued offering music rolls until December 31, 2008. The last new-issue piano roll that came off the assembly line was the company's 11,060th, a version of "Spring Is Here" by Rodgers and Hart recorded by pianist Michael T. Jones.

Nancarrow's late work employed canons (in which a melody is overlaid upon itself using staggered entrances, as in "Row, Row, Row Your Boat" or "Frère Jacques") with a previously unrealized level of complexity. In his *Study No. 40*, for example, twelve different superimposed melody lines each move at a different tempo. (It's worth noting that the eccentric English composer Kaikhosru Shapurji Sorabji [1892–1988], who was credited in the *Guinness Book of Records* as writing the longest piano work in history, created impossibly difficult pieces that contained nearly as many notes as Nancarrow's. Amazingly, several pianists, including the equally eccentric John Ogdon, managed to record Sorabji's mammoth *Opus Clavicembalisticum*, written in 1930.)

Today, Nancarrow's focus on super-performance continues in the music of composer Noah Creshevsky (b. 1945), who calls his approach "hyperrealism." Creshevsky, whose background included studies with famed French teacher Nadia Boulanger and composer Luciano Berio and a close association with composer Virgil Thomson, had always been fascinated by the idea of transcending human limitations. "I had an uncle," he remembers,

> who did magic tricks. And I hounded him about how he did them. When I finally learned the answers, I was disappointed, because the tricks became commonplace. Boulanger talked about this: How we lose the wonder of childhood and, as artists, have to recapture it somehow in a new, "informed" second childhood. Music ought to be magic, and I'm always aiming for something that goes beyond the ordinary—I don't even want to be able to put my finger on it.
>
> I take materials that are recognizably of this world—real

instrumental and vocal performances—and exaggerate them electronically, creating performances that normal human beings are incapable of producing. As a student, I remember hearing compositions by Liszt that were criticized for their empty virtuosity, but I was always intrigued by that supreme degree of technical accomplishment. My music pushes virtuosity to new levels, resulting in sounds that are lifelike and yet not real.

I like that point which hovers between reality and the magical.

It's a good description of that ineffable state to which the Alchemists aspired, where music and enchantment find common ground.

CHAPTER 9

The Rhythmitizers

PART 1 *The American Adventure Begins*

L IFE IS RHYTHM. We breathe out and in, our hearts beat a familiar tattoo, bodily fluids ebb and flow, and, in this, we join a natural world filled with cycles—from the orbits of the planets and the patterns on mollusk shells to the grinding regularity of cricket song. Such repetitive movement can become the respiration of a musical organism. Sometimes nothing else is needed: in portions of Africa, the gnashing, pounding, and chopping of food and the fetching of water each morning turn village life into song.

All over the world, in fact, the beat goes on, insistent, primal, and unending. Composers harness this endless stream of pulses by forming them into recognizable patterns, groups of two, three, or four beats that give music its "meter." Thus they write marches based on a meter of "2," foxtrots based on repeating groups of "4," and waltzes based on a feeling of "3."

It's easiest to perceive these patterns when they are danced. Indeed, musical rhythm might well have begun with the experience of walking, skipping, hopping, and running, activities that grow from the repeated motions of feet, ankles, legs, and knees working in synchrony. Such regularity—like the methodical spacing of columns in ancient Greek architecture—connects music to poetry, which also employs sequences of "feet," predictable arrangements of weak and strong accents that give birth to "poetic meter." Shakespeare's iambic pentameter is an example, where each line contains five "iambs" (conforming to the sound "short-long"):

The Plantation.
Anonymous.

> When in/de-spair/with for-/tune and/men's eyes,/
> I all/a-lone/be-weep/my out-/cast state. (*Sonnet 29*)

Western music, like poetry, sinks comfortably into such cycles, though both musicians and poets embrace many techniques to avoid the feeling of rhythmic monotony. In a poem, these involve the duration of words, the play of syllables, or the difference in effect between lines that stop suddenly and those that run on. Composers use similar devices—changing articulation, setting up contrasts between long notes and short tones, shifting dynamics, repeating pitches, and making us aware of silence—to enliven their musical phrases.

Beethoven sometimes brought a fiery demeanor to his music by purposely upsetting metrical regularity, creating moments of near chaos by placing accents where they didn't "belong." As the twentieth century approached, such rhythmic play in music, known as "syncopation," became a style unto itself. It arose powerfully in cities throughout the great American melting pot, where European, Caribbean, African, and other traditions collided with each other, especially in neighborhoods like the notorious "Five Points" section of New York, situated at the southern end of Manhattan Island.

By the nineteenth century, Five Points was already one of the meanest spots in the city, a shantytown of wooden tenements built in the shadows of tanneries and slaughterhouses, filled with poor immigrants, mostly Irish, and newly freed slaves. Drinking and fighting were common in the streets, which laid claim to New York's greatest concentration of bordellos and its highest crime rate.

Charles Dickens, no stranger to big-city slums, visited in 1842, and found the place repulsive. "Debauchery has made the very houses prematurely old," he observed. "See how the rotten beams are tumbling down, and how the patched and broken windows seem to scowl dimly, like eyes that have been hurt in drunken frays." But a highlight of his American tour also occurred at Five Points, when he dropped by a dance emporium on Orange Street called Almack's.

A little thrill crept through Dickens as he descended the stairs into the establishment's narrow, low-ceilinged room, where he was greeted by "a buxom fat mulatto woman, with sparkling eyes, whose head [was] daintily ornamented with a handkerchief of many colors." It had been the most exotic experience of his trip thus far. But the truly memorable part of the evening didn't begin until a sixteen-year-old black teenager named Juba rushed onto the dance floor and launched into his routine. At that, the joint exploded.

"Instantly the fiddler grins, and goes at it tooth and nail; there is a new energy in the tambourine; new laughter in the dancers; new smiles in the landlady; new confidence in the landlord; new brightness in the very candles," Dickens wrote in his book *American Notes*. The performance must have been breathtaking:

Single shuffle, double shuffle, cut and cross-out, snapping his fingers, rolling his eyes, turning in his knees, presenting the backs of his legs in front, spinning about on his toes and heels like nothing but the man's fingers on the tambourine; dancing with two left legs, two right legs, two wooden legs, two wire legs, two spring legs—all sorts of legs and no legs—what is this to him? And in what walk of life, or dance of life, does man ever get such stimulating applause as thunders about him, when, having danced his partner off her feet, and himself too, he finishes by leaping gloriously on the bar-counter and calling for something to drink . . . ?

Juba's real name was William Henry Lane. Born in Providence, Rhode Island, he had been tutored in the ways of dance by a black jig-and-reel expert, "Uncle" Jim Lowe. But he went well beyond those first lessons, soaking up all the styles of the time by imitating the best moves of his competitors, no matter what their backgrounds. There was a great deal to absorb. Walt Whitman, as a young reporter in old New York, noted how even butchers in their stalls would, in quiet moments, "amuse themselves with a jig, or a break down."

The dance forms that the Irish brought from home included one called *doubles,* which involved "striking the ground very rapidly with the heel and toe, or with the toes of each foot alternately." Such steps, combined with African-American-bred moves like the *shuffle,* gave birth to tap dancing. It was an evolution helped along by commercial promoters who set up dance contests between performers of different ethnicities, insuring a collision of styles, and provoking audience fervor by exploiting the racial divide. Beginning in 1844, Juba and the Irish-American dance phenomenon John Diamond were each paid very large fees to face off in a series of dance exhibitions in the Chatham and Bowery theaters.

The high-stepping, foot-stomping styles of these men were not just fun to watch. As they beat time with their feet, they also produced a special kind of rhythmical music. Irish jigs and English clog movements combined with minstrel steps and other dances to generate fantastic percussive effects, the sounds as mesmerizing as the motions. Some even rivaled the rhythmic sophistication of a popular nineteenth-century entertainer named Pell who demonstrated amazing virtuosity on the percussive "bones." According to *Dwight's Journal,* published in Boston in 1861, Pell created intricate patterns on his "primitive rattle . . . with the most frantic contortions" producing "something entirely without precedent."

Despite that assertion, Pell did have competitors, however, like a black dancer named Tom from Palestine, Texas, who became known for putting a glass of water on his head and "making his feet go like trip-hammers, sounding something like a snare drum," without spilling a drop. When Juba visited England, critics pointed to his remarkable ability to keep exact time, and found in his sounds "the very genius of African melody," as if he were replicating the hypnotic thumps, whacks, and claps of an indigenous drum ensemble. (Even earlier in Great Britain, according to William Thomas Parke's *Musical Memoirs* of 1830, "Negro tambourinists" were in demand to teach their techniques to "belles of distinction who were anxious to display Turkish attitudes." Tambourines were, after all, one of the trappings of Turkish Janissary bands. In 1804 in Edinburgh, the acknowledged master of the instrument was a teacher named Robert Crichton.)

Before long, piano players were displaying some of the same rhythmic qualities in their performances that dancers and percussionists had used with so much success. In saloons and sporting houses, a new sensation called *ragtime* took hold. ("Negroes call their clog dancing 'raggin,' " reported one commentator in 1889, proposing an origin for the name.) It percolated around the country, from cities in the Midwest and the Northeast all the way to the port of New Orleans. Ragtime's prominent feature was a kind of rhythmic schizophrenia—a catchy jag in the melody produced accents in the "wrong" places, putting it at odds with the pianist's rock-solid left hand, which kept a regular, marchlike accompaniment, moving along as if nothing were amiss.

From where exactly did these odd disruptions of the normal accent scheme come? Dance was always a big influence. Black composer Will Marion Cook (1869–1944) suspected that rag's origins could also be found in visits made by black sailors to Asian ports, particularly to Turkey, where odd rhythms were in the air. Others pointed to Spanish dances like the bolero as an ancestor to the style. The influx of Caribbean culture into New Orleans was an important key, coloring the fabulous stylings of Jelly Roll Morton (1885–1941). Trombonist George Filhe described how, in 1892, young musicians would take the ordinary dances of the day, such as quadrilles and schottisches, and "swing" them, adding greater rhythmic propulsion; some of their elders, he said, were turning to Mexican music as a way of injecting excitement into their programs. (The first mariachi record in the United States was made in 1903 in Chicago.) Decades later, one of New York's top piano attractions, Walter "One-Leg Shadow" Gould, made his reputation by similarly taking Civil War–era schottisches and "sprucing them up."

If the origins are a bit hazy, one thing is certain: the sense of rhythmic excitement in this music was potent. It "sends one's blood tingling," said bandleader Martin Ballmann in 1912. Another commentator, Hiram K. Moderwell, concurred: "I felt my blood thumping in tune," he explained, "my muscles twitching to the rhythm." Newspaper columns were filled with reports of arms and legs spasming to the music, as if electrically shocked. German writer Gustav Kühl, among others, complained that the music was not anything like a respectable Strauss waltz, but rather "like a balking horse that is impossible to master."

Kühl's analysis notwithstanding, European influences abounded, especially in this music's straightforward structures and trite harmonic conventions. This was predictable: numerous all-black bands—Frank Johnson's, James Hemmenway's, and Isaac Hazzard's in Philadelphia; J. W. Postlewaite's in St. Louis; and Walter F. Craig's orchestra in New York—had long served as the musical pillars of upper-class socials, where the bill included old-fashioned dances like cotillions, quadrilles,

Jelly Roll Morton

waltzes, and polkas. Those proper musical models became firmly ingrained in the popular imagination, and difficult to escape. Nevertheless, the new musical genre, filled with infectious "muscle-twitching" rhythms, had an indelible impact.

Many of its leading lights could be found in St. Louis's Chestnut Valley district, home to ragtimer Tom Turpin's famous Rosebud Bar. Besides Turpin, pianists in the area included Scott Joplin, Louis Chauvin, Arthur Marshall, and ragtime composer Charles H. Hunter. The Rosebud held annual contests to find the best ragtime player. New York's Tammany Hall was the scene of another contest (sponsored by *Police Gazette* magazine) that bestowed the title of "Champion Rag Time Pianist of the World" on someone named Mike Bernard in January of 1900. The most significant ragtime piano conclave, though, took place in 1893 at the Chicago World's Fair, where W. C. Handy, Scott Joplin, abolitionist Frederick Douglass, and author W. E. B. Du Bois were among the celebrities attending.

The fair helped establish Chicago as *the* place to be, and State Street quickly became home to some of the best musicians of the day. Jelly Roll Morton, Scott Joplin, and Porter King collaborated on writing the "King Porter Stomp" there. Young white musicians like Benny Goodman, Bix Beiderbecke, Tommy Dorsey, Paul Whiteman, and Bunny Berigan would soon follow as "black and tan" cabarets (where white patrons and black artists cohabited) sprouted up, run by the likes of Jack Johnson, the world's first black heavyweight boxing champion. Chicago's South Side, in nurturing the careers of outstanding pianist Earl Hines, bandleader Cab Calloway, and singers Ethel Waters and Alberta Hunter, soon became known as the "Broadway of the Black Belt." By the 1920s, remembered musician Eddie Condon, there was so much hot music in Chicago that you could stand on a South Side corner, "hold an instrument in the middle of the street and the air would play it."

As ragtime proliferated, the population most responsible for its success turned out to be middle-class white women, in a replay of the Victorian-era piano boom. According to ragtime expert Max Morath, these women were "keyboard-trained in the European manner, participating in America's booming quest for culture. It was mainly our grand-mothers who purchased those colorful rags in million-copy lots."

Ragtime was rather genteel in comparison to the more rambunctious styles that would soon follow. But as early as 1913, a back-lash had already set in. "Can it be said that America is falling prey to the collective soul of the Negro through the influence of what is popularly known as 'rag time' music?" asked a letter to the *New York Herald*, reprinted in the *Musical Courier*. It was a kind of music, claimed the writer, "symbolic of the primitive morality and perceptible moral limita-tions of the Negro type."

Despite that resistance, the music got hotter, and more popu-lar, as it blossomed into early jazz. Lafcadio Hearn, a Greek-born journalist who moved to New Orleans, noted in 1917 that the word "jaz" was commonly used by Southern blacks to mean "to speed things up or make them more exciting," before being adopted by the Creoles to describe a kind of music that featured bouncy, ragged rhythms and accents in unexpected places. Milton "Mezz" Mezz-row, a white Chicagoan born in 1899, expressed the burning inten-sity with which young urban musicians of every color embraced these swinging syncopations when he described roaming the streets and clubs "all jammed up and full of energy, restless as a Mexican jumping bean . . . I felt like I wanted to jump out of my skin, hop off into space . . . I was maneuvering for a new language that would make me shout out loud and romp on to glory. What I needed was

James P. Johnson

the vocabulary. I was feeling my way to music like a baby fights its way into talk." As jazz took on wilder rhythms and greater displays of virtuosity, a new generation of pianists also pushed the art to greater heights. They flourished especially in New York, remembered piano icon James P. Johnson (1894–1955). "The other sections of the country never developed the piano as far as the New York boys did," he explained.

> The reason the New York boys became such high-class musicians was because the New York piano was developed by the European method, system, and style. The people in New York were used to hearing good piano played in concerts and cafés. The ragtime player had to live up to that standard . . . New York developed the orchestral piano—full, round, big, widespread chords and tenths—a heavy bass moving against the right hand. The other boys from the South and West at that time played in smaller dimensions . . . Luckey Roberts was the outstanding pianist in New York in 1913—and for years before and after.

THE EUROPEAN CONTRIBUTION TO JAZZ

There are many more connections between the classical and jazz traditions than are commonly recognized. Even the rhythmic lilt of jazz has correlates in the Baroque practice of playing classical melodies in uneven rhythms, using such figures as the "hornpipe" and "scotch snap." In France, the practice was known as *notes inégales* (unequal notes), and it's possible that this technique influenced musical development in New Orleans. Even the "blue" notes that became associated with jazz can be found in early British sources, such as *The Fitzwilliam Virginal Book*. Theorists commonly labeled these bluesy clashes "cross relations" (the English call them "false relations"). Immigrants brought this sensibility to America, especially in settlements populated by former Englishmen, such as Appalachia and the backwoods of the South, where country blues fiddling took root.

Ragtime's shift into more intricate jazz styles was spearheaded by figures like pianist and composer Eubie Blake (1883–1983), a onetime "buck dancer" (a minstrel dance style) and member of the vaudeville team of Sissle and Blake, who learned piano by sitting at the feet of accomplished performers and watching their fingers. By the age of fifteen he was playing at Aggie Shelton's bordello in Baltimore, and his *Charleston Rag* of 1899 served as the foundation for the East Coast "stride" piano style (so called because the player's left hand "strides" insistently and rapidly between the lowest piano tones and the instrument's midrange).

Dance remained a constant inspiration. Back in New Orleans at the turn of the twentieth century, pianist Tony Jackson (1876–1921) even danced while he played. Teams like Buck and Bubbles (Bubbles—his real name was John W. Sublett—was chosen by George Gershwin to create the role of Sportin' Life in *Porgy and Bess* and gave tap-dancing lessons to Fred Astaire) and the Nicholas Brothers (with their legendary acrobatic style) performed at the great jazz spots, including Harlem's Cotton Club. Indeed, for the musicians, rhythmic flair became just as important *off* the bandstand as on it, remembered James P. Johnson. "All of us used to be proud of our dancing—Louis Armstrong, for instance, was considered the finest dancer among the musicians," he recalled. "It made for attitude and stance when you walked into a place, and made you strong with the gals. When Willie ['The Lion'] Smith walked into a place, his every move was a picture."

Buck and Bubbles

Some of the dazzling figures now executed by keyboardists could also telegraph "attitude," particularly when they embodied a powerful rhythmic current, as they did in boogie-woogie, a style based

Meade "Lux" Lewis

on rollicking left-hand bass patterns that churned over and over like the gears of a train at full throttle. Indeed, there was always an implied association between boogie style and rustic locomotives, with classic works in the genre carrying titles like *Honky Tonk Train Blues* (by Meade "Lux" Lewis, 1927) and *Choo-Choo* (by Duke Ellington, 1926). (There are classical precedents to those left-hand techniques as well, like the rocking broken-chord pattern used by Mozart known as "Alberti Bass." As Willie "the Lion" Smith explained, "The truth is that the familiar boogie figures can be heard in several of the old operatic scores. It wasn't anything new." But the differences are plain: Mozart's sense of classical decorum is quickly demolished in the face of boogie's explosive energy.)

The term "boogie" had been used as early as 1913 at musical rent parties, at which performers raised money to help friends pay the bills. Admission was inexpensive, though partiers had the opportunity to spend more on refreshments, such as pots of chitterlings and pigs' feet and jugs of corn whiskey. "A makeshift bar in the hallway [sold the booze] in half-of-a-pint portions called 'shorties,' " reported one eyewitness. "Then there would be goings-on until daybreak, and rent next day for the landlord." These affairs didn't always maintain the highest musical standards. Musician Romeo Nelson described the scene this way: "You could get away with anything—just hit the keyboard with your elbow and fists, it didn't make no difference to them, they were so drunk by then." But the insistent rhythmic foundation of rent-party piano gave revelers just what they were looking for.

The style started to pop up everywhere. Wilbur Sweatman jumped on board the rhythm train with a *Boogie Rag* in 1917. W. C. Handy, composer of "St. Louis Blues," said he had encountered it in Memphis even earlier, at the turn of the century. Willie "the Lion" Smith reported that he first heard it in Atlantic City in 1914, played by someone known as Kitchen Tom. And trumpeter Bunk Johnson found it in New Orleans, where it was played in bars and barrelhouses. "A barrelhouse," he explained, "was just a piano in a hall. There was always a piano player working when I was a kid. I'd go into a barrelhouse and play 'long with them piano players 'til early in the morning."

This raw, energetic music, sometimes called "barrelhouse and boogie," soon spread to honky-tonks all around the country. It even began to serve as the test of a pianist's mettle. According to Little Brother Montgomery, the Louisiana pianist who arrived in Chicago in 1928, it was impossible for a pianist at that time to get work unless he could play the "Chicago Fives," in all likelihood *The Fives* by Texans George and Hersal Thomas, a piece that contained all the musical gestures of the day: boogie-woogie, ragtime, swing, and the blues. (As it spread, each region of the country developed its own name for the boogie genre. In Mississippi, it was known as "Dudlow Joe.")

Just ten years later, thanks to record producer John Hammond, boogie was heard from the stage of New York's Carnegie Hall in a concert that featured singer Big Joe Turner (1911–1985), along with Pete Johnson (1904–1967), Albert Ammons (1907–1949), and Meade "Lux" Lewis (1905–1964), a formidable trio of pianists who soon after took up residence at Barney Josephson's Café Society, the Greenwich Village haunt of wealthy sophisticates that advertised itself as "The Wrong Place for the Right People."

But boogie wasn't the only musical train roaring down the track. Another "show-off" piano style arose, not coincidentally, with the burgeoning popularity of two new mechanical devices: piano rolls (which hit a peak in sales between 1919 and 1925) and the newfangled invention known as the record player. This was "novelty piano," which often resembled an over-the-top parody of ragtime, with rapid alternations between the hands, flashy patterns running up and down the keyboard, and lots of whimsical filigree (a feat made easier when the source was a piano roll, since additional holes could always be punched by an editor, adding the equivalent of an extra hand or two into the already busy musical texture). Pianist Zez Confrey (1895–1971) was at the center of the novelty storm, with compositions like *Dizzy Fingers*, *Stumbling*, and *Giddy Ditty*. His *Kitten on the Keys* (1921) sold over a million sheet-music copies in its first year, and Confrey performed at the historic Paul White-man concert in 1924 that premiered Gershwin's *Rhapsody in Blue*. Gershwin's own use of novelty effects, in both his piano rolls and published arrangements, shows the pervasive allure of the style.

INDUSTRIAL AMERICA helped spread the word. Small, out-of-the-way communities in the middle of the country, like the Quaker town of Richmond, Indiana, produced a crop of homegrown jazzers who were also catching the bug. Richmond was headquarters for Gennett Studios, one of the small companies that sprang up to reap the rewards of a new, blossoming market in recorded sound. Pianist Hoagy Carmichael (composer of "Star Dust") recalled:

> In the farmlands among the Indiana-Iowa corn, and from the cow-pasture universities, there sprouted a beardless priesthood of jazz players and jazz composers. Instead of buttermilk and Black-stone, we were nurtured on bathtub gin and rhythm . . . It just happened, like a thundercloud. It may sound sentimental to say that young men caught fire in a quest for beauty, that they dedi-cated themselves to its realization, starving and striving, laugh-ing, dreaming, and dying. So it's sentimental, but I think it's true.

Indeed, things got so musically hot in the Midwest that a Nebraska columnist in the late 1920s wrote blithely that "if you want to see some sin, forget about Paris and go to Kansas City." Locals like pia-nist Franklyn Taft Melrose ("Kansas City Frank," who was men-tored by Jelly Roll Morton) established solid jazz credentials.

Gennett, built along a river gorge and railroad tracks, grew as a division of the Starr Piano Company, which by 1915 was producing fifteen thousand instruments annually. Driven by an entrepreneurial spirit (in 1906, Starr was still marketing a small player piano for apartments called "The Princess," which reached a height of just four feet four inches), the company's owners took advantage of ongoing battles over the provenance of the phonograph, which had been invented by Thomas A. Edison in 1877 but subsequently improved upon by various competing parties. As the courts became mired in an attempt to untangle the legal rights to the machine, Gennett decided to offer their own record players and discs beginning in 1916.

By 1922, the Gennett studio, a single-story, grey wooden building set on a concrete floodwall against the Whitewater River, was producing important jazz, blues, and country records. Its roster included Wendell Hall, a folk singer who wore hillbilly garb; fiery speechmakers from the Ku Klux Klan; and comedy troupes (the "Gennett Laughing Record" featured a group of people convulsing uncontrollably at a series of flubbed violin solos).

But the label is best remembered today for its astounding cache of early jazz greats, each making a side trip to record at Gennett while performing in Chicago. Among these were the New Orleans Rhythm Kings, Jelly Roll Morton, and Earl "Fatha" Hines (whose recording debut occurred at the Gennett facilities in 1923, while he was with Lois Deppe's orchestra).

W. C. Handy and his business partner, Harry Pace, started a recording company in New York called Black Swan Records at around the same time. In a play for customer loyalty, their advertisements declared that "all other colored records are by artists only passing for colored." For a while, the blues crest triggered by Mamie Smith and Willie "the Lion" Smith's "Crazy Blues" of 1920 served them well. But the firm lasted only three years. Perhaps word got out that despite their marketing claims, they were actually using white performers with assumed names; more likely, they were simply less-than-savvy businessmen.

B OTH RAGTIME and novelty piano were highly stylized forms, with a fairly rigid catalog of musical gestures. But jazz is a centrifugal force: always pushing outward against the boundaries. The next generations of Rhythmitizers really cut loose, with fingers flying in a swirl of adventurous energy.

PART 2 All That Jazz

JAZZ PIANISTS took the playful spirit of ragtime and boogie and injected a new earthiness. Suddenly, the music seemed to wink at its listeners, as if acknowledging an erotic spark at the heart of every performance. Writer Eudora Welty captured the essence perfectly in *Powerhouse*, her tribute to Thomas "Fats" Waller (1903–1943):

> He is in motion every moment—what could be more obscene? There he is with his great head, fat stomach, and little round piston legs, and long yellow-sectioned strong big fingers, at rest about the size of bananas. Of course you know how he sounds—you've heard him on records—but still you need to see him. He's going all the time, like skating around the skating rink . . . Then all quietly he lays his finger on a key with the promise and serenity of a sibyl touching the book.
>
> Powerhouse is so monstrous he sends everybody into oblivion.

Waller and his close friends James P. Johnson and Willie "the Lion" Smith formed the triumvirate at the center of the powerful Harlem "stride" school of piano playing. The Lion (a name he earned through his fearless soldiering in the Great War) had a nickname for each of his colleagues: Johnson, who "was kind of naïve and easygoing," became "The Brute"; Waller was "Filthy." They were inseparable, and each became a big draw in the black-and-tan clubs, establishments referred to by gossip columnist Walter Winchell as "sepia sin spots," and at Harlem rent parties, where the playing had now reached new levels of virtuosity. "It got so we never stopped and we were up and down Fifth, Seventh, and Lenox all night long

hitting the keys," remembered Smith. "We even had a booking agent—old Lippy [Boyette] . . . On a single Saturday he'd book as many as three parties for us and we'd alternate between them."

The friendly competition pushed each musician to develop a personal style. "My way was to get a cigar clenched between my teeth," related Smith, "my derby tilted back, knees crossed, and my back arched at a sharp angle against the back of the chair. I'd cuss at the keyboard and then caress it with endearing words; a pianist who growls, hums, and talks to the piano is a guy who is trying hard to create something for himself." Each party drew a different kind of crowd, from "formally dressed society folks" to truck drivers, gamblers, and entertainers. But none could compare with those thrown by Park Avenue socialites, who began inviting the troika to their events after the Harlem musicians forged a lasting friendship with pianist/composer George Gershwin.

Fats Waller

Gershwin was a frequent patron of the Harlem clubs, and deeply admired the musicianship of all three pianists. He put the word out to his acquaintances, who often made use of their talents. Yet it wasn't always smooth sailing. The three pianists would often be doted over by partygoers and inspected like rare birds from a dis-

tant shore: "We felt like a couple of whores being interviewed by a high school reporter," said Smith. At one particularly fancy party given in 1924 to celebrate the premiere of Gershwin's *Rhapsody in Blue*, they found themselves adrift at the bar. Gershwin had typically seated himself at the piano and was threatening to stay there all night. (Once he wondered aloud if his music would still be performed in a hundred years. "It will be if you're still around!" murmured his friend Oscar Levant.) The Lion was forced to take action. "I finally went over and said to Gershwin, 'Get up off that piano stool and let the real players take over, you tomato.'" The good-natured star simply smiled and vacated his spot.

Smith felt right at home with Gershwin. The two had grown up in similar surroundings, and the Lion had even learned Yiddish as a young boy while working for Jewish shopkeepers. Indeed, he eventually converted, and late in life advertised his services in Harlem as a Jewish cantor.

Willie "the Lion" Smith and Duke Ellington

W HEN JAZZ IMPROVISERS competed in contests for the crown of top player (known as "cutting sessions"), Smith, Johnson, and Waller were incomparable. That is, until they met a virtually blind pianist from Toledo, Ohio, who had arrived in New York in 1932 as an accompanist for singer Adelaide Hall. "Tatum! You can't imitatum!" wrote critic Barry Ulanov of the great Art Tatum (1909–1956), whose keyboard pyrotechnics left every musician within earshot breathless and dispirited.

WHAT WILLIE "THE LION" SMITH TAUGHT ME
ABOUT STRIDE *by Mike Lipskin*

The left hand in stride gives the piano its own full rhythm section, often a necessity before jazz bass and rhythm guitar proliferated. The style was inaptly named, based on the fact that the left hand tends to "stride" or alternate between the low section of the piano and chords around the middle of the keyboard. But stride is a musical language that uses many devices—riffs, special harmonies, and mixed meters, such as 3/4 against 4/4, and 6/8.

The left hand may play single notes, octaves, full tenths with inner voicings, or arpeggiated chords, with either the top or bottom note being played first. Alternations may further alter the pattern by emphasizing the first and the third beats rather than the normal second and fourth. Various critical rhythmic tensions and releases also appear, sometimes by means of a dynamic rise and fall over a period of measures. All of this, combined with intricate right-hand melodic improvisations, occurs within a rocking, swing beat.

When one first attempts stride after hearing a James P. Johnson or "Fats" Waller display, it's as if you've disassembled your entire car and have the pieces all over the floor just as somebody drives by in a Ferrari. Any jazz pianist attempting the style must listen to the masters and practice it over a period of years, long enough so that the performer does not have to think about each left-hand alternation but can anticipate the music in whole sections or choruses.

Willie "the Lion" Smith's business card

Why do some pianists seem preoccupied with speed rather than substance, often attempting to play a James P. Johnson composition more quickly than he did, rushing faster and faster, as if trying to catch a train? The result always sounds tense and mechanical. It takes time and study to delineate all the musical elements of the style. When you hear the real thing it's as good as jazz piano can get.

"I did double glissandos in sixths, and double tremolos," bragged James P. Johnson. "These would run other ticklers [piano players] out of the place at cutting sessions. They wouldn't play after me . . . I could think of a trick a minute . . . Playing a heavy stomp, I'd soften it right down—then I'd make an abrupt change like I heard Beethoven do in a sonata. Once I used Liszt's *Rigoletto Concert Paraphrase* as an introduction to a stomp." For Tatum, all that was child's play.

Put the finest jazz pianists in a room, remarked jazz icon Teddy Wilson, and Tatum would make them all sound like amateurs. When he played, the piano often resembled a tennis court, with streams of notes shot from one end of the keyboard to the other like blistering ground strokes across an imaginary net. A lob from the bass might be answered by a cascading volley from the treble, each hand hurtling blindingly fast figures at the other in a musical and athletic tour de force. For anyone who challenged him, it was instantaneous "game, set, and match." But his phenomenal note-perfect runs and implausible leaps were just the beginning.

As writer Mait Edey pointed out, "his aim was not [merely] to construct new lines over a given [chord] progression, but to play or suggest the melody of the tune chorus after chorus, erecting a massive structure of countermelodies, fluid voicings, substitute chords, and sometimes whole substitute [chord] progressions."

It all added up to an astonishing command of the music and the instrument. Guitarist Les Paul recalled an after-hours jam session in a Harlem mortuary. Tatum observed for a while, and then asked if one of the piano's F-sharp keys was stuck. "I says, 'Yeah,' " reported Paul. "And he says, 'Is that E stuck?' I said, 'Yeah, it's down, too.' He said, 'Any others down?' I said, 'No, those are the only two.' He says, 'OK, get me another beer.' So I got him another beer, and finally he says, 'Well, I'm ready to go up there.' So when he got up there, boy, he blew everybody away, and whenever he'd make a run . . . with his other hand he'd pull those two keys up so they were ready to go down." (The pianist would sometimes use the same multitasking trick with a glass of beer. But the idea wasn't new. Classical virtuoso Leopold de Meyer used to reach ostentatiously for a bouquet of flowers and bring it to his lips whenever his right hand had half a bar of rest. It drove his female admirers wild.)

Every pianist who encountered Tatum had a war story to tell. Young Count Basie (1904–1984), who, despite prolific gifts as a "stride" player (he took lessons from Fats Waller), developed a sparse, tasteful sound with maximum poise and minimal exertion (the short, light melodic fragments and "fills" that became his signature perfectly counterbalanced the heft of the band,

Billie Holiday accompanied by Art Tatum

and made his playing instantly recognizable), made the mistake of sitting down at a piano in a Toledo club in the late 1920s. "That's when I got my personal introduction to a keyboard monster by the name of Art Tatum," he remembered. "I don't know why I sat down at that piano . . . I just don't know what made me do what I went and did. I went over there and started bothering that piano. That was just asking for trouble, and that's just exactly what I got. Because somebody went out and found Art.

"That was his *hangout* . . . They brought him in there, and I can still see him and that way he had of walking on his toes with his head kind of tilted . . . 'I could have told you,' one of the girls at the bar said.

" 'Why didn't you, baby? Why didn't you?' " pleaded Basie.

When the Harlem striders met up with Tatum, they discovered that same sinking feeling. Stride pianist Donald Lambert (1904–

Count Basie and his band, 1943, with singer Dorothy Dandridge

1962) once made the mistake of offering a public challenge, and when Tatum first arrived in New York, Fats, Johnson, and the Lion felt compelled to have a go at him as well. Maurice Waller, Fats's son, described the event. Each man took a turn at the piano, and they strutted their stuff with utter confidence. The terror from Toledo went last. Launching into the pop hit "Tea for Two," his left hand offered a rock-solid beat while his right played dazzling arpeggios and intricate harmonies; finally, he brought the theme to a roaring climax. James P. made another attempt, playing "Carolina Shout" "as if his hands were possessed by a demon. But it wasn't good enough," said Maurice. Then Waller pulled out all the stops with his showpiece, "A Handful of Keys." But Tatum swept them off their feet with a version of "Tiger Rag." Johnson made a final attempt with his arrangement of Chopin's *Revolutionary Etude*. "Dad told me he never heard Jimmy play so remarkably," wrote Maurice Waller. "But the performance fell short. Tatum was the undisputed king."

The great classical virtuosos Sergei Rachmaninoff and Vladimir Horowitz were also awestruck. Horowitz tried his own hand at an arrangement of "Tea for Two" (as did Russian composer Dmitri Shostakovich in a 1928 work he entitled *Tahiti Trot*). Yet even he couldn't match Tatum's pianistic brilliance. Pianist Steven Mayer recorded note-for-note transcriptions of Tatum's improvisations, and has performed them on programs that feature both Tatum and Liszt. Though the two piano giants operated in different rhythmic worlds, their melodic ideas and technical tricks seem remarkably similar. Perhaps that's why jazz pianists with solid classical training—like Oscar Peterson and the formidable two-fisted player from Detroit, Sir Roland Hanna (1932–2002)—found his approach so gripping.

Sir Roland Hanna

Not all the piano stylists were male, of course. Throughout the 1930s and later, the public came to know such piano celebrities as Estrild Raymona Myers, known as Ramona (1909–1972), who performed with bandleader Paul Whiteman and played duo piano with Gershwin; Hildegarde Loretta Sell, known simply as Hildegarde (1906–2005), who started out as part of an act entitled Jerry and Her Baby Grands and went on to fame in Paris and London, playing at the coronation of King George VI and capping her career with an eightieth-birthday concert at Carnegie Hall; and Dana Suesse (1909–1987), dubbed "the Girl Gershwin" by *The New Yorker*, who wrote a string of hit songs as well as concert pieces (many recorded superbly by pianist Sara Davis Buechner), including *Concerto in Three Rhythms*, which Suesse performed in 1932 with Paul Whiteman. (American pianist Peter Mintun works to keep the contributions of all these women alive.)

Billy Taylor

LEARNING FROM TATUM
by Billy Taylor

The question when you heard Tatum was: "Who are those two guys?" I'm convinced that one of the reasons he became so formidable is that in his youth, the player piano was very much a part of everyone's consciousness. It was in many of the houses in my neighborhood when I was growing up. And when Tatum first heard the player piano, he was listening to rolls on which people had added extra notes after the fact. But he didn't think about those things. He just figured out how to create the same effect with just two hands.

From the time I heard my first Tatum recording, he was my idol. I was always trying to analyze the things he was doing. Of course, I couldn't play like that, though I could play like Fats Waller and Teddy Wilson. It wasn't until late in my career that I finally started trying some of the things he did—like a technique I developed of having a "conversation" between my right and left hands.

That trick developed from the time I would take him out to bars here in New York. We'd all stand around all night waiting for him to play. Finally, after hours, he'd play something and then, in the middle of a solo he'd reach up for a beer without stopping. There was no interruption in the music. I filed that away and thought, "One of these days I'll try that." It occurred to me that if I practiced emulating some of the things he did with his left hand, I could build up enough technique to pull it off.

He told me one time about how he had sent a message to the New York stride players: "Tell James P. and Fats Waller that I'm coming." Being battle-ready was one of the requisites for success in that world. Sometimes, this toughness can lead to amusing situations. For example, Mary Lou Williams organized a jazz festival in Pittsburgh and asked me to put together all the piano players for a session during which they would talk and play. And it resulted in Earl Hines and Duke Ellington playing two pianos together. But for some reason they were not in sync rhythmically and I heard this as soon as they started. And I'm sure they did too, but neither one would give in to the other. It was just plain stubbornness. And it was one of the funniest things I ever heard.

Several women could easily challenge Waller, Johnson, and Smith for musical depth and technical pizazz, including Hazel Scott (1920–1981), Dorothy Donegan (1922–1998), and the ever-evolving Mary Lou Williams (1910–1981). "I'm the only living musician that has played all the eras," boasted Williams to pianist Marian McPartland (b. 1920) on McPartland's acclaimed radio program, *Piano Jazz*. "Other musicians lived through the eras and they never changed their styles." Indeed, moving through all the historical periods from boogie, stride, and swing through bebop

Hazel Scott

and beyond, Williams's restless pursuit of the new made her, in the words of Duke Ellington, "beyond category."

Each of these players, and many others, created a separate strand in the great jazz tapestry. Rhythm still reigned; as poet Langston Hughes put it in "Juke Box Love Song," pianists continued to "take Harlem's heartbeat / Make a drumbeat / Put it on a record, let it whirl." But as formidable musicians built upon jazz's early foundations, the art form began to sprout many branches.

PART 3 *Rock Solid or Teetering on the Brink*

Mary Lou Williams

THE RHYTHMS that had invigorated jazz wound their way like vines through these musical genres and flowered into hybrids. Jazz, blues, country, and Latin American rhythms combined to create the earth-shaking style known as rock 'n' roll. (The Spanish *habanera*, which had earlier found its way into the music of Scott Joplin and Jelly Roll Morton, was ever-present. "If you can't manage to put tinges of Spanish in your tunes," claimed Morton, "you will never be able to get the right seasoning.")

Rock 'n' roll's earliest hits—such as Bill Haley's 1954 version of "Shake, Rattle and Roll," and Fats Domino's 1955 recording of "Blue Monday"—are drenched in both boogie and the habanera. Jazz musicians were its foundational artists; young jazz pianist Phineas Newborn Jr., performing on tour with a band led by his father, Phineas Newborn Sr., helped create the musical backup for rock pioneer Jackie Brenston.

Even this style's name had a blues and jazz legacy. The singing Boswell Sisters (Martha, Connie, and Helvetia) recorded a song with the title "Rock and Roll" in 1934, though they claimed that the title reflected the "rolling, rocking rhythm of the sea." When blues singer Trixie Smith recorded "My Daddy Rocks Me (with One Steady Roll)" in 1922, and Duke Ellington recorded "Rockin' in Rhythm" in 1931, they had something a bit coarser, and closer to the spirit of rock 'n' roll, in mind.

With the birth of rock, the cultural warning alarms went off, just as they had for jazz. *The New York Times* quoted noted psychiatrist Dr. Francis J. Braceland that rock 'n' roll was a "communicable disease." *Time* compared gatherings of its youthful celebrants to "Hitler's mass meetings." In Newport, Rhode Island, the music was banned from the naval station due to a "beer-bottle-throwing, chair swinging riot" at a Fats Domino concert, which Rear Admiral Ralph D. Earle Jr. blamed on the performance's "frenzied tempo." Some of the response was certainly racially motivated. As Elvis Presley, the king of rock 'n' roll, told the *Charlotte Observer* in 1956, "The colored folks been singing and playing it just like I'm doing now, man, for more years than I know. I got it from them."

The music, though, often flowed freely across racial boundaries. "Blueberry Hill," one of "Fats" Domino's (b. 1928) hits, had been introduced by Gene Autry and also achieved success in a recording by the Glenn Miller Orchestra; the Platters' "Smoke Gets in Your Eyes" was penned by Jerome Kern and Otto Harbach for the 1933 operetta *Roberta*. But there was an inevitable sense in the black community that white performers were exploiting their musical language—and, of course, black jazz and rhythm-and-blues musicians had been shamelessly swindled throughout the decades. Ray Charles (1930–2004), a fabulous rhythm-and-blues pianist and perhaps the most soulful singer of his era, saw it differently, though: "I believe in mixed musical marriages, and there's no way to copyright a feeling or a rhythm or a style of singing. Besides, it meant that White America was getting hipper."

Nevertheless, it was alarming for some to witness pop singer Pat Boone (b. 1934) achieve spectacular success with a version of Domino's "Ain't That a Shame." The face of a vanilla, middle-of-the-road America, Boone, with his white buck shoes and clean-cut persona, signaled membership in a very different club than that of the rockers. That 1955 hit had been Antoine "Fats" Domino's biggest success.

Five feet two inches tall and 224 pounds, Domino grew up in New Orleans idolizing another Fats—Waller. His early shows included a finale in which this big man would shove the piano across the stage as the band played "When the Saints Come Marching In." But by the early 1950s he had moved beyond clownish antics with three million-selling records: "The Fat Man," "Goin' Home," and "Going to the River." The magazine *Ebony* summed up his electrifying appeal this way: Elvis and Pat Boone may make the kids "flop around like headless chickens," it said, but when Fats Domino "builds to a climax, riding along on the locomotive-like beat of a seven-man combo, pandemonium erupts. Teenagers shriek and contort their bodies; their limbs jerk in spastic rhythms; their eyes roll" and they shake "like leaves." That latter image seems awfully close to that of headless chickens, but perhaps it was a matter of degree. The crowds did seem to lose control in his presence: Fats Domino performances sometimes required police intervention. "I don't know why music should make anybody fight," he lamented, genuinely perplexed. "It makes me happy even when I'm feeling bad."

Fats was a happy man indeed, and he showed no ill will toward Pat Boone. At a concert in New Orleans he invited the white singer up on stage to sing "Ain't That a Shame" with him. Alluding to the extra income he received from Boone's smash recording of his song, Fats pointed to a finger on his hand: "This man bought me this ring with this song," he announced.

Other rock piano dynamos included "Little Richard" Penniman (b. 1932), who according to producer Robert "Bumps" Blackwell was the only performer he ever met "who would beat the piano so hard he'd break an eighty-gauge [sic] piano string." Little Richard's "frantically charged piano playing and raspy, shouted vocals on such classics as 'Tutti Frutti,' 'Long Tall Sally,' and 'Good Golly, Miss Molly,' " announced the Rock and Roll Hall of Fame, "defined the dynamic sound of Rock and Roll."

And then there was the aforementioned Jerry Lee Lewis, nick-named "the Killer." Lewis's appeal also stemmed from manic energy. The more he lost control, the happier his fans became. As journalist Andy Wickham wrote, "Presley shook his hips; Lewis raped his piano. He would play it with his feet, he would sit on it, he would stand on it, he would crawl under it, and he would leap over it." Critics of the music and the lifestyle were aghast. But nothing speaks like success. Jerry Lee claimed there were almost as many zeroes on his checks as there had been F's on his third-grade report card. His style relied mostly on boogie-woogie figures, along with aggressive glissandos and country music sounds that imitated gui-tar strums, "bent note" effects, and "sliding tones" (known to gui-tarists as "hammer-ons" and "pull-offs"), a style that also came to be associated with Nashville pianist Floyd Cramer (1933–1997).

B Y THE 1960s, rock had smoothed over its edges, dropping the "and roll" portion of the label, and incorporating some of the lyrical qualities associated with the Great American Songbook. Some rock pianist-songwriters, like Neil Sedaka (b. 1939), Carole King (b. 1942), and Barry Manilow (b. 1943) veered far from the edginess of rock's origins, while others, like Elton John (b. 1947), Billy Joel (b. 1949), and Stevie Wonder (b. 1950) continued to reshape and refine the tradition.

The Spanish-tinged rhythms that fed rock's percussive fervor became the foundation of New Orleans piano, a complex blend with as much zest and brazenness as the city's celebrated gumbo. The father of this style was Henry Roeland Byrd (1918–1980), known as both "Professor Longhair" and "Fess." Fess's recipe (not unlike that for gumbo) threw in a little of everything—a pinch of barrelhouse, a dash of gospel, and even a touch of calypso. The mix was delectable. He was inducted into the W. C. Handy Blues

Hall of Fame in 1981 and into the Rock and Roll Hall of Fame in 1992. The famous New Orleans club Tipitina's was named after one of his most acclaimed recordings. It is still a center of this type of music.

WRITING MY MUSIC *by Billy Joel*

A lot of my songs began as an exercise for the piano, something that could be played on its own. I think of how Mozart must have approached his music. Writing in sonata form satisfied his need for melody and variation; [he had] something that led away from the theme, which I call a bridge; and then he reiterated and concluded it. I think this goes back to my piano lessons, all that Kuhlau and Mozart and Clementi; their melodies can easily end up as songs.

Remember that group in the 1960s that took a Bach melody and turned it into a hit song [that started,] "How gentle is the rain . . ." ["A Lover's Concerto" by the Toys]? Then there was a version of a Mozart sonata, sung by a group called the Tymes: "Somewhere, my love waits for me." I'm writing my own classical pieces, to turn into rock and roll songs.

The master wizard is Beethoven. He's the one I keep going back to over and over again. I discover secrets about music by what I call "breaking the Beethoven codes." His harmonies are filled with things you don't notice. There are times when I'll think, "He did this on the bottom, underneath the chord," and the hair will stand up on my arms.

One of the things you like about this kind of music is its variation, its shadings, nuance, and subtlety. Rock and roll, on the other hand, obliterates. That's the essence of rock. [But] its sexual energy, passion, angst, rage are in classical music too. I guess it's a matter of maturing to the point that you're ready to hear something other than the same three-chord songs over and over.

Among Professor Longhair's descendants were Huey "Piano" Smith (b. 1934), who exerted a huge influence on rock players with rollicking numbers like "Rockin' Pneumonia and the Boogie Woogie Flu"; stylist Allen Toussaint (b. 1938); the short-lived James Booker (1939–1983); and Mac Rebennack (b. 1940), also known as "Dr. John."

The next generation of New Orleans musicians introduced an even greater level of technical command. Among them was the phenomenal blind pianist Henry Butler (b. 1949), who absorbed the exciting rhythmic interplay between right and left hands trademarked by Professor Longhair and brought it to new levels of complexity, often giving the illusion, as in his piece *Orleans Inspiration,* that more than one player is performing.

*Professor
Longhair*

SPANISH RHYTHMS MOVED northward as well, through Puerto Rican, Dominican, and Cuban immigrants. They burst onto the dance scene in New York with the fiery mambo, cha-cha, and merengue, then settled in the 1960s and 1970s into a style known as "salsa" ("sauce," as in the multilayered blend that gave the music its special flavor). "The piano assumes a unique role in the Latin tradition," explains Grammy Award–winning Latin-jazz pianist Arturo O'Farrill.

In the beginning, it served, as early jazz piano did, as a kind of parlor instrument. One of the purveyors of the style was Amer-

ica's Louis Moreau Gottschalk, who began to write with different syncopations than those used by Scott Joplin or Jelly Roll Morton, rhythms influenced by things he heard in Havana. Another influence was Cuban Ignacio Cervantes [1847–1905]. But the piano did not become a distinctly different voice until music in Puerto Rico and Cuba became more folk-oriented.

In the mountains of those countries, roving bands of troubadours, accompanied by guitar and percussion, would improvise, in a tradition that continues to this day. Of course, pianos don't travel well into the mountains. So, back in the city, the piano began to mimic the guitarists' arpeggios [chords broken up into single-note melodies] and raggedy, offbeat patterns. These figures were called *montunos,* which comes from the Spanish word for "mountains."

As the style moved farther and farther away from the polite parlor tradition, it became wildly popular. Today, the sound of the montuno is the first thing people think of when we use the phrase "Latin music."

Mac Rebennack ("Dr. John")
LISA HOULGRAVE

Leaders among the contemporary crop of Latin musicians include Cuban pianist Chucho Valdés (b. 1941), who, says O'Farrill, brought "supervirtuosity—a Lisztian technique—to Latin music. He comes from the Russian classical school of piano technique, which all Havana conservatories practice. Gonzalo Rubalcaba [b. 1963] is also an extraordinary technician, and often regarded as Valdés's protégé." From the island of Puerto Rico, two brothers, Eddie Palmieri (b. 1936) and Charlie Palmieri (1927–1988), came to represent Latin music's move toward modernism.

E ACH OF THESE styles was built on compelling rhythmic patterns. But one other twentieth-century approach that had
nothing in common with these more traditional frameworks seeped
into both the jazz and classical traditions.

In the classical world, it manifested itself in the unsettling
rhythms of Bartók and Stravinsky. In the jazz world, it surfaced
in the music of Dave Brubeck (b. 1920). His 1959 album *Time Out*
featured improvisations on tunes written not in comfortable meters
of three or four, but in five (the phenomenally popular *Take Five* by
saxophonist Paul Desmond), seven, and nine.

Brubeck claimed that his childhood experiences served as
the source of those weird time feels. He grew up on a forty-five-
thousand-acre ranch, he said. When "your father sends you to fix
a fence or start an engine, you are alone," he recalled. "The sound
of those little gas engines—*Chu Chu Chu! Gitcha! Gitcha! Bu Ah
Uh!*—you never knew what they were going to do next. And when
the horse would bring me somewhere, there was no one to talk to.
So I became aware of the gait of the horse." He simply tuned in to
all the rhythmic play going on around him.

"And then, I [also] heard a recording made by the Denis-Roosevelt
expedition in the Belgian Congo," he explained, referring to film-
maker Armand Georges Denis's and his wife's, Leila Roosevelt's,

ABOVE LEFT
Chucho Valdés

ABOVE RIGHT
Eddie Palmieri
TAD HERSHORN

Dave Brubeck

venture to the region in 1935–1936. "And these rhythms were so complicated! I thought the sound was unbelievable. And I felt that jazz should reflect its African roots. But at first, most of the jazz musicians objected to what I was doing with unusual meters."

Indeed, he was often accused of failing to "swing," an overused and often misunderstood term. ("Swing" is sometimes described as a sense of forward propulsion, but it has more to do with a feeling of organic unity; something swings when its rhythmic, harmonic, and melodic aspects all combine in a way that naturally fits the style of the music. Every great musician, jazz or classical, embodies it in his or her own distinctive manner.) But audiences loved the freshness of Brubeck's vision, and eventually most of his detractors also came around.

CHAPTER 10

The Melodists

PART 1 *Straight from the Heart*

M ELODY IS THE part of the music we leave the concert hall humming. Composers may "develop" it through crafty variations, fragment it into small odds and ends, or cover it with a thick blanket of harmonies. But melody, in its simple, naked form, is perhaps the thing audiences crave most. Liberace, a twentieth-century piano personality with a huge television following, used melody as his formula for success: "My whole trick is to keep the tune well out in front," he said. "If I play Tchaikovsky, I play his melodies and skip his spiritual struggle."

Most popular works are abundant in tunefulness, even without the helpful tampering of a television star. But not all melodies are alike; some are cool and cultivated, others filled with passion and allure. Composers may create bouncy jingles, as effervescent as vintage Champagne, or stark, angular cries built of icy threads of sound.

These differences show up era to era. Modern tastes embrace an unsentimental, just-get-to-the-point sort of lyricism: simple, soothing, and fashionably laid back. The great Romantics, however, like Chopin, Tchaikovsky, and Rachmaninoff, composed long, soaring phrases. In their unsettled expanse, they mirrored the endless yearnings of a generation of broken hearts. The short-lived, remarkably prolific composer Franz Schubert (1797–1828) is a spiritual forefather of this group.

Makers of beautiful tunes are often disparaged; American composer Ned Rorem once remarked that Debussy is held in higher regard than his fellow Impressionist Maurice Ravel simply because Ravel wrote prettier melodies. An 1869 program note for the Royal Philharmonic Society by Sir George Macfarren is similarly revealing in regard to Schubert, calling him "ill trained, nay, all but uneducated in the mechanism of composition," and yet with "such an affluence of ideas as has enriched few of the greatest masters." He was a fountain of good tunes, claimed Macfarren, but "failed in technical skill for their development." This was in response to Schubert's free-floating imagination, which made his forms more elastic. In retrospect, the critique of compositional weakness is off-target; perhaps this composer's greatest talents were in his ability to milk a theme while creating the perfect textures to match it. Indeed, in Schubert, it is often the musical atmosphere that lingers in the memory. "Schubert's Sonatas," wrote novelist Elfriede Jelinek, "contain more forest hush than the forest itself."

He was no Liszt or Paganini. Schubert was shy and unglamorous, with a "round, plump, somewhat swollen face," according to Heinrich Kreissle von Hellborn, set off by a low forehead, "pouting lips," and a "stumpy nose." (His nickname was "Little Mushroom.") His music, even at its splashiest, is not meant to dazzle; it looks inward. "He was to music its great heart, as Beethoven was its great mind," wrote H. L. Mencken.

Still, Schubert's emotions were consistently tempered by a classical restraint. "He never allowed violent expression in performance," wrote his contemporary Leopold von Sonnleithner. "Everything that hinders the flow of the melody and disturbs the evenly flowing accompaniment is . . . contrary to the composer's intention and destroys the musical effect."

Schubert once told his friend Josef Hüttenbrenner, "I have come into the world for no purpose but to compose," and it certainly seemed that way to his teachers, who were dumbfounded by his talents. "If I wanted to instruct him in anything, he already knew it," said Michael Holzer, who was content merely to watch over his young ward "with silent astonishment." Vienna's revered Antonio Salieri, the court musical director, happily took him on as a composition student.

THE SINGING PIANO IN MOZART AND SCHUBERT *by András Schiff*

Schubert was one of the best melodists of all time, and probably the greatest composer of song. If you want to understand his piano music, you must approach it through his songs—just as you have to approach Mozart's piano works through his operas. In Mozart's keyboard pieces, each theme is like a character. I see his C minor Fantasy, for example, as a miniature version of *Don Giovanni*. In seven or eight minutes, you have the overture, the arias, the various character roles, and the great finale.

Both composers require us to make the piano sing. Of course, they were aware of the instrument's shortcomings: you play a note on the piano, and the minute you hit it, it starts to diminish. There is no way to avoid this. The piano cannot sustain a long note, or make it swell. It

Franz Schubert, lithograph of 1846 by J. Kriehuber (1801–1876)

can't produce a perfectly smooth legato—a real singing voice. Yet the art of piano playing rests on the ability of a musician to create the illusion of these things. Why does Beethoven write a crescendo on a long note at the end of the first movement of his *Les Adieux* Sonata when it is impossible to achieve on a piano? As a performer, you have to use your powers of imagination to convince yourself that it really is possible. (There are also extramusical ways to convince an audience, but they involve visual cues that won't work in recordings.)

Unfortunately, many people have the wrong idea about how these ends are achieved. Pianists often think that creating an ideal legato in Mozart's long passages of sixteenth notes means playing them evenly—it's what the piano competitions honor. But it's wrong. These melodic lines should never sound like a necklace of even pearls, because some of the notes are more important than others—they may represent the basic harmony, or act as leading tones, or serve as "guest notes" (a term I use for tones that stick out as dissonances). Such passages need to be shaped.

The illusion of singing is equally important when playing Schubert, where each piano work is actually a song without words. Perhaps calling him a melodist simplifies the matter, because he is also a genius of harmony, of modulations, of drama. But his songs give us important cues and associations that help when interpreting the piano pieces, because they combine music and poetry—they tell a story. And we can learn to recognize certain types of musical figures from these stories when they appear in the piano music as well, so we might say: "Ah, this is like the movement of the brook in *Die schöne Müllerin*." Schubert's musical language has its own grammar—filled with commas, question marks, and exclamation points. The songs open the door.

But fame was elusive. He sent one of his greatest songs, "Der Erlkönig," to the publisher Breitkopf and Härtel and they simply returned it . . . to the wrong Schubert! The recipient, another man named Franz Schubert who lived in Dresden rather than Vienna, sent word to the publisher that he was keeping the music in order to learn who had submitted "that sort of trash" with *his* name on it. Nevertheless, a coterie of admirers in Vienna began organizing "Schubertiads," all-Schubert musical evenings. "There was a grand feeling and dancing" afterward, reported Franz von Hartmann about one such event, where Schubert and his friends continued to talk and drink into the night.

In Schubert's very short life he managed to compose over six hundred songs, a handful of symphonies, chamber music, operas, and piano sonatas. His marriage of text and musical accompaniment created unforgettable images, such as "Gretchen at her spinning wheel, the father and child galloping through the haunted night, restless love beneath the pelting of the pitiless storm," wrote Sir W. H. Hadow in the 1904 *Oxford History of Music*, in reference to some of the composer's most famous songs. In them, explained Hadow, music and poetry "are no longer two but one, a single indivisible utterance of lyric thought." There is something deeply poetic even about his purely instrumental music. His great B-flat Piano Sonata, D. 960, the last of his works in the genre, is a journey that encompasses transcendent calm, distant rumbles, expansive, sunlit landscapes, triumphal fanfares, and dark forebodings, all within the first few minutes of the first movement.

Schubert requested that he be buried near Beethoven, the towering figure who had eclipsed all who followed, especially in Vienna, and comparisons between the two were inevitable. Each had pushed music into strange new territories. But Beethoven deliberately shocked listeners as he stormed the barricades of musical form. Schubert simply wandered down wayward roads, not a musical warrior so much as someone exploring a maze, captivated by the journey and filled with wonder at every step.

THE THEME of strangeness runs through the life and music of another great melodist, who spent his early years idolizing the man he referred to as "my only Schubert." Robert Schumann (1810–1856) was the archetypical Romantic, a tormented soul who burst on the scene like a shooting star, then plunged into insanity, illness, and an early demise. Novelist Gustave Flaubert's definition of the

Robert Schumann

artist as "a monstrosity—something outside nature" suggests the flavor of Schumann's life.

He had his first major breakdown at the age of twenty-three. Even earlier, at nineteen, he seriously injured a finger while using a mechanical contraption to achieve greater flexibility, and lapsed into a month of heavy drinking, during which he suffered tremors, confusion, blackout spells, and nightly hallucinations. The gruesome remedy recommended for these physical ailments was known as "animal baths," and involved sticking his hand into the innards of slaughtered creatures. It brought on further psychic torment, and of course his hand remained crippled.

He was enthralled by music, and by the fantasy worlds of the writers E. T. A. Hoffmann and Jean Paul. He left law school and sought out Friedrich Wieck—the piano teacher (and father) of famed child prodigy Clara Wieck—who promised to make him a Paganini of the piano. But Clara, nine years his junior and an established performer, captured nearly all of her father's attention. It was an unhappy collaboration: teacher and student were often at odds. Wieck wanted Schumann to become "more manly" and to abandon his "unrestrained fantasy." That wasn't going to happen; Schumann was by nature a dreamer. He confessed to his diary that he had always felt trapped "between form and shadow." In the face of this pressure, he produced imaginary companions—Florestan, the freewheeling, passionate improviser, and Eusebius, the introspective poet—to express the splintered parts of his ego. They would soon inhabit his music.

When Wieck took his daughter on an extended performance tour, Schumann looked elsewhere, reaching out to Johann Nepomuk Hummel (1778–1837), who had been Mozart's most gifted student. Though Schumann had studied Hummel's exercises and admired them, the choice was a peculiar one. Unlike Schumann, Hummel was a melodist who emphasized restraint and purity over emotion. Schumann's sensibilities had placed him on the other side of the piano-playing spectrum, with Wieck's own favorite model, John Field (1782–1837), considered a "singer among pianists." Hummel was not interested. He called the music Schumann sent him "distinctive" but "somewhat bizarre." (Later, reviewing Hummel's Etudes, op. 125, Schumann, under the guise of Florestan, retaliated by lamenting their absence of "imagination.")

So Schumann stayed with Wieck. And when Wieck returned home with the now fifteen-year-old Clara, something new sparked the household dynamic; the pair had unwittingly brought Cupid along with them. Robert's Piano Sonata in F-sharp minor, op. 11 (influenced by Hummel's work in the same key), was the first sign that something had changed. It was a musical valentine dedicated "to Clara by Florestan and Eusebius" and based partly on a theme she had composed, along with a love song, "To Anna," written by Schumann while he was still a teenager.

Thus began one of the great love stories in music history. Wieck did everything in his power to stop it, even going to court to prevent their marriage. But Robert and Clara were inseparable. Even after his death in 1856, she remained the chief interpreter of his music, becoming a solemn musical "priestess" who dressed in black and devoted all her efforts to her late husband's memory.

Clara had a lot of practice in fulfilling the role of faithful servant. Her mother, Marianne, one of Wieck's former students, had assisted her husband and bore him five children during their eight years of marriage—before leaving him for one of Friedrich's former teachers. At that point, Clara became the gleaming trophy of his life's work, and she dutifully performed on command. By the age of nine, she had played in the Leipzig Gewandhaus; at age twelve she performed in Paris. In Vienna, at eighteen, she gained the admiration of Paganini, Chopin, Liszt, and Mendelssohn, who reported he was "wholly astonished" by her. (Paganini was, in Wieck's eyes, a musical god, unrivaled in technical accomplishment and in the ability to move an audience. Clara had first played for him many years before, in 1829, at the age of ten, "on an old, very poor piano with black keys," and he promptly announced that she had a calling for the art.)

On that Viennese trip, newspapers reported a new confection being served in local restaurants: "torte à la Wieck." "It was recently advertised in the *Theaterzeitung* with the comment that it was an ethereal, light dessert that played itself into the mouth of the eater. Isn't that a laugh?" she wrote to Robert. Austria's great poet Franz Grillparzer wrote a hymn of praise after hearing her play the "Appassionata" Sonata, entitled "Clara Wieck and Beethoven."

Clara also composed, but Wieck discouraged her attempts at what he considered a manly art. "I once believed that I possessed creative talent," she wrote in her diary in November of 1839, "but I have changed my mind about this idea; a woman must not wish to compose—no one has yet been able to do it, should I be destined for it?" Nevertheless, the handful of works she left behind show an exquisite talent. Reviewing Clara's *Soirées musicales* (written 1834–36), Robert declared that they revealed "a life effulgent and tender, apparently responsive to the slightest stirring . . . [with] a wealth of unconventional resources, [and] an ability to entangle the secret, more deeply twisting threads and then to unravel them, something one is accustomed to expect only from experienced artists—and males!"

Schumann's own music contained more secret, twisting threads than a spy novel. He embedded codes in almost every work, often referencing his love of the moment or scenes from his favorite literature. His early *Abegg Variations*, op. 1, used the name of his dancing partner at a Mannheim ball, Meta Abegg, for its theme (A, B-flat, E, G, G). *Papillons (Butterflies)*, op. 2, portrayed scenes from Jean Paul's novel *Flegeljahre*, musically rendering such images as an "aurora-borealis sky full of crossing, zig-zag figures," and "a giant boot that was sliding around, dressed in itself." In *Carnaval*, op. 9, he took the letters of the birthplace of Ernestine von Fricken, a momentary romantic obsession, and combined them with those letters in his own name that could be translated into music notation. Ernestine's town was Asch—in German musical nomenclature, A,

E-flat, C, and B natural—and Schumann's name was rendered as Scha (E-flat, C, B natural, and A). The themes created from these combinations permeate the piece, and even appear in a cryptic chart in the printed music entitled "Sphinxes."

Sphinxes

He placed musical references to Clara in his works as well. His *Davidsbündlertänze* (*Dances of the Confederates of David*), written after Clara pledged herself to him, consists of a set of dances, each signed by either Florestan or Eusebius; he claimed that Clara could be found passing lightly all through it. The title was named for a band of crusaders, partly imagined and partly real, conceived by Schumann to fight against the forces of artistic ignorance, just as David had fought the Philistines. Even his *Novelettes* are allusions to Clara; he decided that the name *Wieckettes* wasn't pleasant sounding, so he used the name of another Clara he knew, the singer Clara Novello, to form the title.

PLAYING SCHUMANN *By Emanuel Ax*

If you want a definition of the Romantic in music, Schumann was it. Everything he wrote was over the top. The music can be incredibly passionate or superbly quiet—he'll go as far as he can in any direction.

Compare him to someone like Chopin, and you realize that while Chopin was a genius and unbelievably inventive, he had a French side, which expresses itself in a sense of balance and restraint. There is a kind of structure in his brain that gets transmitted through the music. With Schumann, the structure is there, but you're not meant to be aware of it. The music just seems wild and impulsive, and the foundation is often hidden. Playing it becomes an adventure.

The Sphinxes chart in Schumann's Carnaval

Schumann constantly surprises with mood swings, unusual structures, and changing textures. His music is beautiful, but, as Hummel noted, there is always an element of the bizarre at its core. "I am very pained that Robert's compositions are not recognized as they deserve to be," wrote Clara in an early diary. "I would very much like to play them but the public does not understand them." The sounds, though warm and sincere, are often filled with references to a mysterious fantasy world beyond the notes. Schumann's *Humoresque*, op. 20, even contains a line that is not to be played; it is printed as an implied "inner" melody, revealed only to the performer. A clue to such mysterious games might be found in the verse by critic Friedrich Schlegel that the composer attached to his Fantasy in C, op. 17: "Through all of the tones that sound in this colorful earth-dream, there emerges one ethereal tone for him who listens in secret."

That ethereal tone proved his undoing. As his mental instability progressed, Robert began hearing a single note drumming incessantly inside his head. On February 10, 1854, it dissolved into music "more wonderfully beautiful and played by more exquisite instruments than ever sounded on earth." He tried to write down this theme sent to him by "the angels." But on February 27, the voices turned demonic, and he threw himself into the Rhine. Schumann entered an asylum in March, never to emerge again.

A DEVASTATED CLARA WAS comforted after her loss by the composer who had become an intimate of the Schumanns after Robert first heard his formidable music and dubbed him "Athena springing fully armed from the head of Zeus." Johannes Brahms (1833–1897) was indeed impressive even in his youth, though the forward-looking cognoscenti found little to like about his attachment to the formal practices of the past. The critic of Leipzig's the *Signale*, in a review of Brahms's First Piano Concerto, gave voice to the claim that the composer was too academic and unemotional, describing his music as "waste, barren dreariness." In Boston, critic Philip Hale proposed that the city's new Symphony Hall mark a special door with the words "Exit in case of Brahms." Tchaikovsky offered the cruelest cut of all: Brahms, he said, was nothing but "a giftless bastard," and he found it annoying "that this self-inflated mediocrity is hailed as a genius." Schumann seemed prescient when he declared that Brahms was "another John the Baptist, whose revelations will puzzle many of the Pharisees, and everyone else, for centuries."

Why the many dismal reviews? The prevailing winds were against him. Brahms drew on the technical mastery of Bach, Handel, and Palestrina, as well as Beethoven (who trumped them all), at a time when the classical world was tossing out the old forms and embracing free-flowing emotion, as exemplified by the music and polemics of Richard Wagner (1813–1883). (Wagner had his critics, too, of course—Clara Schumann, for one. And the venerable Italian composer Gioachino Rossini, though cautioning that one could not judge a Wagner opera after just a first hearing, nevertheless quipped, "I certainly don't intend on hearing it a second time.")

According to Clara, Brahms spoke of "how the old masters had the freest form, while modern compositions move within the stiffest and most narrow limits." Indeed, the twentieth-century revolutionary Arnold Schoenberg wrote an essay, "Brahms the Progressive," to link his own twelve-tone technique, in which every aspect of a piece is derived from a single thematic kernel, with the tightly controlled mastery found in the music of Brahms.

The charges against Brahms of being too cerebral, dry, and complex were made in the context of a culture war, with Wagnerian forces arrayed against a group seen as too elitist and, not coincidentally, too Jewish. One critic complained of Brahms's use of "Jewish-temple triplets." Another lumped him with Eduard Hanslick (whose book *The Beautiful in Music* argued that music was not directly expressive of emotions and should be valued purely for its formal elements) along with other members of "the music-loving and music-making Jewry." Brahms, who was of course not Jewish, found the whole trend repugnant. "I can scarcely speak of it," he said, "it seems so despicable to me."

Despite the accusations, he was not a product of the conservatory.

Young Brahms

At the age of ten, he was playing the piano in public, often in waterfront bars and bordellos. By twenty, he had written several major piano works, all of them, wrote *New York Times* critic Harold C. Schonberg (expressing the vacillation that even sincere fans seem to bear), "serious and thick, with rumbling basses, awkward figurations, and an almost complete lack of charm. But they radiated bigness; there was something monumental about them." They were also filled with gorgeous melodic ideas, gripping rhythmic innovations, and daunting piano acrobatics. His two piano concertos are fiendishly hard. Pianist and composer Anton Rubinstein pointed to Brahms's biggest problems: "For the drawing room, he is not graceful enough," he claimed, "for the concert hall not fiery enough, for the countryside not primitive enough, for the city not cultured enough."

Heartwarming melodies could break through Brahms's natural austerity like a ray of sunshine piercing the clouds. In the piano Intermezzos, lyrical themes seduce the ear and stir deep emotions, despite the intellectual elements (like his trademark asymmetrical phrases) that always threaten to intrude on the state of reverie.

Brahms remained undeterred. He would often brandish a rapier wit against a world that was frequently unsympathetic. During a rehearsal of one of his quartets, the violist asked if he liked their tempos. "Yes," said Brahms, "especially yours." Once, when a lady gushed, "How do you write such divine adagios?" he replied, "My publisher orders them that way."

But when he was with the Schumanns, all was different. Robert embraced him from the beginning, introduced him to important musicians as well as to his very first publisher, and even insisted that the young man move into their home. Brahms became devoted to the couple, and was at Clara's side when Robert tried to commit suicide. Following Schumann's death, he fell in love with her. Nevertheless, from all appearances, the relationship remained platonic.

According to a grandson, Ferdinand Schumann, Brahms, who visited Clara in 1894 and 1895 (now transformed, he noted, from a handsome, slim composer into "a corpulent little gentleman" with a half-red, half-grey mustache, a high voice that sounded "as if it were cracked," and long hair that fell "rather low over the back of his coat collar"), told her that by this time he no longer composed for the public but only for himself, and confessed that after the age of fifty, his creative powers had begun to diminish. Nevertheless, reported Ferdinand, Brahms still rose as early as seven in the morning, accompanying his fingers on the piano keyboard with "peculiar sounds—one might call them a sort of gasping, grumble or snoring." Clara remained steadfast, of course. "Brahms is without a rival," she argued when others proffered comparisons. "[He] stands alone among the living." They passed away only months apart.

The older Brahms

THE MUSICAL REPUTATION of Felix Mendelssohn (1809–1847) fell victim to the same forces that had belittled Brahms, but with more dire results. In May of 1877, the *Musical Times* published an article expressing dismay over it. "There have been signs lately," it warned, "that Mendelssohn is becoming the favorite object of mud-throwing." The composer had died only thirty years earlier. During his lifetime he had stood at the peak of the musical world, yet his legacy was then quickly fading.

His talent had been evident early on. As a precocious child he astounded Goethe by playing a Mozart autograph at sight, then performing from a nearly illegible manuscript by Beethoven. Witnesses reported encountering a boy—in "a tight-fitting jacket, cut very low at the neck, and over which the wide trousers were buttoned; into the slanting pockets of these the little fellow liked to thrust his hands, rocking his curly head from side to side, and shifting restlessly from one foot to the other"—who could play from memory any Bach fugue, and repeat note-for-note the music of Weber's opera *Der Freischütz*, three or four days after first hearing it. His earliest compositions were written before his tenth year.

Adulthood only fulfilled the promise. Pianist and conductor Hans von Bülow told an acquaintance that if he wanted his son to prove that he has "learned a good deal as a pianist, I would ask him for a Mendelssohn *Song Without Words*." The inventor of that short musical form, Mendelssohn, was, in the view of virtuoso Anton Rubinstein, the man who "saved instrumental music from destruction."

And yet, especially after his death, he was increasingly regarded as a lightweight. Sir George Grove gave as much space in his famous *Dictionary of Music and Musicians* to Mendelssohn as he had to Beethoven and Schubert. Nevertheless, he lamented the composer's alleged lack of depth: "Who can wish that that bright, pure, aspiring spirit should have been dulled by distress or torn with agony?" he wrote. "It might have lent a deeper undertone to his *Songs*, or have enabled his Adagios to draw tears where now they only give a saddened pleasure."

That quality of classical restraint, which led to accusations of superficiality, was natural to him, and also evident in Mendelssohn's piano playing. His teacher Ignaz Moscheles, a former student of Clementi, had little influence in the matter. "This afternoon . . . I gave Felix Mendelssohn his first lesson," he wrote in 1824, "without losing sight for a moment of the fact that I was sitting next to a master, not a pupil." Despite Grove's carping, many found this conservative approach a virtue. Jenny von Gustedt called Mendelssohn's pianism "just like the man himself: no feeling that tended towards the bizarre, no disharmony that was not gently absorbed, no virtuoso displays to make us dizzy. Hummel seemed to me to play with more fire, with more external passion, but one did not feel, as one did with Mendelssohn, that his playing was so deeply heartfelt."

The twentieth-century literary and social critic Lionel Trilling described the trend away from the "sentimental" (Gustedt's "heartfelt") to an approach based on conflict (Grove's "distress") as the beginning of modernity's embrace of "authenticity." In our own time, there is no higher praise than being called "authentic." But in Mendelssohn's day, sentimentality was the coin of the artistic realm. Complex works of Beethoven and Schubert took second place in popularity to opera fantasies, paraphrases, and small poetic fragments that seemed perfect, independent little worlds of the heart.

Felix Mendelssohn

Songs Without Words were the embodiment of that sentimental ideal, and Mendelssohn was the father of the form. Actually, he and Wilhelm Taubert, both students of pianist Ludwig Berger, each wrote a series of instrumental "songs" in 1831, but Taubert based his music on specific texts and images, while Mendelssohn refused, he said, to be imprisoned by words; he believed they were inadequate to the musical experience. Comparing Taubert and Mendelssohn, Robert Schumann explained that the former was "inspired by poems, while the latter perhaps conversely should inspire one to write poetry." (Today, Italian pianist Roberto Prosseda [b. 1975] is a tireless advocate of Mendelssohn's music, and the discoverer of several dozen previously unknown works. His renderings of these pieces, including many unpublished *Songs Without Words,* have been both musically elegant and beautifully recorded.)

For many, Mendelssohn's work continues to inspire. If his pieces were not exactly cutting-edge, his mastery of music's structural intricacies was formidable, and the composer himself viewed such technical skill as the only legitimate basis of art. Once, Robert Schumann told him about the existence of a large telescope, and conjectured that "if the inhabitants of the sun gazed at us through a telescope, we should look something like worms in a cheese. 'Yes,' replied Mendelssohn, 'but *The Well-Tempered Clavier* would still command their respect.' " His reverence for Bach's abilities far outweighed any interest in being radically innovative or groundbreaking. Indeed, Mendelssohn explained to composer Johann Christian Lobe that the very word "groundbreaking," which connotes clearing a path that no one had ever walked before, was nothing but hollow praise; to be desirable, he claimed, "this new path would have to lead to much more beautiful, more charming territory. For just clearing a new path can be done by anyone who knows how to wield a shovel and move his legs."

What poisoned Mendelssohn's standing most of all was the shovel wielded by Richard Wagner in an attempt to bury the man's reputation, followed by more than a century of German musicologists who continued to pile on the dirt. The tool Wagner used was a despicable essay released three years after Mendelssohn's death on "Judaism in Music." Wagner's aim, he claimed, was to cleanse German culture of elements that were foreign to what he considered its true nature. Hence, his attack on Jews like Mendelssohn, whose rootlessness and strange ways, including "synagogue rhythms" and ornate melodies, inspired an "instinctive revulsion" in gentiles.

Neither the family's name change to Bartholdy, nor Mendelssohn's championing of the music of J. S. Bach—he revived and conducted the *St. Matthew Passion* in its first performance since Bach's death in 1750—failed to inoculate him against the rampant anti-Semitism of the time, which crept into the correspondence even of his friends Robert and Clara Schumann. His musical successes would have continued in any case. But the death of his talented sister Fanny on May 14, 1847, was more than he could bear. (Her compositions reveal another case of a major female talent limited by lack of opportunity.) Less than six months later, Felix succumbed to a series of strokes, his life and career ended at the tender age of thirty-eight.

A S T H E S E S T Y L I S T I C battles raged on, one great melodist remained above the fray with a brilliant musical voice all his own. Frédéric Chopin (1810–1849) embodied the spirit of his era (and his homeland) with such singular imagination and lyrical brilliance that colleagues could only echo Robert Schumann's critical assessment: "Hats off, gentlemen—a genius." He changed forever the way the piano was played.

Schumann described Chopin's music as "cannons buried in flowers," a sonic garden filled with strange and exquisite flora, and imbued with a mysterious potency. Chopin's friend and rival Franz Liszt found a "deep melancholy" in these elegant works, saturated with the long-suffering Polish spirit. As pianist Piotr Anderszewski put it, in Chopin "you have the Slavic soul in all its breadth and depth, its generosity—the expression of a whole continent extending eastward—all dressed up in an impeccably tailored French suit . . . Perfectly cut. European. Western. But what screams and wailing are stifled within!"

Indeed, Chopin left Poland at a time of national mourning. Many of its cultural leaders had fled in the wake of the failed 1830 "November uprising" in Warsaw against Russian domination. And, like Chopin, most of them—such as poets Juliusz Slowacki and Adam Mickiewicz, both national treasures—headed to Paris.

Who could blame them? Francis Hervé's *How to Enjoy Paris* extolled the virtues of the city:

> The merry dance, the sprightly air of those who pass, the dazzling lights, the company, two or three deep, who line the way,

seated on chairs, under gay canopies reading, drinking, smoking, and laughing, in the midst of them several well dressed ladies, of great respectability, just descended from their carriages, and these, rattling on the stones, with the noise of fruit-women, tumblers, footmen and their lasses, the most obsequious apologies for molesting the toes of the seated spectators, many of whom come for no other purpose than to enjoy the endless bustle.

Little wonder Paris was quickly supplanting Vienna as the artistic capital of the world. By 1828, life there included such amenities as gas lighting, horse-drawn buses, and cafés with large plate-glass windows. The town was filled with celebrities—poet Heinrich Heine; painter Eugène Delacroix; writers Victor Hugo and Honoré de Balzac; virtuoso pianists Franz Liszt, Sigismond Thalberg, and Friedrich Kalkbrenner; composers Giacomo Meyerbeer, Gioachino Rossini, Hector Berlioz, and Luigi Cherubini. (Chopin was so impressed on first hearing Kalkbrenner—a man Mendelssohn dismissed as nothing but a "little fish patty . . . an indigestible sausage"—that he actually considered taking lessons. But Kalkbrenner's suggestion to Chopin that he cut some passages from one of his piano concertos seemed dead wrong, and alarmed the composer's Warsaw teacher, Józef Elsner. Luckily, his family dissuaded Chopin from studying with Kalkbrenner, an act that might have robbed him of his uniqueness.)

Chopin's French father had suggested England or America as likely prospects for a career. But in Paris, Prince Valentine Radziwill introduced him to the wealthy Rothschilds, and his social and financial future seemed assured. He took on students from the richest families. (Unfortunately, his most promising, a young Hungarian named Carl Filtsch, died of tuberculosis at the age of fifteen.) His performances were instant successes, though he quickly learned that the large concert hall was not for him; he was no Liszt, and played best in more intimate surroundings.

His student Carl Mikuli reported that Chopin could not bear the sound of piano pounding, and compared it to a barking dog. He once said that "concerts are never real music; you have to give up the idea of hearing in them the beautiful things of art." (In the next century, pianist Glenn Gould would create a scandal by taking much the same position.) Berlioz described Chopin's sound as softness in the extreme, "so that one is tempted to go close to the instrument and put one's ear to it as if at a concert of sylphs or elves." But what he lacked in ferocity, Chopin more than made up for in poetic refinement. "The tone, though small," reported Liszt, who admired the delicacy of Chopin's playing, "was absolutely beyond criticism, and although his execution was not forcible, nor by any means fitted for the concert room, still it was perfect in the extreme."

Chopin was, in a sense, a crooner of the piano keys. That's why he found the operatic melodies of his friend Vincenzo Bellini (whose lyrical gifts earned him the label "the Swan of Catania") a prime inspiration, along with the music of Mozart and Bach. In order to produce what Liszt described as Chopin's "perfection" of sound, he developed an entirely new technique at the keyboard. Alfred Hipkins, who tuned pianos for Chopin in London, described how his left-hand arpeggios "swelled or diminished like waves in an ocean of sound." That nuanced smoothness was achieved through a variety of unorthodox moves, such as placing his thumb on the black keys, or allowing a single finger to slide from one key to another (as in the playing of many jazz pianists today). Composer Stephen Heller said that Chopin's "slim hands" would "suddenly expand and cover a third of the keyboard like a serpent opening its mouth to swallow a rabbit whole."

Chopin's ease in navigating the keyboard was also assisted by advances in the construction of the piano, such as Sébastien Érard's 1808 "repetition action" and his aforementioned 1821 double escapement. It was like adding power steering and brakes to an old-model car, making it responsive to the slightest touch. In fact, Chopin found Érard's pianos "too insistent"—"You can thump it or bash it, it makes no difference," he claimed—and preferred the more natural feeling of the piano built by Pleyel, which he described as having a "silvery and slightly veiled sonority and lightness of touch."

Chopin's rhythmic approach startled contemporaries. Some of his compositions, like the Polonaises and Mazurkas, had their origins in Polish dance. He had been an avid and accomplished

Frédéric Chopin

social dancer back home in Warsaw. But even when performing a dance rhythm, his sense of time, like his tonal shading, was stunningly fluid. It caused such consternation among his colleagues that Meyerbeer once became embroiled in an argument with him over how many beats he was playing in one of his Mazurkas, whose rhythm is based (like the waltz) on groups of three. According to Wilhelm von Lenz, a pupil of Chopin, Meyerbeer declared that the music sounded as if it were in a meter of two, not three. "I had to repeat it while Chopin, pencil in hand, beat time on the piano; his eyes were blazing," reported Lenz. But the German composer could not be persuaded. "Only once have I ever seen Chopin lose his temper," recalled Lenz, "and it was at that moment."

A MODERN PIANIST PLAYS CHOPIN *by Garrick Ohlsson*

Chopin is often misunderstood as a sort of sickly creator of delicate piano works—a salon composer who dipped his pen in perfume to write nocturnes for lovesick Contessas. Yes, his music has a ravishing surface beauty, yet there is depth, drama, and mastery within. For all the improvisatory quality—and his music does sound spontaneous, as if it fell from the heavens—he worked like a tortured soul to capture just the right spirit in every piece.

He stands at the very cusp of Classicism and Romanticism. If you don't bring to his music a strong sense of the structure, it comes out as magic and moonlight—but you'll get sick of it quickly. If you *only* have the structure and miss the magic, it becomes unbearably awful.

And being true to Chopin does not mean that you must play at the volume of a whisper, as he did. When he writes *forte* (loud) or *fortissimo* (extremely loud), I don't think they were metaphors. He meant them. As a large-framed performer myself, I take comfort in knowing that he loved the way Liszt played his Etudes. Like all the pianists of my generation, I grew up on Rubinstein, Horowitz, and Rachmaninoff—and that wasn't small-scale playing!

He was refined and aristocratic . . . but passionate. And his great love affair with novelist George Sand set tongues wagging across Europe. She was born Aurore Lucile Dupin before assuming the title Baroness Dudevant through marriage. By the time Chopin first met her, however, she had become notoriously independent, cultivating a persona that included, along with her masculine nom de plume, several gender-bending traits, like wearing men's clothes and smoking cigars. Her initial effect on Chopin did not induce songs of love. "What a repulsive woman Sand is!" he remarked to Liszt. "But is she really a woman? I am inclined to doubt it."

Many, however, had already fallen under her spell. Heine found her incredibly attractive. Her features, he reported, have a "Greek regularity. Their form . . . is not hard, but softened by the sentimentality which is suffused over them like a veil of sorrow. The forehead is not high . . . and the delicious chestnut-brown curly hair falls parted down to the shoulders."

Chopin was finally conquered at a party at which George was the guest of honor. She clearly had designs on the young genius, and used the occasion to abandon her usual outfits for a white dress with a red sash—the Polish national colors. And Chopin fell hard: "She looked deeply into my eyes while I played," he reported. "It was rather sad music, the legends of the Danube; my heart danced with her . . . And her eyes in my eyes, somber eyes, singular eyes, what were they saying? She was leaning on the piano and her embracing gaze flooded me."

Musician and biographer Frederick Niecks regarded them as perfectly suited, since "he is so lady-like, and she is such a perfect gentleman." And for a while, the relationship worked very well, though some jumped at the chance to blame the composer's dissonances and violations of traditional rules on their romance. "The entire works of Chopin present a motley surface of ranting hyperbole and excruciating cacophony," ranted one London reviewer, but there was, he explained, an excuse for these delinquencies: "He is entrammeled in the enthralling bonds of that arch-enchantress, George Sand, celebrated equally for the number and excellence of her romances and her lovers." As Chopin's health declined year by year, George cared for him. During a particularly bad patch, she took Chopin to Majorca, where he composed his beautiful Preludes even as death crept nearer.

Bad health had plagued him from the start. His sister Emilia succumbed to tuberculosis at the age of fourteen. "She caught a cough, started spitting blood . . . turned so pale that one could not recognize her," he remembered. Both Emilia and Frédéric had been forced to go to a health resort in 1826 to drink "metal" waters and goat's milk, and to receive vapor inhalations, and two years later, Chopin was rushed to a resort again for a cure. As he created his greatest works, the disease continually waxed and waned, threatening his very existence.

CHOPIN'S MUSICAL ORIGINS

Some of Chopin's musical ideas had their seeds in his early training in Warsaw, where a music magazine reported that "in almost every home with ambitions for education, one finds a grand piano from Vienna, Dresden, Berlin or Breslau, and often someone who plays it very well." (As in the rest of Europe, however, the player was usually female.) Early compositional models he learned at that time had a big impact. One of his teachers, Vaclav Würfel, published a *Collection of Introductions (Preludes) in All Tones for the Pianoforte.* Chopin followed suit with his own now-famous op. 28 Preludes, which also owed a debt to Hummel (especially in its arrangement of keys). Many of the unusual harmonic shifts and musical figures in his music (and the peculiar fingerings he used to play them) can also be traced to his childhood experiences: in theoretical studies, organ playing, and his teacher Józef Elsner's philosophical bent toward music as the "language of emotions." Other mainstream composers also exerted an influence: Chopin's Fantaisie-Impromptu is clearly influenced by an Impromptu by Moscheles, and Bach emerges in the counterpoint that fills his works with increasing sophistication from mid-career onward.

Perhaps that vulnerability contributed to the ethereal beauty of his music (much of which later became the basis for pop songs, like "Sincerely Yours" and "I'm Always Chasing Rainbows"). Observers described his melodies metaphorically as "the tall lily in the fountain that nods to the sun," or as a sound from the lips of a "slender-hipped girl with eyes of midnight." One called his Nocturnes (that wistful genre invented by the equally subdued Romantic John Field) "reveries of a soul fluctuating from feeling to feeling in the still of the night." (It was just such over-the-top prose that prompted scholar and pianist Charles Rosen to begin writing his own liner notes in defense of more sober scholarship, thus launching one of the great music-book-writing careers of the twentieth century.) His songful music reaches out in long, elastic phrases, adorned with intricate filigree; its chief quality is a flowing gracefulness, tinged with poetic yearning.

Toward the end of his short life Chopin visited London, where he loved the women, the horses, and the public squares, though he complained that, unlike Paris, with its abundant pissoirs, there was "nowhere to pee." He tried to disguise himself as a Monsieur Fritz from Paris, but once he played at a soirée in the home of piano maker James Broadwood, everyone in attendance instantly recognized the sound and his secret was out. Later, after breaking up with Sand,

and with Paris in a revolutionary fervor, he returned to London, seeking shelter from Queen Victoria. Unfortunately, the London air proved nearly fatal.

Others took up the job of looking after the besieged artist. He decided to travel to Scotland at the urging of two women fans; hearing of his plans, Henry Broadwood (James's son) purchased three first-class train tickets for the journey: one for Chopin, one for his servant, and a third for the pianist's feet, so he could put them up when he was tired.

But his health continued to decline. "Tomorrow I return to Paris—scarcely able to crawl, and weaker than you have ever seen me," he wrote to George Sand's daughter, Solange, in November of 1848. "Why doesn't God finish me off at once, instead of killing me by inches?" The following October, while in Paris, his wish was finally granted.

PART 2 *Breezy and Unflappable*

THE MUSIC OF Frenchman Erik Satie (1866–1925), a model of wistful simplicity, embodies an emotional aloofness typical of the French, and of modernist melody. Part of Satie's charm stems from the composer's unflappability: "Jazz speaks to us of its suffering and we don't give a damn. That's why it's beautiful, real," he once wrote. Forget about heart-on-your-sleeve sentimentality and emotional angst. He raised nonchalance to an art.

Satie was just thirteen when his family sent him to the Paris Conservatory, where he developed a dread of academia; his teachers judged him one of the *least* promising in the class. Yet his best-known piano works, like the three *Gymnopédies* (two of which were later orchestrated by Claude Debussy), still move us with their childlike directness and, as his first publisher put it, a "penchant for reverie." American composer John Cage, who found human willfulness so repugnant that he dreaded even the masterworks of

Beethoven, summed up Satie's contribution in a single sentence: "You can't understand why something that absurdly simple should be so fascinatingly beautiful." Nevertheless, Satie's plainness, like Picasso's sparse strokes that somehow convey a complete picture, was drawn from a deep well of experience: it is, as T. S. Eliot put it in the last of his *Four Quartets,* "a condition of complete simplicity/ (Costing not less than everything)."

If Satie's music was blissfully free of the pushiness associated with more "willful" composers, his personality wasn't. While playing piano at the infamous Paris cafés Le Chat Noir and L'Auberge du Clou (where he first met Debussy in 1891), he adopted an affected bohemian lifestyle and sharp-edged irreverence that led him to pen musical works with names like *Genuine Flabby Preludes (for a dog)* and *Dried Up Embryos,* along with a book called *Memoirs of an Amnesiac.* (Rossini, who gave up composing opera at the age of thirty-seven, established a precedent for these absurdist piano pieces in the 1860s with a series of works dubbed *Sins of My Old Age.*) He dressed from head to toe in grey velvet, for which he earned the nickname "the Velvet Gentleman," and invented his own church, fantasizing rituals involving 1,600,000,000 black-robed supplicants. When the director of the Paris Opéra ignored his submission of a ballet score, an infuriated Satie dispatched his seconds to challenge the man to a duel. He was once imprisoned for sending an insulting postcard to a critic.

Satie's predilection for nonsense surfaced even before the rise of Dada, an absurdist art movement born in the shadow of World War I. Yet Satie perfectly embodied its glorification of the ridiculous. When Debussy told him he should pay more attention to form, his defiant response was a piano work called *Three Pieces in the Form of a Pear.* He poked fun at classical piano eminences like Muzio Clementi, composing a spoof on the latter's famous C Major Sonatina, which he called *Sonatine Bureaucratique*—for which he changed the common tempo marking of *vivace* (fast) to *vivache* (*vache* being French for "cow").

Perhaps Satie's back was always up because the criticisms of his work seemed endless. European music in his day was moving

a mon cher Erik Satie
Jean Cocteau
1920

*Erik Satie by
Jean Cocteau*

toward greater complexity and ever larger and more luscious sonorities, which led some to accuse him, by comparison, of a kind of artistic poverty. "Satie was in the position of a man who knows only thirteen letters of the alphabet," claimed writer Contamine de Latour, "and who decides to create a new literature using only these, rather than admit his own deficiency."

When he finally took this view to heart and pursued studies at the Schola Cantorum under composer Vincent d'Indy, he was accused of having abandoned his genuine style in favor of one that was too learned and artificial. In an address called *In Praise of Critics*, he dealt with the subject bluntly. "Last year I gave several lectures on *Intelligence and the Appreciation of Music Among Animals*," he said. "Today I am going to speak to you about *Intelligence and the Appreciation of Music Among Critics*. The subject is very similar." Still, he had his supporters, including Debussy and Ravel. On January 16, 1911, they showed their appreciation of his work by organizing a concert in Satie's honor; at the event, Ravel performed Satie's exquisite *Second Sarabande*. And suddenly, many fickle Parisian insiders who had been ridiculing Satie began to praise him.

His turn to churchly activities plunged him into the study of Gregorian Chant, Medieval sacred songs that flowed in long, arching phrases, like soft, rolling hills. Like those ancient chants, Satie's melodies seemed to float without a clear sense of direction. That quality, coupled with his gently colorful harmonies that hovered like billowing clouds, anticipated by more than a decade the experiments of Debussy and other French "Alchemists."

Yet, beneath the rarified airs and tomfoolery, listeners couldn't fail to recognize a tender spirit at this music's center. Composer Georges Auric attended a performance of Satie's 1917 collaboration with Cocteau and Picasso—the ballet *Parade,* which marked the birth of surrealism—and summed up the qualities that placed Satie in the pantheon of musical greats: "Like that of Picasso, his art does not attempt to seduce us by means of a brilliant and lively evocation," he said. "As if seeing him for the first time he shows us the quintessence of the individual human being."

S ATIE'S DREAMY MUSICAL wanderings and pastel hues permeate one of the longest piano melodies ever written, composed by his compatriot Maurice Ravel (1875–1937) for the slow movement of his Piano Concerto in G. Ravel, like Debussy, often wrote music of vivid imagery, such as his Lisztian *Jeux d'eau (Water Games)* of 1901, a portrait of dancing streams, described by pianist Alfred Cortot as "liquid poetry," and the "Ondine" movement from his 1908 *Gaspard de la nuit (Gaspard of the Night)*, which portrays a nymph attempting to lure a mortal to her underwater lair. But the never-ending melody of this concerto movement, like the sweet, melancholic theme of his *Pavane pour une infante défunte (Pavane for a Dead Princess)*, seems, through its expansiveness and plaintive beauty, to suspend time.

Ravel announced that his intention in the Piano Concerto was to create "light-hearted" music, not aimed at "profundity or at dramatic effects." Pianist Marguerite Long, who premiered the work, nevertheless found the pensive second-movement melody—"where," she complained, "one has no respite"—incredibly difficult. "I told Ravel one day how anxious I was . . . to be able to maintain the *cantabile* [singing style] of the melody of the piano alone during such a long, slow, flowing phrase," she reported. " 'That flowing phrase!' Ravel cried. 'How I worked over it bar by bar! It nearly killed me!' "

On the surface, Ravel's melodies were delicate and graceful, shaped by a host of musical flavors, from his combined Swiss, French, Spanish, and Basque heritage along with his contacts

with Indonesia and other far-flung cultures. (His robust, scintillating harmonies, especially in *Gaspard de la nuit*, presage modern jazz as well.) Ravel's teacher Gabriel Fauré (1845–1924)—a master of the art song and of piano compositions that seem as diaphanous as spun sugar—also helped cultivate his lyrical gifts. (Aaron Copland regarded Fauré as the greatest composer of his time—the "Brahms of France.") Then there was Ravel's unfailing aristocratic demeanor, which endowed his music with fastidious detail and perfect posture. (Stravinsky called him the "Swiss watchmaker" of music.)

But his Piano Concerto in G hints at yet one more musical shadow, in phrases that wind sinuously through musical detours more suggestive of Harlem streets than of Parisian boulevards. Those bluesy inflections that surface in Ravel's writing—slinky, brash, and seductive—were written in homage to America's George Gershwin (1898–1937).

Maurice Ravel

RAVEL WAS JUST one among many hypnotized by Gershwin's melodic gift. After hearing "The Man I Love," English composer John Ireland (Benjamin Britten's teacher) told a friend, "That, my boy, is a masterpiece—a *masterpiece*, do you hear? This man Gershwin beats the lot of us . . . Who wants another symphony if he can write a song like that? Perfect, my boy, perfect. This is the music of America; it will live as long as a Schubert Lied, a Brahms waltz."

Gershwin nonetheless yearned to write those great symphonies, works that would "catch a glimpse of our skyscrapers . . . feel that overwhelming burst of energy which is bottled in our life . . . hear that chaos of noises which suffuses the air of our modern American city," he said. For much of his life, he felt inadequate to the task. "The European boys have small ideas but they sure know how to dress 'em up," he told Broadway songwriter Vernon Duke, in explaining why he began studies with Joseph Schillinger (who developed a scientific method of composition) long after he had already achieved international recognition. Elements of that training with Schillinger can be found in Gershwin's masterpiece, *Porgy and Bess,* which, Duke later commented, caused the raising of the "highbrows' eyebrows." It also appears in abstract, modernist experiments like his "I Got Rhythm" *Variations,* where the melody is expanded incrementally with mathematical calculation.

Like Schubert, Gershwin was critically attacked for his lyrical bounty, as if it offered proof of weak musicianship. In fact, critic Irving Kolodin declared Schubert and Gershwin "as much alike as any two composers I can think of." There were obvious differences, of course. Schubert was socially withdrawn, his music inner-directed. Gershwin thrived on celebrity and glitter, his art full of swagger and high spirits.

Gershwin's musical roots were, after all, established in the teeming immigrant culture of New York City. George (Yakov Gershovitz) and his lyricist brother, Ira (Israel Gershovitz), came of age when dance halls served as a communal hub, and the streets were a proving ground for popular entertainers. (In 1907, thirty-one dance establishments could be found on New York's East Side between Houston and Grand Streets. And even though the *Forward* warned Jewish girls against evil "professors" who taught "unbridled Coney island . . . dances," they were a magnet for the young.)

That neighborhood, one of many in which the Gershwins temporarily settled, was hopping. Comedian George Burns was an instructor in Bennie Bernstein's Dancing School at Second Street and Avenue B; in off hours, his Pee Wee Quartette, formed with three other boys, sang in backyards and saloons, and then passed around the hat. It's no wonder that George's melodies, growing from this vibrant atmosphere, strut and stride with such cheerful insouciance.

As a youngster, George studied intently with a teacher named Charles Hambitzer, but his musical ideas were largely shaped by the sounds he heard around him—player pianos, dance bands, Jewish

cantillation, and popular song. When the family moved uptown, he listened outside Harlem nightspots to learn the vernacular of important black musicians like James Reese Europe.

Europe, a hero in Harlem as the leader of a World War I musical troupe that worked the front lines, famously created the Clef Club Orchestra—a group of over one hundred musicians that included violins, cellos, basses, percussionists, numerous mandolins and banjos, twenty-three guitars, and eleven pianos. Commenting on this strange instrumentation, the bandleader explained how it enhanced the ensemble's unique charms. The "steady strumming accompaniment" from all the mandolins and banjos gave them a sound similar to a Russian balalaika orchestra, he noted. And the multiple pianos were, he said, "sufficient to amuse the average white musician who attends one of our concerts for the first time. The result, of course, is that we have developed a kind of symphony music that, no matter what else you may think, is different and distinctive, and that lends itself to the playing of the peculiar compositions of our race." The Clef Club Orchestra performed at Carnegie Hall in 1912 for the benefit of the Music School Settlement for Colored People. It was

George Gershwin at the piano

perhaps the first time that popular music had entered that venerable concert venue, and for the occasion, segregated seating was suspended. Europe's "symphonic jazz" was a forerunner of many things to come.

Gershwin became a musical sponge, soaking in the French modernism of Debussy and Ravel, the Romantic virtuosity of Franz Liszt, the atonal experiments of Alban Berg, and a range of popular keyboard styles, including song-plugger piano (which he used for his early job, selling sheet music), novelty piano (exemplified by tricky, "finger breaking" ditties such as Zez Confrey's *Kitten on the Keys*), and the Harlem swing made famous by Fats Waller, Willie "the Lion"

Smith, and James P. Johnson, who became his friends and mentors.

All of this made him a very splashy musician, and he was quick to show it. George's friend Oscar Levant remarked, "An evening with Gershwin is a Gershwin evening." The music that brought him to international attention combined all of these elements into an inspired musical tapestry.

The turning point for him was a landmark event in New York's Aeolian Hall organized by bandleader Paul Whiteman—the so-called King of Jazz (who actually couldn't play jazz)—at a concert billed as "An Experiment in Modern Music." Other events around the same time had already focused attention on jazz as serious music. One was presented by the singer Eva Gauthier, who included such popular hits as "Swanee" and Irving Berlin's "Alexander's Ragtime Band," accompanied by George at the piano, on an otherwise straightforward recital program. Another was an afternoon concert sponsored by the League of Composers, with members of Vincent Lopez's orchestra serving up jazzed-up excerpts from *Carmen* and *H.M.S. Pinafore*.

Whiteman's show was splashier and more ambitious. It began

Gershwin's hands

with a rendition of "Livery Stable Blues," which *Musical America* described as "exciting and very stupid," then continued with a fantasy on the "Volga Boatmen's Song," Edward MacDowell's *To a Wild Rose*, Elgar's *Pomp and Circumstance*, and piano pieces by Zez Confrey. A demonstration of the relationship of jazz to "good music" revealed the thematic connections between the "Hallelujah Chorus" and "Yes, We Have No Bananas." The high point, however, was the premiere of two works composed especially for the event: *Four Serenades* by operetta composer Victor Herbert and *Rhapsody in Blue* by George Gershwin. George hadn't been sure what to call his piece until his brother told him about an afternoon spent at an art gallery studying the paintings of Whistler. Ira liked some of Whistler's descriptive titles, such as *Nocturne in Black and Gold* and *Arrangement in Grey and Black* (better known as "Whistler's Mother"). Why not a *Rhapsody in Blue?* he asked.

Musical "rhapsodies" are works that seem stitched together— patchworks of ideas—and this one was a musical potpourri containing examples of everything Gershwin had learned. One section, he reported, was sparked by a train ride "with its steely rhythms, its rattlety-bang." Others basked in Lisztian love themes, or hinted at raucous Jewish dances from the old country. The piano writing combined virtuoso figurations à la Liszt and Confrey, set alongside a bouquet of melodies that featured the bluesy wails that form a natural connection between black spirituals and Jewish prayer.

Rhapsody in Blue set off a chain reaction that can be felt to this day. The critics remained true to form. Two weeks earlier, Pierre Monteux had conducted Stravinsky's *Rite of Spring* in its New York debut, and critic Daniel Gregory Mason disdained both composers, calling them "Tweedledum and Tweedledee." *The New Republic* carped that Gershwin and Whiteman were ushering in the "vanilla epoch of jazz." Nevertheless, during its first year alone, *Rhapsody in Blue* was performed eighty-four times by Whiteman's band. Sales of the recording with Gershwin at the piano totaled a million copies.

Though reviewers often faulted his technique and sense of form, audiences clamored for his tunes. Composer Arnold Schoenberg

got to the heart of the matter in a tribute written after Gershwin's untimely death. There were a number of so-called serious composers who disdained Gershwin, he said: men "who learned to add notes together. But," added Schoenberg, "they are only serious on account of a perfect lack of humor and soul."

SUPREME MELODISTS ALSO arose in the mainstream jazz world, including pianists with a Mozartian elegance, like Teddy Wilson (1912–1986), whose delicate touch and unfailing tastefulness put him in high demand as a collaborator with Louis Armstrong, Lena Horne, Benny Goodman, and Ella Fitzgerald; and Nat "King" Cole (1919–1965), a graceful player who also entranced the world with his singing style.

Nat "King" Cole

Oscar Peterson wrote of the effect Wilson's playing had on him as a youngster "in the throes of personal musical upheaval." When he heard Wilson play, he said, "I could feel his love of the instrument flowing through every phrase and run, that impeccable touch giving a crystalline sound to what he played. He could swing so hard at times that the pulsation was almost overwhelming. Yet on other occasions he would touch a song with such delicacy that each note became like a single raindrop."

George Shearing (1919–2011) became famous for a technique that gave extra prominence to his melodies by supporting each individual tone with a full harmony played in parallel motion by both hands. In this "Shearing sound," the melody appears as both the top and bottom notes of these rich chords. The device was pioneered by Milt Buckner (1915–1977) and used to good effect by many others, but it remains forever associated with this blind London-born pianist who infused his work with a broad knowledge of the classical repertoire.

But perhaps the most astounding Melodist in the history of jazz piano was Bud Powell (1924–1966). As one of the founders of "bebop," a style that featured an endless string of winding phrases played at breakneck speed, he gained a reputation as someone who could hold his own even with the master of the form, saxophonist Charlie "Bird" Parker. The "bop" revolution had begun, in fact, as a trial by fire, as Parker, Dizzy Gillespie, and other musicians at the time set out to create a kind of music that only members of their inner circle could perform, eliminating pretenders to the throne. The new complexity was a shock to many: Gillespie, whose fluid, high-pitched improvisations set a new technical standard for trumpeters, was reprimanded by a club owner for playing "Chinese music." The innovations perfectly suited Powell's rapid-fire approach, however, and his fertile imagination.

Though plagued by psychiatric problems and a history of erratic behavior, Powell became a model for melodic invention, reflecting the kind of aesthetic that had been cultivated by masters of the Baroque. That earlier epoch prized creative flair in the manipulation of melody; J. S. Bach could spin out tunes and toss them to and fro like so many balls in the hands of an expert juggler. Powell's own sense of invention seemed equally limitless.

Pianist Bill Evans once paid tribute to Powell's artfulness by citing his "artistic integrity . . . incomparable originality, and the grandeur of his work." If he had to choose a single musician as emblematic of these traits, said Evans, it would have to be Powell. Recordings of such Powell classics as *Tempus Fugit, Parisian Thoroughfare, Un Poco Loco, 52nd Street Theme,* and *Dance of the Infidels* are a living testament to Evans's assessment.

Bud Powell, in exploiting his melodies through seemingly endless variations, proved that lyrical genius observes no distinctions of race, class, or historical period.

CHAPTER 11

The Cultivated and the Vernacular

T HE FOUR BASIC sounds served as primary colors for pianists, but these could be blended in various proportions to create many hues (just as printers combine four simple ink colors—cyan, magenta, yellow, and black—to produce an entire rainbow on the printed page). And like painters who employ different brushstrokes and contrasts of light and darkness to enhance their color palettes, keyboard musicians had all sorts of techniques at their disposal to conjure an entire world of sound through their fingertips.

In the myriad styles developed by the Alchemists, the Melodists, the Combustibles, and the Rhythmitizers, the piano managed to cross cultural boundaries, attracting audiences for such disparate works as Gottschalk's *Siege of Saragossa*, Monk's *In Walked Bud*, and Beethoven's "Hammerklavier." Its ease in shifting between the "cultivated" and the "vernacular" traditions made it ripe for appropriation by the Holy Rollers, the high rollers, and the rock 'n' rollers, many of whom made their music far from the clubs and concert halls.

Church directors had begun adopting the piano by the mid-nineteenth century, when hymnists like William Batchelder Bradbury discovered that the unobtrusive instrument was well suited for choir accompaniment. Bradbury's thousand-voice children's choir at the Broadway Tabernacle in New York City set the stage for the efforts of many others, like Charles M. Alexander of Tennessee, who became known as "the Father of Evangelical Pianism." According to Alexander's wife, "the quick, incisive notes of a piano held the singing of a large crowd together . . . and [unlike the organ] did not detract from the value of vocal harmonies"—that is, it didn't swamp the efforts of the singers.

The good word spread. Alexander's collaboration with evangelist R. A. Torrey led to a series of revival meetings in Australia during 1902. T. Shaw Fitchett, publisher of the first Australian Alexander hymnal, offered an eyewitness account:

> Climb up by stairway and ladder to the top of the organ and look down. You see a tiny frock-coated figure standing on a little red island in the midst of a sea of faces. To his right and left are grand pianos, and between them a cabinet organ . . . A few silver notes float up from the pianos. They are faint but unmistakable—the preliminary bars of the "Glory Song," and there is a thrill of recognition . . . one word, "Ev'rybody," comes floating up, to be chased by such a volume of melody that the roof rings to the shout: "Oh, that will be glory for Me!"

Back in the United States, Billy Sunday, a professional baseball player turned minister, electrified believers with sensational oratory and, beginning in 1910, had the additional help of piano inspiration under the musical direction of Mr. Homer Rodeheaver. *Musical America* reported in 1917 that the two pianists playing under Rodeheaver must have been twelve feet tall, because their extraordinary sound was of such "orchestral power." But Billy Sunday's best-known pianist, Bentley D. Ackley, turned out to be a heavy cross to bear. He drank heavily, denounced Rodeheaver, threatened to expose the profession of evangelism as a hoax, and sued his employer—eventually winning $20,000 in court in 1914. Of course, to forgive is divine: once the legal battle was resolved and his pockets were filled, Ackley rejoined Rodeheaver and Sunday and resumed his musical duties at their programs.

Meanwhile, in a different part of town, pianists ministered to clients with more earthly needs—joining a long and venerable history in support of the world's oldest profession. From the nineteenth century onward, most pleasure houses had traditionally sported a piano. Philosopher Friedrich Nietzsche recorded a visit to one during which he was overcome by a panic when "surrounded by half-a-dozen apparitions in tinsel and gauze, looking at me expectantly. For a moment I was speechless," he remembered. "Then I made instinctively for the piano as being the only thing with a soul present."

Johannes Brahms, among others, famously played in similarly sordid settings. As the tradition flourished on American soil, it offered employment to many a jazz pianist, sometimes substantially shaping their styles as well. The rollicking New Orleans sound that grew out of Storyville—the town's notorious red-light district—was partly a result of the disrepair of the instruments in these bawdy houses: musicians had to find ways to force music out of those battered remnants whose keys often failed to sound, and playing very full harmonies and doubling up on melodies and bass lines was one way to do it.

PLEASURE HOUSE PIANO, CIRCA 1869 *by George Ellington*

There is a piano in the room, which is played by a man hired for the purpose. Nothing but popular and lively music is played. Only the songs of the period find favor in the eyes of the class of people who patronize these establishments. During the war, "When This Cruel War Is Over," "John Brown," "We'll Fight for Uncle Sam," "Red, White and Blue," etc., were the popular songs of the day. At the present time Offenbach's music is much in favor, and such songs as "Up in a Balloon," "Tassels

on the Boots," "Rollicking Rams," "Bells Will Go Ringing for Sarah,"
"Not for Joe," "Champagne Charlie," etc.

FROM *The Women of New York, or the Under-World of the Great City*
BY GEORGE ELLINGTON

Along with well-known artists such as Jelly Roll
Morton and Champion Jack Dupree, who both
emigrated from the region, New Orleans locals
like Willie "Drive 'Em Down" Hall, Kid
Stormy Weather, and Tuts Washington set
the standard. Up north in Sedalia, Missouri,
honky-tonk musician and cornet player Scott
Joplin also played in brothels and social
clubs, though a bit more sedately, emphasizing melody over hot rhythms. (His delicate
demeanor may have resulted from the fact
that his piano technique left something to
be desired, but perhaps the humidity in Sedalia was also kinder to its instruments.) These
establishments offered an invaluable opportunity
for pianists of the underclass to develop their talents.

Joplin, a member of the first postslavery generation in the United States, composed ballet and opera scores
as well as piano rags. (He received his boyhood musical training
in Texarkana, Texas, through free lessons from a German-Jewish
immigrant named Julius Weiss.) The tender and melancholy
Mexican-tinged *Solace*, made famous through the film *The Sting*, is
but one example of his ability to write sinuous, sentimental tunes.
One of his operas, *Treemonisha*, includes arias and recitatives that
bear no resemblance to the ragtime style at all. Ironically, his most
famous piece, *Maple Leaf Rag*, is perhaps his least melodic. "Most of
his melodies are enchanting," relates ragtime expert Max Morath,
"but the *Maple Leaf Rag* is rhythmic. You really can't hum it. In
that regard, its popularity is a trick of fate." In 1976, Joplin received
a posthumous Pulitzer Prize.

Scott Joplin from the cover of The Cascades

233

Mrs. H. H. A. Beach

Regional styles that embraced "vernacular," or colloquial, elements—giving as much weight to folk materials as they did to high-brow artifice—grew everywhere from such self-contained communities, each inflected with local dialect, dance, color, and history. Even many composers steeped in European schooling brought popular themes and rhythms into their works (Haydn and Beethoven were early examples). Americans like Anthony Philip Heinrich (1781–1861), Mrs. H. H. A. Beach (1867–1944, otherwise known as Amy Beach), Charles Tomlinson Griffes (1884–1920), and Arthur Farwell (1872–1952) were still wedded to European models, but they worked intensely to bring an American character to their music. Of them, Beach was the most Romantic; Griffes, the purist Impressionist, as exemplified by his most famous piano piece, *The White Peacock* (1915); and Heinrich, the most eccentric.

Born in Bohemia, Anthony Philip Heinrich lost his inherited fortune in the Napoleonic Wars and journeyed on foot through North America, settling in a log cabin in Kentucky, where he began producing jarring, episodic music with titles like *The Dawning of Music in Kentucky, or the Pleasures of Harmony in the Solitudes of Nature.* This compendium takes well-known tunes like "Hail, Columbia" and "Yankee Doodle" and places them alongside an endless, often bizarre, volley of notes; the composer himself described the outcome as "full of strange ideal somersets and capriccios."

Indeed, he could easily fit the "Combustibles" paradigm. John Hill Hewitt, in his book *Shadows on the Wall*, described the scene when this wild-eyed composer visited the White House to give a private performance for President Tyler:

We were shown into the parlor. The composer labored hard to give full effect to his weird production; his bald pate bobbed from side to side, and shone like a bubble on the surface of a calm lake. At times his shoulders would be raised to the line of his ears, and his knees went up to the keyboard, while the perspiration rolled in large drops down his wrinkled cheeks . . .

The composer labored on, occasionally explaining some incomprehensible passage, representing, as he said, the breaking up of the frozen river Niagara, the thaw of the ice, and the dash of the mass over the mighty falls. Peace and plenty were represented by soft strains of pastoral music, while the thunder of our naval war-dogs and the rattle of our army musketry told of our prowess on sea and land.

The inspired composer had got about half-way through his wonderful production, when Mr. Tyler arose from his chair, and placing his hand gently on Heinrich's shoulder, said: "That may all be very fine, sir, but can't you play us a good old Virginia reel?"

Had a thunderbolt fallen at the feet of the musician, he could not have been more astounded. He arose from the piano, rolled up his manuscript, and taking his hat and cane, bolted toward the door, exclaiming: "No, sir; I never plays dance music!"

I joined him in the vestibule . . . As we proceeded along Pennsylvania Avenue, Heinrich grasped my arm convulsively, and exclaimed: "Mein Gott in himmel! De peebles vot made Yohn Tyler Bresident ought to be hung! He knows no more about music than an oyshter!"

Heinrich's piano works were championed in the twentieth century by pianist Eugene List.

Arthur Farwell wrote pieces of a simpler melodic nature, often basing his music on Native American themes, and he founded a publishing venture, the Wa-Wan Press, to promote this practice. By the early twentieth century, other classically trained composers, such as William Grant Still (1895–1978) and, across the ocean, the British composer Samuel Coleridge-Taylor (1875–1912), began to introduce elements of black culture into Western classical music.

Charles Ives

EUROPEAN-INFLUENCED American romantics like Edward MacDowell (1860–1908) and Ethelbert Nevin (1862–1901) are remembered mostly for their attractive, homespun miniatures (MacDowell's lovely *To a Wild Rose* and Nevin's *Narcissus* are piano-teacher favorites). Nevertheless, MacDowell's larger works are compelling and virtuosic. Still, they are relatively tame in comparison to the music of New England mavericks like Charles Ives (1874–1954), Carl Ruggles (1874–1971), and their associate Henry Cowell; a thread of American vernacular material runs through much of their music.

Ives was a visionary whose pioneering musical techniques—such as superimposing musical strains of vastly different keys and tempos on top of each other—set the stage for many composers who followed. He inherited some of these from experiences as a child in New England, where his father directed holiday marching bands to start off from opposite ends of the town and then musically collide when they met in the central square. His revolutionary inclinations also manifested in Ives's approach to the insurance business, where he made his fortune. The driving force in each instance was a knotty personality steeped in moral certitude—that families without wealth deserved protection against calamity, for example, and that "beauty in music is too often confused with something that lets the ears lie back in an easy chair."

Despite his unsentimental stance toward musicians, critics, and the public, Ives always had a soft spot for his country and his region's proud history. Quotes from familiar tunes and hymns—like "Columbia, the Gem of the Ocean" and "Aura Lee"—abound even in his most dissonant music, and a tenderness and nostalgia are evident throughout. Listening to his music is like wandering through a memory box filled with old photos, sing-along songbooks, political pamphlets, yellowed poems, the bass drum of a big brass band, remnants of an old watering hole, and perhaps a pair of boxing gloves. He paid musical tributes to American literary figures he admired: his Second Piano Sonata (*The Concord Sonata*) has movements dedicated to Ralph Waldo Emerson, Henry David Thoreau, the Alcotts, and Nathaniel Hawthorne. Pianists William Masselos (1920–1992) and John Kirkpatrick (1905–1991) were staunch advocates of Ives's piano music, bringing it to a public that had been largely unaware of his existence.

Composers Aaron Copland (1900–1990), Virgil Thomson (1896–1989), and Leonard Bernstein (1918–1990) also represented an American school that prized melody and accessibility above experimentation (though both Copland and Bernstein had their craggy moments). Copland and Thomson studied with the renowned French teacher Nadia Boulanger. But Copland, a Jew from Brooklyn, and Thomson, a faintly anti-Semitic midwesterner, shared few musical traits. Copland's populist instincts gave rise to a sound now associated with America's wide-open vistas. His film music (like the themes from *Our Town*, which he arranged for piano) could be heartbreaking in its innocence and yearning.

Aaron Copland

Thomson, whose fame rests more on his reputation as a critic than as a composer, was, on the other hand, an elitist with a sharp wit; nevertheless, his piano "portraits" of people were rendered in a musically simple, even naïve (not to say boring) fashion. While in Paris, he joined forces with the highly eccentric writer and cultural figure Gertrude Stein (biographer Jack Lord, best known for his exquisite little book about sculptor Alberto Giacometti, noted that Stein reminded him of "a burlap bag filled with cement and left to harden"); her nonsensical lyrics, combined with Thomson's hymn-like melodies, resulted in some of the most peculiar "operas" (such as *Four Saints in Three Acts*) ever written.

Bernstein easily outshone his compatriots, with a spectacular career in conducting, lecturing, and composing for Broadway, film, and opera, as well as for the concert stage. His most successful music reflects an easy lyricism and a rhythmic stride, along with an eclectic embrace of the classical, pop, and jazz traditions all at once.

Latin rhythms, which permeated classical music in the South American regions since the nineteenth century, fostered in each nation a particular sound print. In Argentina, a key ingredient was the tango—influenced by both the habanera and the milonga—which captivated American pianist Louis Moreau Gott-

schalk as he toured in 1867. By 1910, it was sweeping the cafés of Buenos Aires and becoming a sensation in New York clubs like Bustanoby's Domino Room, where movie heart-throb Rudolph Valentino danced the night away while composer Sigmund Romberg played the piano. Leading newspapers such as the *New York Mail* described the new dance craze as "an immodest and basely suggestive exercise tending to lewdness and immorality," but, like jazz and rock, it fired up the popular imagination.

ABOVE
Tango dancers from Erik Satie's Sports et divertissements, *drawings by Charles Martin*

OPPOSITE
Alberto Ginastera with pianist Barbara Nissman

Such stains on the tango's reputation contributed to composer Astor Piazzolla's (1921–1992) reluctance to admit his involvement in the style when he was studying in Paris with Nadia Boulanger. (A popular aphorism has it that every small American town can claim both a Walmart and a student of Boulanger's.) As Piazzolla told it, he initially showed her his symphonies and sonatas. "It's very well written," she said. "Here you are like Stravinsky, like Bartók, like Ravel, but you know what happens? I can't find Piazzolla in this." So she pried into his personal life. "It wasn't easy to lie to her," he admitted, but he tried to hide the fact that he was a bandoneón (a hand-held instrument related to the concertina) player who performed tangos in cabarets. "Finally, I confessed and she asked me to play some bars of a tango of my own," he remembered. "She suddenly opened her eyes, took my hand and told me: 'You idiot, that's Piazzolla!' And I took all the music I composed—ten years of my life—and sent it to hell in two seconds."

Piazzolla's unique view of the tango combined the music of the streets with his love of Bach, along with the influence of his Argentine teacher, composer Alberto Ginastera (1916–1983), who produced music of feverish rhythmic energy and intense pungency, along with moments of ravishing melodic beauty. Among purists who objected to Piazzolla's tampering with the form, he became known as the "assassin of the tango." But his musical personality was always compelling, and he continues to rank as one of the most beloved composers of the late twentieth century. One of his former band members, pianist Pablo Ziegler, continues the tradition.

GINASTERA'S EVIL MUSIC

The progressive rock group Emerson, Lake & Palmer adapted the fourth movement of Alberto Ginastera's First Piano Concerto for their 1973 album, *Brain Salad Surgery,* under the title *Toccata.* Keyboardist Keith Emerson met with Ginastera at his Swiss home to share the results. When the composer responded, "Diabolical!" Emerson misunderstood, thinking Ginastera was displeased, and he was ready to drop the project. But the composer had simply meant that the music was frightening—which, he later explained, truly captured the essence of his original. So all went forward as planned.

Other countries developed their own unique musical personalities. Brazil's most revered composer, Heitor Villa-Lobos

(1887–1959), also studied in Paris, where jazz, Eastern sounds, and rhythmic vitality were all in vogue. Nevertheless, his art remained homespun, embracing the Brazilian personality in all its flamboyance, restlessness, and eroticism: "My music," he claimed, "is natural, like a waterfall." In his series of *Bachianas brasileiras*, Villa-Lobos combined the rhythms and colors of native Brazilian dance with lessons learned from the example of Johann Sebastian Bach. A meeting with pianist Arthur Rubinstein in 1918 resulted in a string of vibrant, folk-inflected piano works of extraordinary virtuosity, with score markings like "infernal" and "faster still."

THE SPIRIT OF SOUTH AMERICAN MUSIC *by Gabriela Montero*

The power of South American music lies in its vividness in portraying the sounds, rhythms, and colors of the continent's landscape—the birds and fauna are so rich and diverse, nature almost engulfs you—and the romanticism and passion of its people. Rhythm is incredibly important. We love to dance, and we have this in our blood. Latin people are very connected to their emotions. So in the music, you always hear the stories of great loves and losses—often of joy and tragedy at the same time. The combination makes it both bittersweet and appealing, because in some way, we can all relate to this poetic narrative.

Many Europeans were bitten by the same bug. The graceful Norwegian composer Edvard Grieg (1843–1907); Spain's Enrique Granados (1867–1916), Manuel de Falla (1876–1946), and Isaac Albéniz (1860–1909); and the Armenian composer Komitas (1869–1935) all represented tunesmiths profoundly shaped by the traditions of their homelands. The sound of Spanish music—often as dramatic and colorful as a painting by Goya, with intimations of flamenco guitar and the intoxicating rhythms of peasant dance—has now become a mainstay of contemporary jazz artists as well.

Next door, in France, composers like Gabriel Fauré and Francis Poulenc (1899–1964) represented their country's artistic spirit in a bouquet of delicate and fanciful works. Fauré's palette of colors and gossamer textures often reflect the perfumed air of a Paris salon. Poulenc is full of playfulness and biting irony, yet his flowing melodies are also a sonic soufflé (Ravel admired Poulenc's ability "to write his own folksongs").

Each of the world's nations, from Asia to Scandinavia and the lands beyond, contributed its own flavors into this great musical stew. But two nations took center stage: the brooding, emotionally intense Russians and the analytical, academically inclined Germans. Their influence is still felt.

CHAPTER 12

The Russians Are Coming

T HEIRS BECAME one of the most powerful pianistic "schools" of all time. As conservatories were springing up all over Europe—Paris in 1795, followed by Milan, Naples, Prague, Brussels, Geneva, Florence, Vienna, London, The Hague, Leipzig (established in 1843 by Mendelssohn), Munich, Berlin, and Cologne—the one that made the most profound impact was the St. Petersburg Conservatory, founded in 1862 by Anton Rubinstein (1829–1894) and Theodor Leschetizky (1830–1915). It instantly came to symbolize what Leschetizky described as the Russian musical spirit: prodigious technique wedded to passion, dramatic power, and extraordinary vitality. St. Petersburg eventually graduated such remarkable figures as Tchaikovsky, Rachmaninoff, Prokofiev, and Shostakovich, though Rubinstein resigned his conservatory post in 1891 to protest racial quotas instituted by Alexander III (imposed because Jews were winning too high a percentage of the annual prizes).

The Russian tradition had been forged through two musical luminaries of the Romantic era. Franz Liszt imparted rhapsodic fire and dazzling technique. John Field's tune-based dreaminess fostered a love for the lyrical. In Anton Rubinstein, the first great Russian pianist to step onto American soil, audiences got both.

The man was so shambling and awkward that some witnesses compared him to an elephant. Others called him a bear. In any case, reported writer Sacheverell Sitwell, "He had something animal about his downcast, shaggy head and the shape of his limbs and back." But Rubinstein was a pianistic force to be reckoned with. It was said that as a young prodigy, he had been kissed by Liszt and proclaimed his successor. And he was ready to assume the mantle.

Anton Rubinstein

When his ship arrived in New York in 1872, more than two thousand people gathered to greet the pianist and escort him to his lodgings with a torch-lit parade. Outside his windows at the Clarendon Hotel, members of the Philharmonic serenaded him with Wagner, Beethoven, and Meyerbeer. (Apparently, no one at the Philharmonic realized just how much Rubinstein despised Wagner. After attending the 1865 premiere of *Tristan und Isolde* in Munich, he threatened to commit suicide. "If that is music," he argued, "what object have I in living any longer?" Luckily, in New York he restrained himself.)

Rubinstein became known as the "shaggy maestro." He had a face like Beethoven's (Liszt called him "Van II") with a scowling demeanor and an extravagant accumulation of unkempt hair. When he bowed, his tresses fell in his face, and according to one report, they "constantly rebel[led] at being imprisoned behind the ears" when he played. It sparked comparisons to the biblical Samson.

Rubinstein
Plays for the
Czar *(detail)*,
*by F. Luis Mora,
was one of the
first paintings
commissioned for
the Steinway art
collection.*

He was an impetuous performer, bringing even jaded orchestra members to "a certain wild and unaccustomed enthusiasm." His opening concerts lasted an agonizing two and a half to four hours, yet throughout the evening his magnetism was unfailing. Here was a pianist, wrote musicologist H. E. Krehbiel, who "stirred up emotional cyclones wherever he went and scattered wide the wrecks of discriminating judgment." That suspension of "discriminating judgment" was a lucky thing for Rubinstein, because his performances were usually so riddled with mistakes that when Liszt protégé Moriz Rosenthal (1862–1946) heard the Russian play an absolutely faultless recital, he feigned concern. "Poor Rubinstein!" he said. "His eyesight is failing."

In New York, the pianist got lost in his own D minor Piano Concerto. "He shook his locks, wove appropriate harmonies and sequences with his great paws, and until he finally found himself, he kept on improvising," remembered one witness. Yet, as critic Eduard Hanslick noted, Rubinstein continued to fascinate because his virtues arose from "a source rapidly drying up" in the music world—"robust sensuality and love of life." Like Proust's grandmother, who said she loved all that was natural in life—"Rubinstein's mistakes, for example"—the public remained adoring.

Not everyone went along with the crowd. Even the admiring Hanslick complained that Rubinstein's programs were often "too much for even the strongest nerves." Clara Schumann derided his playing in 1857: "The piano often sounded awful," she claimed, "like glass, namely when he made his frightful tremolandos [stormy "shakes" in which the tones are made to tremble] in the bass—truly ridiculous, but they delighted the public." Rubinstein reported in his autobiography that even Liszt, the perpetual bearer of goodwill, had received him coldly. (In Liszt's case, the reason was extra-musical: Rubinstein had obtained a letter of introduction from the Russian ambassador and used it without checking the contents. It turned out to be a gripe by the ambassador about having to engage in "the tedious duty of patronizing and recommending our various compatriots in order to satisfy their oftentimes clamorous requests. Therefore we recommend to you the bearer of this letter, one Rubinstein.")

Rubinstein could be coldly unsympathetic himself. Josef Hofmann (who would eventually be recognized as one of the world's greatest pianists) played for him. "Did you start?" Rubinstein asked after listening to a few measures. "Yes, Master, I certainly did," replied Hofmann. "Oh," replied Rubinstein. "I didn't notice."

When Rubinstein started, everyone noticed. Newspaper correspondent George W. Bagby, who witnessed a performance by the pianist (familiarly known as "Ruby"), recounted the experience in a literary piece called "Jud Brownin Hears Ruby Play": "Well, sir he had the blamedest, biggest catty-corneredest pianner you ever laid eyes on—something like a distracted billiard table on three legs . . . When he first sit down, he peered to care mighty little about playing, and wished he hadn't come. He tweedle-eedled a little on the treble, and twoodle-oodled some on the bass—just fooling and boxing the thing's jaws for being in the way." But once things got going, Bagby was swooning along with the rest of the crowd:

> The house trembled, the lights danced, the walls shuck, the sky split, the ground rocked—heavens and earth, creation, sweet potatoes, Moses, ninepences, glory, tenpenny nails, Samson in a 'simmon tree—Bang!!!
>
> With that bang! He lifted himself bodily into the air, and he came down with his knees, fingers, toes, elbows and his nose, striking every single solitary key on the pianner at the same time. The thing busted and went off into seventeen hundred and fifty-seven thousand five hundred and forty-two hemidemi-semi-quivers, and I knowed no mo' that evening.

Vladimir de Pachmann

Hyperbole aside, a look at Rubinstein's programs confirms how much more than tweedle and twoodle was going on. His final recitals in New York (a group of seven) included works by J. S. Bach, C. P. E. Bach, Handel, Scarlatti, Mozart, Schubert, Weber, Mendelssohn, Schumann, and more. The second concert alone included six difficult Beethoven sonatas. At the end of his last performance, the audience rushed to the stage and tore at his clothes in an effort to gather souvenirs; women wept and tried to embrace him. But when he left, he vowed never to do it again.

With the piano firm Steinway backing the tour, Rubinstein had booked 215 concerts (at the staggering fee of two hundred dollars each) in 239 days! "The receipts and the success were invariably gratifying," he wrote, "but it was all so tedious that I began to despise myself and my art." Years later he was asked to repeat the tour, but he refused, saying the conditions were inimical to art—"One grows into an automaton, simply performing mechanical work; no dignity remains to the artist, he is lost." Still, he admitted, "the proceeds of my tour in America laid the foundation of my prosperity. On my return I hastened to invest in real estate."

OTHERS WERE EAGER to replace him. One of the wildest, least predictable, and most mesmerizing was Vladimir de Pachmann (1848–1933). Born in Odessa, his looks and the music for which he became best known inspired critic James Huneker to dub him "the Chopinzee." He not only looked like a chimp, he chattered like one too. He'd talk animatedly and mutter throughout his recitals, commenting on the music as he played and, at times, insulting the audience. According to biographer Mark Lindsey Mitchell, "If it was summer, he would pretend to mop his brow; if it was winter, he would shake his fingers to suggest that they were too cold to allow him to play. 'Bravo, de Pachmann,' or 'C'est joli,' he would say if his playing pleased him; 'Cochonnerie, cochonnerie!' if he felt that he had 'played like a pig.' "

He would gaze into the distance and announce that Chopin was in the room, or lecture his adoring listeners on their lack of expertise. Once, when a woman was fanning herself in the front row, he complained, "Madame, I am playing in 3/4 and you are fanning in 6/8." He "ordered one latecomer to 'sit down' in so peremptory a fashion that the unfortunate woman almost sank through the floor," reported the April 1912 edition of *Musical America*.

He just couldn't control himself. Once during a Leopold Godowsky recital, he rushed to the stage and began instructing the performer—a man whose technical mastery was so impeccable, he famously rewrote Chopin's fiendishly difficult Etudes to make them even harder—on how to play the piano. It was outlandish. But audiences ate it up.

In 1899, writer Willa Cather attended one of his concerts with a friend who had become a Pachmann student. The sound was so ravishing, Cather reported, that her companion had "utterly collapsed" by the time the pianist reached Chopin's Third Prelude. His playing, she wrote in the December 30 issue of the *Courier*, was "full of tantalizing pauses and willful subordinations and smothered notes cut short so suddenly that he seems to have drawn them back into his fingers again." Clearly, there was magic at work.

T HE TWENTIETH CENTURY found many of Russia's pianists settling into American conservatories, including New York's Juilliard School and Philadelphia's Curtis Institute, as a ruling elite. (American pianist Lucy Mary Agnes Hickenlooper [1880–1948] realized the value of a Slavic name and successfully transformed herself into Olga Samaroff, becoming perhaps the most powerful musical educator of her time. She married conductor Leopold Stokowski before he had achieved celebrity status and helped push his career to new heights.)

On the concert stage, however, Russian virtuosos began to reveal a diversity of approaches rather than a monolithic school. There had, after all, been other, less volatile musical influences within the Russian musical world. Sigismond Thalberg, for one, also visited St. Petersburg but, according to Friedrich Wieck, he had to leave after becoming embroiled in a quarrel with one of the tsar's favorite officers, during which he used intemperate language (apparently, a not uncommon occurrence). "I feel sorrier for Henselt," remarked Wieck, about another European transplanted to Russia; "they say he is not happy with his wife."

Indeed, German pianist Adolf von Henselt (1814–1889), a student of Hummel, spent forty years instructing students as the official imperial court pianist. His playing, according to his student Bettina Walker,

> suggested a shelling—a peeling off of every particle of fibrous or barky rind; the unveiling of a fine, inner, crystalline, and yet most sensitive and most vitally elastic pith. With this, it suggested a dipping deep, deep down into a sea of tone, and bringing up thence a pearl of flawless beauty and purity; something, too, there was of the exhalation of an essence—so concentrated, so intense, that the whole being of the man seemed to have passed for the moment into his finger tips.

He used to tell his students to imagine they were sinking their fingers in dough.

And Theodor Leschetizky, co-founder of the St. Petersburg Conservatory with Anton Rubinstein, had been a protégé of Beethoven's student Carl Czerny (with whom Liszt had also studied). Leschetizky was a tough man to please. He was known to walk beneath his students' windows after dinner to learn if they were following his instructions.

Renowned pianist Ignaz Friedman (1882–1948) arrived for his audition with Leschetizky armed with a letter of recommendation from his teacher, Hugo Riemann. But after playing, he was told, "Don't bother with the piano, you will most likely play the tuba better." The experience of another future star, Benno Moiseiwitsch (1890–1963), was no better. "After I had played," remembered the virtuoso pianist, "he remarked casually, 'Well, I could play better with my feet than that.' " Nevertheless, the teacher took them both on. Leschetizky claimed there were three indispensables to becoming a virtuoso pianist: one had to be Slavic, Jewish, and a child prodigy. (This was very odd, especially since Leschetitzky was a Catholic, but the statement was no stranger than Vladimir Horowitz's pronouncement that there were only three kinds of pianists: Jewish, gay, or bad. Horowitz himself fit the first two categories, and occasionally also the third.)

Two Russian pianists from early in the twentieth century, and two from the generation following them, reveal the range of styles that evolved from these influences.

Firebrand Vladimir Horowitz (1903–1989), fleeing his homeland in the wake of the 1917 Revolution, made his way through Europe with a string of triumphs. Anton Rubinstein would have been proud. In 1925, when he played the Tchaikovsky First Piano Concerto in Hamburg as a last-minute replacement for an ailing musician, conductor Eugen Pabst was so astonished by the power and speed of his playing that he left the podium mid-performance to watch Horowitz's hands. Booked for two recitals in small halls in Paris, Horowitz found the response so spectacular that he had to play five concerts, the last one at the Paris Opéra. American manager Arthur Judson heard him in Paris in 1928 and signed him up immediately for a tour of the United States.

While Horowitz's approach was electrifying, Sergei Rachmaninoff's (1873–1943) playing was described by observers as having been shaped by more restrained, classical sensibilities—the music projected through the "cold white light of analysis." Of course, he could also soar musically. Critic Harold Schonberg wrote that "only the very greatest vocal artists—a Lotte Lehmann or an Elisabeth Schumann—could shape a phrase with equal finesse and authority."

In Rachmaninoff's hands, said composer Nikolai Medtner, "the simplest scale, the simplest cadence" acquired "its primary mean-

Vladimir Horowitz

ing." What made his performances especially beautiful was the sense of inevitability he brought to an interpretation. Horowitz, on the other hand, was an emissary of the unexpected, often accused of distorting the music—of ignoring the composer's intentions in pursuit of added excitement; he was no mere interpreter, but a musical hurricane that held the audience spellbound by the force of his personality.

Horowitz's American debut at Carnegie Hall featured the Tchaikovsky First Piano Concerto again, this time with Thomas Beecham conducting. "I chose the Tchaikovsky because I knew that I could make such a wild sound," Horowitz told author David Dubal, "and I could play it with such speed and noise. I very much wanted to have a big success in the United States." But Beecham, who was also making his debut that night, had a different conception, one that was, in Horowitz's view, too self-absorbed and too slow. At the event, feeling that time was running out and anxious to make an impression, Horowitz made his move in the last movement, like a thoroughbred in the final stretch of a race. "I wanted to eat the public alive," said Horowitz, "to drive them completely crazy. Subconsciously, it was in order not to go back to Europe . . . So in my mind I said, 'Well, my Englishman, my Lord, I am from Kiev, and I'll give you something.' And so I started to make the octaves faster and very wild." According to *The New York Times*, "The piano smoked at the keys."

Sergei Rachmaninoff

The conductor fought to keep up, but he had been taken by surprise, and the situation quickly became hopeless. Horowitz later said, without a hint of remorse, "We ended almost together." His American career was assured.

Sergei Rachmaninoff was in the audience that night, and he wasn't pleased. Horowitz reported that Rachmaninoff told him, "Your octaves are the fastest and loudest, but I must tell you, it was *not* musical. It was not necessary." So Horowitz recounted the story of how the performance had unfolded, and Rachmaninoff's perpetually dour expression lightened. "But Rachmaninoff could always find something to complain about in any performance," said Horowitz. Except for the stunning individuality and spectacular technique both possessed, the two pianists had little in common. Yet they would become lifelong friends.

Rachmaninoff had set out to be a composer, scoring an early success with his most famous piece, the Prelude in C-sharp minor. It became an albatross around his neck. When England beckoned in 1898—where the prelude was published under various titles, including *The Burning of Moscow*, *The Day of Judgment*, and *The Moscow*

Waltz [sic]—it was chiefly on the strength of that one hit. Everywhere he went people demanded to hear it. James Huneker reported that it was still an audience favorite in 1918. "The Rachmaninoff 'fans,' " he wrote, "and there were thousands of them in the audience, clamored for the favorite piece . . . But the chief thing is the fact that Rachmaninoff did not play it. All Flapperdom sorrowed last night, for there are amiable fanatics who follow this pianist from place to place hoping to hear him in this particular Prelude, like an Englishman who attends every performance of the lady lion tamer hoping to see her swallowed by one of her pets."

In addition to that Prelude, Rachmaninoff created some of the most memorable tunes of our time. Several were turned into pop hits, including "Full Moon and Empty Arms" and "All by Myself," both taken from themes from his Second Piano Concerto. His wordless song "Vocalise" is simply breathtaking. And the sweeping eighteenth variation from his *Rhapsody on a Theme of Paganini* for piano and orchestra—in which the composer held a mirror to Paganini's Twenty-fourth Caprice, rising upward wherever Paganini descended and vice versa, yielding a gorgeous, soaring melody—became a favorite of Hollywood filmmakers.

The road had not been easy. His First Symphony was an utter failure (composer César Cui said it "would have delighted the inhabitants of hell"), and soon after its disastrous premiere, Leo Tolstoy reacted to his work by asking, "Is such music needed by anybody?" Rachmaninoff was plunged into a deep depression, relieved only by treatments from hypnotist Nikolai Dahl. As those psychic clouds dispersed, he created his incredibly successful Second Piano Concerto, and dedicated it to Dahl. His subsequent triumphs in America and his growing popularity led some musicians and critics to regard his work as superficial—merely pretty.

Horowitz had been attracted to a very different sort of Rachmaninoff piece: the formidable, intense, and technically daunting Third Piano Concerto. It was just the kind of showpiece that allowed him to shine. Before they ever met, the composer heard from virtuoso violinist Fritz Kreisler that "some young Russian plays [your] Third Concerto and the Tchaikovsky Concerto like nothing I ever heard, and you have to meet him." So the day after arriving in New York, Horowitz received an invitation from Rachmaninoff to visit.

THE SPIRIT OF RUSSIAN MUSIC *by Ilya Itin*

It's difficult to describe the spirit of Russian music, because within the tradition there are so many different personalities. But the general perception of the Russian soul as something dark, heavy, tragic, sometimes explosive but also lyrical, has some merit. Russians tend to go to extremes of ecstatic joy or deep depression.

I think this is all connected to the country's history. There have been horrors over the centuries, and there is much to cry about. At the same time, Russian art, literature, music, and theater have always been extremely important to the people, more than in a free society, probably because there was no other outlet for public thinking and sharing. That's why there is a saying that in Russia, a poet is more than a poet.

We think of Russian composers like Mussorgsky and Tchaikovsky, Rachmaninoff and Scriabin as embracing their national character. But even Stravinsky, who eventually adopted an international language, was in the Russian tradition of figures like Pushkin who wanted to be a part of the greater European civilization.

There is, of course, more than just one Russian piano tradition. Even to this day, Moscow and St. Petersburg have an uneasy relationship. Speaking simplistically, Moscow pianists are said to play with lots of pedal and lots of gestures. St. Petersburg pianists are described as playing with no pedal, and always looking at the keyboard. This is an exaggeration, of course, but there is a grain of truth in it. Properly speaking, despite various exceptions, the Moscow school seems to develop playing that is free, and very concerned with color and virtuosity. It is extremely outgoing. The St. Petersburg school is seen as more introspective: detail oriented, focused on structure and other intellectual aspects of the art of the piano.

Of course, this was truer in the past. Today, all those stereotypes are less accurate.

They wasted no time. Rachmaninoff began by playing Medtner for Horowitz; then, off they went to the basement of Steinway
Hall, where they had their choice of pianos for a run-through of
Rachmaninoff's Third Concerto. The composer played the orchestra part on one, while Horowitz played the solo part on another.
"He swallowed it whole," said Rachmaninoff. "He had the courage,
the intensity, and daring that make for greatness." Those qualities
remained Horowitz trademarks his entire life, despite some long
absences from the stage. Other pianists held him in awe, baffled by
his peculiar flat-finger technique, the way the little finger of his right
hand seemed held in a perpetual curl, the speed and accuracy of his
performances, the immensity of his sound, and the painterly way
he had of shading and blending the harmonies he played. Eventually, he had his Steinway rigged so that the action had a hair-trigger
response. But that couldn't account for the speed of his playing:
his student Gary Graffman (b. 1928) reported that this made the
instrument even more difficult to handle for ordinary musicians. He
was simply a talent for the ages.

I F HOROWITZ AND RACHMANINOFF represented fire and
ice, Sviatoslav Richter (1915–1997) and Vladimir Ashkenazy
(b. 1937), leaders in the next generations, offered a more complex
and very modern face to this country's musical heritage. Both were
philosophically opposed to the excesses of Romantic piano style.
What marked them most as quintessentially Russian was a stub-
born streak of independence—cultivated in a totalitarian climate
that made every thinking person an "outsider"—along with phenomenal technical command and an unyielding intensity.

Richter, unlike Henri Herz entertaining at the gold mines, or
Anton Rubinstein rousing the crowds in New York, found the
commercial trappings of his profession repulsive. When he visited
America in 1960 at the behest of the Soviet government, he hated
the "noise, the cheap culture, the advertising," and thought about
"how happy I'd have been if only I'd missed the train."

A reclusive, weighty figure with a doleful temperament and

steel-like will, he despaired of music's loss of innocence from the corrupting force of the concert world. Richter's concept of a perfect recital was to play spur-of-the-moment, without fanfare, in a small, unlit room for a handful of listeners. Little wonder his ideal tour turned out to be of Siberia, that cold stretch of geography—its name means "the sleeping land" in Turkic—whose bleak isolation became an endless horror for men and women sentenced to live there. Between 1929 and 1953, the Soviet authorities shipped more than eighteen million political outsiders to Siberia to endure the deprivations of the Gulag. Ironically, Richter's six-month sojourn across the Urals and Siberia in 1986, when he was well over seventy, driving to small villages and performing for an audience with no classical experience, was a fantasy come true.

"Did you ever see him perform Schubert's B-flat Sonata?" pianist Charles Rosen once asked. "He closed the piano and lowered the lights, and you got the impression you were one of five people in a small room listening to him. And he played it so slowly, which gave it a feeling of even greater intimacy. Richter was the most intelligent pianist I knew."

Sviatoslav Richter

"A concert should be a surprise," Richter told producer Bruno Monsaingeon. "It loses all its freshness if you tell the audience in advance that they should expect something special: It prevents them from listening. That's why I now play in the dark, to empty my head of all non-essential thoughts and allow the listener to concentrate on the music rather than on the performer. What's the point of watching a pianist's hands or face, when they really only express the effort being expended on the piece?"

Emil Gilels

In his desire to distill the concert experience down to an ideal essence, he even gave up the process of selecting his instrument. "[One] reason why I played badly in America," he claimed, "was because I was allowed to choose my own piano. I was presented with dozens and I spent all the time thinking that I'd chosen the wrong one. Nothing is worse for a pianist than to choose the instrument on which he's going to have to perform. You should play on whichever piano happens to be in the hall, as though fate intended it so. Everything then becomes much easier from a psychological point of view." And what if the instrument turns out to be disastrous? "You have to believe, more than St. Peter, that you'll walk on water," he said.

Largely self-taught, Richter performed in clubs as a teenager, accompanying singers, violinists, circus acts, and amateur stagings of operatic scenes. Then, at twenty-two, he played for legendary teacher Heinrich Neuhaus at the Moscow Conservatory. Neuhaus's students included such world-class artists as Emil Gilels (1916–1985)—who told admirers during a concert tour of the United States, "Wait until you hear Richter"—and Romanian pianist Radu Lupu (b. 1945), who won such major competitions as Leeds and the Cliburn. But the teacher reportedly confessed that in Richter he had found the pianist he had been waiting for all of his life.

Richter once described Neuhaus as the man who taught him "how to make silences sound," a skill he put to expert use. "I devised a little trick" when playing the Liszt Sonata, he reported. "You come on to the stage and sit down. Without a motion, and in silence, you count up to thirty. And then there's a kind of panic in the audience. What's going on? And only after that long silence, [you play] that first G. Of course it's theatrical, but in music, an element of surprise is essential. Many pianists serve you a menu of dishes you know in advance. But the unexpected is what makes an impression."

There was, of course, one inescapable constant in Richter's life: the totalitarian state. And, like most Soviet artists, he rode a pendulum between obedience and rebellion. He remembered playing at Stalin's funeral—a long fugue by Bach, at which the audience hissed. He was playing on an upright piano, he recalled, and the pedals weren't working. "I couldn't play under such conditions," he said. "I stuffed a score under the pedal to make it work. Meanwhile I saw people running all around. They thought I was planting a bomb. The whole thing was repulsive." The police escorted him away.

Richter with Neuhaus

Pianist Vladimir Ashkenazy won prizes in the Chopin Piano Competition in Warsaw and the Queen Elisabeth Competition in Brussels before sharing first place in the 1962 Tchaikovsky Competition with British pianist John Ogdon (1937–1989). But the indignities and constraints of the Soviet regime became unbearable for him and he escaped with his Icelandic wife to the West, where his piano and conducting careers still flourish.

He has reported that Richter "magnetized" him—"He created his own inner world. There is a feeling of spontaneity, of creating in the moment." At the same time Ashkenazy demonstrated an independent streak from the start by determinately avoiding Neuhaus as a teacher.

THE PIANO AND POLITICS

The piano was used as a political tool well before Richter performed at Stalin's funeral (at the behest of the authorities), or (as a protest) at the burial of author Boris Pasternak in 1960. Another Iron Curtain artist, the virtuosic pianist György Cziffra (1921–1994), was arrested in the early 1950s and sent into forced labor for attempting to escape Soviet-dominated Hungary, as a result of which he took to wearing a large black wristband while performing.

Pianist Ignacy Paderewski used his stature as a pianist during World War I to bolster the prestige of the Polish National Committee, before becoming his country's prime minister in 1919. Later, as the Second World War plunged his country into grief once again, he raised money for Poland's relief efforts through concerts.

The instrument has most often been used as a political tool by bringing to an event a special sense of occasion. When a peace treaty was being negotiated in Potsdam on July 19, 1945, to end the war, President Truman asked American pianist Eugene List to perform for the gathered world leaders. The president turned pages for him. "If you can imagine," said List, "here was Stalin puffing on his pipe and Churchill with his cigar sort of leaning on the piano. And then I played. I tried to play some Russian music and some American and British, as well as some Chopin for President Truman. Churchill was not a music lover, which surprised me because he was a great writer, and orator, and liked to paint.

"I played the theme of the Tchaikovsky Piano Concerto," List remembered, "and Stalin sprang to his feet and said, 'I want to propose a toast to the sergeant.' I couldn't believe it! I was about twenty-two years old. I didn't know what to do. I was rooted to the spot. The President beckoned to me to come forward to the center of the floor and somebody stuck a glass of vodka in my hand—it was so unbelievable!" The next day, Stalin sent to Moscow for Soviet musicians, to even the score.

Unbeknownst to these heads of state, their fierce enemy Adolf Hitler also had a pianist. Ernst Hanfstaengl (nicknamed "Putzi") had been a student at Harvard University, where he was remembered as a cheerleader as well as "for his thundering renditions of Wagnerian music and the apprehension felt by his hearers for any piano which he attacked." Hanfstaengl joined the Nazis—he claimed that the chant of "Sieg Heil" and its accompanying arm movement was a technique that had been used by American football cheerleaders, and that the Führer had learned it from him. He was playing for Hitler on a regular basis (mostly Wagner) soon after, and published a *Hitler Song Book* in 1924.

"Putzi was to Hitler what harp-playing David was to Saul," reported Louis P. Lochner of the Associated Press. "He eased der Führer out of his frequent fits of depression with his piano playing." Indeed, President Franklin Delano Roosevelt, remembering Putzi from his days at Harvard, sent suggestions for keeping Hitler under control: "Try and use the soft pedal if things get too loud."

(Hanfstaengl reported that besides Wagner, Hitler liked Verdi, Chopin, Richard Strauss, Liszt, Grieg, and Gypsy music, though he disliked Bach, Handel, Haydn, Mozart, Beethoven, and Brahms.)

The piano had actually been a presence all through the war, with American troops receiving Steinway "GI" pianos in the field, airdropped from planes. Steinway created these models for their ability to function in rugged terrain, and soldiers sometimes congregated around them even in battle-ready settings.

The Steinway "GI" piano in the field, 1943

A profound political moment for the piano in America was Van Cliburn's surprising win, in 1958, of the first Tchaikovsky Piano Competition in Moscow. At the height of the cold war, a victorious Cliburn returned home to a ticker-tape parade in New York and cover placement on *Time* magazine.

But perhaps the most remarkable political turnaround in modern piano history occurred in China. The instrument was banned during Mao Zedong's Cultural Revolution (1966–1976). Today, that country is actually at the forefront of producing the next great wave of pianists, and pianos as well.

As a young pianist, he gripped listeners with a combination of Romantic fire and masterful control. As he matured, Ashkenazy came to view the classic Russian approach as too extreme. "There is still a fascination with Russian playing in the West," he declared.

That is, playing with a lot of freedom. But it goes against the grain in certain types of music. What I like about Russian ballet is that the dancers don't necessarily take their steps from the rhythm of the music. It's like a *rubato* [gently holding back or rushing forward] in movement. On the stage it's fine, and it doesn't upset the pattern or basic expression of the dance. But in the Russian way of understanding music, this can be bad . . . You don't need to take big liberties in Mozart or Beethoven or Bach. I think there should be an interpretation that arises from within the music, not so much from a concern with being "free."

He points admiringly to Rachmaninoff, "a composer who knew how to get from point A to point B: He understood that the music had to move in a certain way." Indeed, one of the attributes of Ashkenazy's impeccable playing is its remarkable clarity and freedom from mannerisms. He remains one of the world's great players.

THE ANTI-ROMANTIC STREAM in Russian pianism was most forcefully represented by another important talent to emerge from the St. Petersburg Conservatory. Even as a student, Sergei Prokofiev (1891–1953) exploited the percussive side of the piano. His teacher, the formidable Annette Essipov (one of Leschetizky's four wives) reported in the spring of 1910 that Prokofiev "has assimilated little of my method." But the steel-like touch and technical freedom for which he became known were hallmarks of the Essipov-Leschetizky school.

Neuhaus described Prokofiev's piano style: "Energy, confidence, indomitable will, steel rhythm, powerful tone (sometimes even hard to bear in a small room), a peculiar 'epic quality' that scrupulously avoided any suggestion of over-refinement or intimacy (there is none in his music either), yet withal a remarkable ability to convey true lyricism, poetry, sadness . . . His technique was truly phenomenal, impeccable." As a composer, Prokofiev displayed a brilliant flair for combining percussive and lyrical qualities, and, like many Soviet musicians, he often imbued his music with a biting sense of irony (even calling one set of piano pieces *Sarcasms*). The composer's spine-tingling Piano Concerto no. 3, with perpetual-motion piano lines—grinding away like the ceaseless gears of an industrial mill—remains an audience favorite. His strange and haunting Piano Concerto no. 2 is unique in the literature.

Sergei Prokofiev

Prokofiev's colleague Dmitri Shostakovich (1906–1975), who shared a similar sensibility, suffered the worst that Stalin's government could dish out to artists who failed to toe the party line. His work was panned in *Pravda*, the Communist Party newspaper, with this assessment: "Snatches of melody, the beginnings of a musical phrase, are drowned, emerge again, and disappear in a grinding and squealing roar. To follow this 'music' is most difficult, to remember it, impossible." The composer was so fearful of the authorities that he slept in the hallway outside his apartment so that his family would be untouched should the police come to take him away.

Among his most evocative piano works is a celebrated set of

*Tatiana
Nikolayeva*

twenty-four preludes and fugues, written after he had served as a judge at a piano competition at which a young contestant, Tatiana Nikolayeva, offered to play from memory any of the forty-eight preludes and fugues of Bach's *Well-Tempered Clavier.* She won the gold medal, and subsequently played the premiere of Shostakovich's work when it was completed in 1951. Despite political obstacles, the power of his music proved intractable.

CHAPTER 13

The Germans and Their Close Relations

T HE GERMAN TRADITION presented a foil to Russian extravagance, and its exponents were pegged as the frosty intellectuals of the concert circuit. The approach elevates music's architectural scaffolding (a work's most important harmonies and phrases—its metaphorical plumbing and retaining walls) over subjective emotion and surface beauty.

Hans von Bülow (1830–1894), who set out for the United States after meeting Anton Rubinstein in London after the latter's American adventure ("I have paved the way," Rubinstein declared, painting perhaps a too rosy picture of Bülow's prospects), was a prime example. One reviewer went so far as to describe him as a "musical refrigerator." "Is his playing emotional? Are we moved by it? Do we shed tears?" asked a writer for *Dwight's Journal*. "Not in the least," was the conclusion.

Nevertheless, Bülow's credentials were impressive: he was one

of Liszt's favorite students, and had even married the great pianist's daughter Cosima (only to have her stolen from him by Richard Wagner, for whom, strangely, Bülow's enthusiasm never flagged). Despite the Liszt connection, however, he was steeped in Germanic sobriety and ready to show Americans a thing or two. The piano maker Chickering, hoping to regain some of the momentum they were losing to Steinway at the time, gave financial support for his 1875 concert season.

The trip was beset with problems. Bülow engaged marketing whiz Bernard Ullman. But Ullman labeled their negotiations the "Thirty Years' War." The pianist refused to be billed as Liszt's student and son-in-law. And he wouldn't adjust his programs for the new market. "I do not have the time, I do not have the energy to prepare the 'firework' pieces indispensable for the Yankees," he declared. Chickering would soon be in for its share of trouble, too. But by a stroke of good fortune, in October of 1875, Bülow was able to offer Boston audiences a phenomenal gift: the world premiere of one of the most popular piano works of all time.

The Wagners, with Bülow in tow

It was Tchaikovsky's First Piano Concerto. The pianist who had commissioned it, Nikolai Rubinstein, flatly refused to play the work. "It transpired that my concerto was no good," wrote a seething Tchaikovsky after meeting with Nikolai, "that it was impossible to play, that some passages were hackneyed, awkward, and clumsy beyond redemption, that as a composition it was bad and banal, that I had pilfered this bit from here and that from there, that there were only two or three pages which would do, and that the rest would have to be either discarded or completely reworked." So the composer withdrew the score and offered it to Bülow, who found the music's ideas "lofty, strong, and original," and its form "perfect."

The concerto's reception in Boston was mixed, with one reviewer complaining of the music's "formless void, sprinkled only with tin-klings of the piano and snatchy obbligatos" from the orchestra. Nevertheless, it turned out to be a work for the ages. And as Bülow settled in, America seemed to provide even more comforts than he had enjoyed at home. "With horror I think back on the old rotten European world," he wrote his mother. He would soon change his tune again.

As he embraced his new surroundings, Bülow began to express more than a little hostility toward his fellow immigrants. He put down German musicians for drinking beer excessively. "They do not get drunk like the Irish people," he claimed, "but they drink until their blood becomes sluggish and their brains stupid." Then he attacked German music teachers for ruining education in America. Finally, the remarks got personal: Carl Bergmann, conductor of the New York Philharmonic, was singled out for sloppiness and alco-holism.

The pianist was quick to bite the hands that fed him. In Balti-more, when he discovered that his piano had a sign displaying the name Chickering, he ripped it off, stormed around the stage, and returned to kick it repeatedly. "I am not," he said, "a traveling advertisement." On another occasion, he used a jackknife to scrape off the painted Chickering name on his piano. At a New Year's Eve concert in New York, he had forgotten his knife, so he simply had the piano removed and a nameless one brought in. It stirred up a public storm.

The New York Times agreed with Bülow, and implored piano makers to halt the practice. Why not hang a sign directly on the pia-nist? it asked. Even further: why not display one on members of the audience announcing which piano they were listening to? Theodore Steinway was unimpressed by the hubbub. "The damned artists consider piano makers a cow to be milked," he wrote his brother, William. "I wish I could invent a piano that makes you stupid and seasick—I would donate one to each of them."

Bülow bragged in a letter that in America he played like a god. But as the grueling schedule of concerts went on, his stamina began to fade, along with his reputation. Ullman warned that his programs were far too serious to draw large audiences, and that the press was calling him overly intellectual. Meanwhile, by the second year of touring, the pianist was complaining to a friend that he was beginning to feel like a "suitcase with headaches." Increasingly unhappy with Chickering pianos, he attempted to woo over Steinway. Soon, the concerts and the travel all became a blur.

Finally, he could take no more. "You have no idea how terribly depressing, nauseating, and exhausting this slavery is," he asserted, "which I have entered because of vile mammon." There were 33 concerts remaining of his contracted 172 when he ended the trip, sailing home in June of 1876 to recuperate.

THE BRAND WARS, AT THE BEGINNING

Celebrity performers were important to piano builders' marketing efforts almost from the start. Early on, Mozart endorsed the pianos of Johann Andreas Stein. It didn't hurt that Stein's daughter Nanette, who would one day become Beethoven's favorite tuner, was a Mozart student. "Anyone able to see and hear her play without laughing must be *stone*," Mozart wrote to his father (in a pun on the name *Stein*).

> She sits opposite the treble notes, not in the middle forsooth, for better occasion of throwing herself about and making grimaces. She rolls her eyes and all kinds of nonsense. When a passage occurs twice she plays it slower the second time, when thrice, slower still. When she has a passage to execute she lifts her arm high in the air, and if it needs emphasis she uses the arm not the fingers, taking every care to do it heavily and clumsily. Best of all, however, when it is necessary to change the fingers in a passage which should run as smoothly as oil, she does not worry her head at all, but at the critical moment stops, lifts her hand, and begins again quite at her ease . . . She is eight and a half years old and plays everything by heart.

(It's clear Mozart felt genuine warmth for her. Nevertheless, once settled in Vienna, he purchased his piano from another builder, Anton
Walter.)

Within two decades, Nanette—a founder in 1802, along with her
husband, Johann Andreas Streicher, of the piano company Streicher &
Son—was scrambling to gain Beethoven's endorsement. She wasn't
alone; as his fame grew, instruments began arriving at his flat at such
a fast pace he didn't have time to assemble them all. In 1810, Bettina
Brentano von Arnim wrote to Goethe about her visit to Beethoven: "In
the front room there are from two to three pianos, all legless, lying on
the floor." His home, cluttered with piano parts, had begun to resemble
a warehouse.

Beethoven would constantly pit manufacturers against each other,
switching from Streicher to Walter to Reicha to Érard—the French firm
that sent one of its instruments to him in 1803. Within seven years
he was complaining that the Érard had fallen into disrepair, no doubt
due in part to Beethoven's keyboard approach, which, reported Muzio
Clementi, "was not seldom violent, like himself." When the composer
received a piano from the English firm of Broadwood, he shot off an
effusive thank-you letter that the company used (and still uses) to convince customers that its brand was the choice of the immortal composer. "I shall look upon it as an altar on which I shall place the most
beautiful offerings of my spirit to the divine Apollo," he wrote to Thomas
Broadwood, promising to send the music he would write on it. There is
no evidence that he ever did.

Beethoven had special needs, of course. He implored Streicher "to
adjust one of your pianos for me to suit my impaired hearing. It should
be as loud as possible. That is absolutely necessary. I have long been
intending to buy one of your pianos, but at the moment that would be
very difficult for me. Perhaps, however, it will be possible for me to do
so later on. But until then I should like to borrow one of yours."

Johann Friedrich Reichardt reported that Streicher had "abandoned
the soft, yielding, repercussive tone of the other Vienna instruments,
and at Beethoven's wish and advice has given his instruments greater
resonance and elasticity." As a gesture of his friendship, Streicher also

sent Beethoven ear trumpets, and even proposed an upright piano for him with projecting horns to serve as hearing aids. By that point, though, Beethoven's deafness was too far gone—nothing could help.

Hans von Bülow's departure notwithstanding, many found the German tradition's ability to move the spotlight away from the performer and onto the inner thoughts of the composer admirable. "A performing artist should be in the position of a mountain guide," claimed Austrian pianist Artur Schnabel (1882–1951). "A guide's personality becomes more and more important the higher the climbing goes; but from a certain level onward, he must see to it that his charge, the guided climber, is more concerned with the mountain than with the guide."

This "penetration of the letter and spirit of a composition," wrote pianist and musicologist Konrad Wolff, actually offered musicians and audiences a kind of freedom—not only from the cult of fleeting celebrity, but also from "superficial performances of Mozart as 'a masked ball in rococo costume,' " or Brahms "as 'a man with the 3 B's of beer, beard, and belly.' " Such outward stylistic frills might be appealingly showy, but they missed the point. Pianists, Schnabel believed, are tasked with the moral obligation to reveal artistic truth by digging deep into the structure of a work to justify their interpretive decisions. Why should one passage be louder than another, or faster, or slower? What is the invisible architecture that keeps a musical creation from crumbling? The secrets were hidden in the texts themselves, and in the right hands they could be revelatory, yielding lessons about the very nature of music. This pianist's favorite quotation was from Goethe: "What is the universal? The single case!"

Schnabel, a student of Leschetizky who championed the then-neglected sonatas of Schubert and Beethoven's late works, was no technical virtuoso; in fact, Rachmaninoff allegedly called him "the great adagio [slow movement] pianist." And if his cerebral approach did not please everyone, it mattered little to him. After all, conveying Truth had a higher purpose than ripping your heart open and spilling emotion's messy entrails around the keyboard in the hope that an audience will be stirred. He was, he believed, better than that. "The difference between my programs and those of other pianists," he once said, perversely, "is that mine are boring not only in the first half but also in the second."

The evidence suggests otherwise. As a brilliant young student, American pianist Leon Fleisher studied with Schnabel and years later recalled his teacher's playing of a Beethoven scherzo, "giving a lilt to its lighthearted opening, moving on into more darkly shaded areas, returning to the lilt, playing light as air and with a twinkle in his eye." When Schnabel rehearsed the Adagio of a Mozart piano concerto, says Fleisher, the music was "suspended in midair. It sounded like the language of the spheres."

However, Schnabel's purist persona could be harsh, and he was always uncompromising. "The famous sentence that 'the end justifies the means,' " he asserted, "plainly refers to rotten means, otherwise it would be absolutely superfluous. It is similar to the slogan 'Keep Smiling.' It invites one to smile where normally one would, and should, grumble." For the latter, he certainly had a talent.

Artur Schnabel and family

Other Austro-Germanic players of note included Rudolf Serkin (1903–1991), a pianist who shared Schnabel's rigorous approach to music's architecture, though always rendered with graceful, poetic phrasing and a warm-bodied tone; Chilean-born Claudio Arrau (1903–1991), who studied in Berlin with former Liszt student Martin Krause; and Alfred Brendel (b. 1931), hailed in some quarters as the "new" Schnabel.

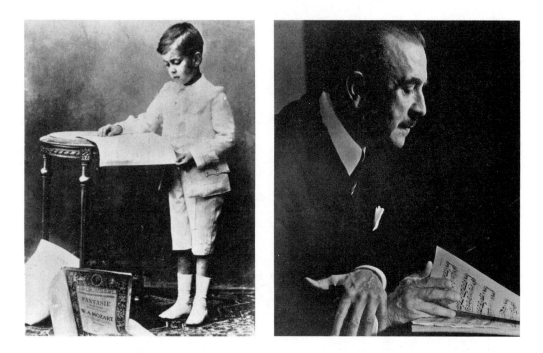

Serkin spent many formative years in Vienna and Berlin, and made his American debut with the New York Philharmonic under the baton of Arturo Toscanini. The critics hailed his "crystalline technique," a combination of power and delicacy. He taught generations of musicians at the Curtis Institute of Music in Philadelphia, and at Marlboro Music, the summer music colony he created in 1951 in the hills of Vermont to nurture the chamber-music tradition, now co-directed by pianists Richard Goode (b. 1943) and Mitsuko Uchida (b. 1948), two of the most formidable modern pianists associated with German repertoire.

Arrau was magnetic. The London *Times* described his playing as "a sort of miracle . . . Like God touching Adam on Michelangelo's Sistine Chapel roof; liquid, mysterious, profound, alive." The pianist's mental concentration alone was so palpable it could fill a hall and rivet an audience.

Leipzig-trained and Swiss-born pianist and pedagogue Edwin Fischer (1886–1960)—who, like Arrau, worked in Berlin with Martin Krause—was an important influence on Alfred Brendel, a pianist both renowned and castigated for his analytical bent. That rarefied reputation was reinforced by his many writings, from poetry with a bizarre, surrealist sensibility to essays arguing for fidelity to the musical text. (Exaggerations about his analytical coolness, he claims, are rampant in the United States but not in Europe. "It's an American trait," he says.)

In fact, much of his scholarly work has been misunderstood. While Brendel's call for faithfulness to a composer's intentions can be taken as the pianist's creed, his written advice suggests a highly subtle approach. "The projection of simplicity can be a very complex business," he reminds us. "An exceptional reservoir of nuances" is required, so that the simplicity does not turn into "emptiness and boredom."

Indeed, his observations reflect as much heart as head: "We follow rules in order to make the exceptions more impressive"; and "a 'psychological' tempo is to be distinguished from the metronomic one." Do your homework, he declares. But keep in mind that "the growing precision of our understanding should enhance, and not diminish, our sense of wonder."

Alfred Brendel with Juilliard student Eun Ae Lee
PETER SCHAAF

Shortly before giving a master class at the Juilliard School in the fall of 2010, Brendel reiterated that position. "The analytical mind is a kind of sphincter for the emotions," he explains. "I don't sit down beforehand and decide what the composer should have done. Even in my writing I don't begin with analysis—it's always in the middle of an essay. My view of performance is very much like Schnabel's. For me the details are all-important because they make the music work as an organic whole."

Minutes later he was demonstrating for students the intricacies of a Beethoven sonata, correcting the balance between their left and right hands, exploiting gradations of articulation, setting a line between discipline and freedom, probing the emotional character of each phrase—and under his hands the piano seemed to mutate into an entire orchestra as Beethoven's overpowering spirit came to life.

NOT ALL OF Leschetizky's progeny followed in the emotionally reserved mold of Schnabel. One of his students galvanized audiences to the point of hysteria, and even sparked a small civil war that required the intervention of the American Congress.

In 1891, Steinway Hall—which had opened in 1866, and quickly became the musical heartbeat of New York City—closed to make way for Carnegie Hall (then called the New Music Hall), and the piano firm marked the occasion by hiring Poland's Ignacy Jan Paderewski (1860–1941) to play three concerts with an orchestra conducted by Walter Damrosch. The longhaired, charismatic pianist created such a rage—Huneker, in the *Musical Courier,* called it "Paddymania"—that Charles F. Tretbar, head of Steinway's concert and artist department, immediately arranged for eighty additional concerts (for a guaranteed $30,000). Audience reaction was so overwhelming that more dates were quickly added. In the end, Paderewski netted $95,000 for his efforts.

His playing had charm marked by a clear sense of proportion, with moments of lightness as well as heartfelt intensity. (Noting that no one could live up to all the hoopla, pianist Moriz Rosenthal wryly commented, "Yes, he plays well, I suppose, but he's no Paderewski.") In the end, the tour was beset with problems. Accommodations were dreadful—those hotels that were actually free of cockroaches and mice wouldn't allow him to practice in his room—and the stress of performing 107 times in 117 days took its toll. The worst experience of the trip came toward the end, though, at the Chicago World's Fair (officially known as the World's Columbian Exposition, in celebration of the four hundredth anniversary of the discovery of America) in May of 1893, where the war that had been simmering between piano makers erupted into a roaring battle.

There had been previous blowups, like the skirmishes between the firms of Steinway, Weber, and Hale in the 1870s. (William Steinway's diary reveals that he had scored a coup in that event by paying *The New York Times* to print a favorable editorial on his behalf.) But they paled in comparison.

The Chicago fair had been plagued with a variety of disputes from the beginning. Sabbatarians brought suit in the courts to prevent a Sunday opening. The event's director created controversy by refusing to hang drawings sent by the Philadelphia Academy of Fine Arts because they were of nudes. The plaster in most of the buildings was still wet at the appointed time for the opening. And a musical struggle of grand proportions was unfolding behind the scenes.

Three years earlier, German conductor Theodore Thomas had moved to Chicago at the behest of business leaders who wanted him to assume leadership of a new permanent orchestra. "I would go to Hell if they gave me a permanent orchestra," replied Thomas, with astonishing prescience. Thus the Chicago Symphony was born. Thomas was also the obvious choice to direct musical activities at the fair, and he invited Paderewski to perform.

No one could have foreseen what happened next. An exhibit area had been set aside for pianos of various makers, each vying for a medal. The East Coast piano brands were better known, but organization officials decided to favor local businesses both in the assignment of display locations and in the rules they established for awarding a prize. Instead of the standard panel of judges used in similar competitions, the winner was to be chosen by just one person: Dr. Florenz Ziegfeld, head of the Chicago Musical College, on whose board sat W. W. Kimball, director of Chicago's largest piano maker.

Chickering of Boston was the first to withdraw. Within two weeks, all sixteen New York firms followed suit. The Chicagoans

A PEACEFUL SOLUTION.
AT THE NEXT WORLD'S FAIR PADEREWSKI WILL PLAY ON ALL THE PIANOS AT ONCE.

expressed outrage, and the dispute spilled over into the pages of newspapers from each of the cities involved. "The pianos of Peoria and Keokuk and Oshkosh will sound much better when they are not compared with the pianos of Boston and Baltimore and New York," wrote *The New York Times* in a snooty editorial. "In the absence of these effete instruments the wild and woolly piano of the West will take all the prizes and its makers may persuade the farmers' daughters of the northwest that it is 'equally as good' as the instruments preferred by pianists."

The man who had come up with the one-person judging system, John Thacher, proclaimed that the Easterners were simply afraid to face the competition. Since outsiders had withdrawn their support, the Chicago piano exhibitors demanded that only *their* pianos be used in the event's concerts.

An 1893 illustration: A PEACEFUL SOLUTION. AT THE NEXT WORLD'S FAIR PADEREWSKI WILL PLAY ON ALL THE PIANOS AT ONCE.

Paderewski had offered to play without a fee, and Thomas had happily booked advertisements for his performance. But recognizing that the pianist would insist on using a Steinway, the director of the fair ordered that posters bearing Paderewski's name be torn down. The *Chicago Tribune* sided with the home team: "If Mr. Paderewski cannot play . . . except on some piano, the manufacturers of which withdrew their exhibits . . . on account of petty spite, then there will be a general willingness to dispense with Mr. Paderewski's playing entirely."

It took an act of the federal government to work things out, and even that required time. First, a special piano committee, appointed by a sitting national commission, was asked to review the situation. They listened to nine hours of testimony and decided that any piano by a nonexhibitor could be removed, "at the point of a bayonet if necessary." Chicago business leaders, still unhappy with the impasse, asked for a meeting of yet another committee—the Boards of Reference and Control—which assembled behind closed doors. They referred the matter to another body, the Council of Administration. And the stalemate continued.

On the day of the opening concert, the council finally reached a decision befitting King Solomon. Paderewski can play on a Steinway after all, they declared, because the music hall was a separate institution from the fair itself; however, as a compromise, Theodore Thomas would be required to display some of the local exhibitors' pianos in the hall, and to use them at his rehearsals.

There were winners and losers. In the end, Paderewski performed, but then canceled his last New York appearances because of fatigue. Thomas was driven out of his job as music director of the fair, and nearly lost the orchestra as well. However, the piano that Paderewski used, now notorious, was placed in the showroom of the local Steinway dealer, Lyon, Potter, where it drew huge lines of people waiting for a chance to see and touch the famous instrument that had caused such a ruckus. That was the kind of marketing success that money can't buy.

CHAPTER 14

Keys to the World

ALL THE WORLD'S A STAGE. Along with Russian extroverts and German introverts, there were purveyors of other regional styles who added their own subtle ingredients to the grand musical stew. Among the offerings, gourmands could sample Polish panache, English earthiness, French charm, Italian refinement, and American spontaneity.

In Poland, the deep melancholy of the country's greatest musical poet, Frédéric Chopin, had a counterpart in a buoyant folk spirit that thrived in towns all along the Baltic Sea. It could also be found in wandering ensembles like the klezmer bands that migrated from Poland through the Ukraine, Lithuania, Russia, and, ultimately, to America. These groups took Near Eastern and European elements, liturgical and secular materials, old traditions and spontaneous improvisations and blended them all into a joyous celebration. That raw vitality could also infect Polish classical performers.

The country's pianism, like the Polish language itself (which over time absorbed parts of Czech, Ukrainian, Turkish, Hungarian, German, Italian, and Latin), incorporated many influences. Those who left at an early age to study and perform abroad, like pianist-composer Leopold Godowsky (1870–1938), who began his career at the age of ten, merged their national sensibilities with those found in newer horizons. Godowsky's approach married Polish sparkle with Germanic precision, all wrapped up in jaw-dropping technical finesse. Heinrich Neuhaus, the legendary teacher of the Moscow Conservatory, was a Godowsky student. He recalled his mentor's "small hands that seemed chiseled out of marble and were incredibly beautiful (as a good thoroughbred racehorse is beautiful, or the body of a magnificent athlete), and see with what simplicity, lightness, ease, logic and, I would say, wisdom, they performed their super-acrobatic task."

Godowsky paid homage to Poland's native heritage by transforming the music of its favorite son into something entirely new, and staggeringly complex. His fifty-three *Studies on Chopin's Etudes* raised the difficulty of Chopin's original versions from the merely treacherous to the nearly impossible. He even combined two well-known Chopin Etudes so that they could be performed simultaneously, the left hand playing one and the right hand the other. Few players can sail easily over his music's hurdles. Yet, for Godowsky, who had yearned as a youngster to study with Liszt, the feat was apparently not very difficult. Critic James Huneker aptly called him "an apparition. A Chopin doubled by a contrapuntalist . . . The spirit of the German cantor and the Polish tone-poet in curious conjunction. He is a miracle worker."

Polish-American Arthur Rubinstein (1887–1982) admitted, "It would take me five hundred years to get a mechanism like Godowsky's." And Rubinstein was no slouch. A bon vivant who relished fine wine, good cigars, and beautiful women, he was often regarded as the yin to Vladimir Horowitz's yang. If the high-strung Russian Horowitz was a lightning storm, Rubinstein, a more Germanic player, was a summer breeze. Fans of each claimed for their favorite the accolade of greatest pianist of the age.

Arthur Rubinstein revisiting his hometown of Lodz, Poland, in 1976

He showered the music and his audiences with warmth. Indeed, his daughter Alina has suggested that when she wanted to feel her father's love, the place to find it was in the concert hall. Over the course of a long career, he evolved from a young piano personality with uneven accuracy into a seasoned artist who approached the repertoire with seriousness, dignity, and an uncanny talent for making it all sound natural. He almost single-handedly changed the way we hear Chopin. In a 1960 article for *The New York Times* Rubinstein wrote of rejecting the common myth of Chopin as "effeminate if appealing, dipping his pen in moonlight to compose nocturnes for sentimental young women." In Rubinstein's hands, Chopin's music became full-bodied and resolute: clearly heartfelt, yet also muscular—in a word, more "masculine." Rubinstein's musical qualities seem to shine through various photos taken of him in action at the keyboard, or dancing through the streets of his birthplace; he radiates the pure joy of life, in a constant celebration of the beautiful.

There was no reckless Russian excess here, but rather tender nobility, playing of emotional sweep tinged with German pensiveness. Little wonder that Rubinstein became a model for the *modern* Romantic player. His sound was tonally inviting, virile, stirring yet unsentimental, his passions an open book on and off the stage. He was also an ideal musical collaborator. Rubinstein's chamber ensemble with violinist Jascha Heifetz and cellist Gregor Piatigorsky became known as the Million-Dollar Trio. As a result of his travels, several composers from Spain and South America—Manuel de

Falla and Heitor Villa-Lobos, among others, from whom he commissioned works—became lifelong friends.

But perhaps the most formidable Polish-American virtuoso was Josef Hofmann (1876–1957). He was born in Podgórze, a fishing village near Kraków, and made his impressive musical debut at the tender age of six; he concertized at New York's Metropolitan Opera when he was only eleven. Despite his youth, he set the town on its ear. "Pianists of repute were moved almost to tears. Some wiped the moisture from their eyes," declared *The New York Times*. As the years went on, his playing grew even more impressive. He performed in Europe, America, and Russia, giving an astounding series of twenty-one concerts in St. Petersburg in 1913, which included 255 compositions.

His style was impulsive—full of subtle and not-so-subtle contrasts—with sonic gradations that ranged from volcanic outbursts to gentle murmurs. Sometimes he exhibited the full scope of these contrasts all at once, effortlessly shaping the individual lines in a busy musical texture as if they were each being rendered by a separate musician. This was pianistic control at its peak. As writer David Dubal pointed out, "His spontaneity was deeply calculated." Yet, his finely etched passagework, the hues he elicited from his keyboard harmonies, his masterful rhythmic flair and puckish sense of play were all simply breathtaking.

Hofmann was regarded by many of his peers as perhaps the greatest pianist of all. Late in life, Rachmaninoff declared him "still . . . the greatest pianist alive *if* he is sober and in form." Sobriety was actually his greatest challenge.

Like Godowsky's, his hands were small. In fact, he had a special piano built with narrower keys to accommodate their limited span. His students at the Curtis Institute of Music, not realizing the keyboard was constructed to be narrower than usual, hit wrong notes whenever they tried to play it, and came to believe the instrument was haunted. (The idea of narrower keyboards has been catching on, especially as a boon to students with very small hands, as a way of preventing strain and injury. At Southern Methodist University, Texas Tech University, the University of North Texas, and the Uni-

versity of Nebraska, some students are using 7/8- and 15/16-size keyboards produced by Steinbuhler & Company of Titusville, Pennsylvania.)

Unlike his teacher, the wild, longhaired Romantic Anton Rubinstein (who first heard him perform at the age of seven and expressed astonishment), Hofmann eschewed flamboyance. Instead, he took on the demeanor of a business executive, and cultivated skills on the tennis court. Along with stupendous musical gifts, he possessed a mind brimming with ideas—his seventy patents included designs for pneumatic shock absorbers for cars and planes, the automatic windshield wiper (which purportedly had its origins in the metronome), and a house that revolved with the sun. Among his students was the formidable Shura Cherkassky (1909–1995), regarded as perhaps the last great Romantic.

Young Josef Hofmann

OTHER PARTS OF the globe exhibited their own particular traits. The stalwart English—hardy, forthright, and free of flashiness—played piano like ideal hosts at an afternoon tea: solidly self-assured and models of propriety. Among the best were the elegant Sir Clifford Curzon (1907–1982), who studied with Wanda Landowska and Artur Schnabel; the muscular Dame Myra Hess (1890–1965); and the phenomenal Solomon, born Solomon Cutner (1902–1988).

They were as upright and dependable as the guards at Buckingham Palace. Their Germanic tendencies were reinforced by a piano-technique guru named Tobias Matthay (1858–1945), whose many books—including *The Act of Touch in All Its Diversity* (1903) and *The Visible and Invisible in Pianoforte Technique* (1947)—offered a method for ease of movement in performance. The results left some observers cold. Of Dame Myra Hess, a student of Matthay,

Virgil Thomson declared, "She is not memorable, like a love affair; she is satisfactory, like a good tailor."

Nevertheless, Hess had many fans on both sides of the Atlantic, and, despite Thomson's assessment, Americans were especially enthusiastic about her gifts. "In England, it is as if people *hope* I will play well," she explained;

"in America they positively *expect* me to play well." Thomson's criticism might have contained a kernel of truth, but she could certainly muster the fire, especially in a big concerto.

Her friend, critic and conductor Arthur Mendel, made an interesting observation about these diverging views of her playing. Lamenting the differences between what he considered to be her less-than-inspiring recordings and his recollections of hearing her live, Mendel concluded that in person Hess emitted a kind of charismatic spark that went beyond the music and reached into the listener. "I think," he wrote, "[that] performance for her was *essentially* communication to an audience." She certainly had a talent for winning over a crowd. According to one charming but probably apocryphal story, someone noticed the pencil marking "L.U." scattered throughout her printed music, and inquired what it stood for. The initials turned out to represent the words "look up"; they were a reminder for the pianist to gaze heavenward at key moments in order to convey the impression that she was under the spell of divine inspiration.

Sir Clifford Curzon

Hess became the inspiration for an entire nation during World War II. When London's National Gallery was emptied of art to protect it from German bombs, Hess organized a series of concerts in the space; one thousand people showed up for the opening concert instead of the expected fifty. Her ongoing presentations there, which continued throughout the fighting, became a symbol of the enduring spirit of Londoners in the face of terrible adversity. In

1941, a grateful King George VI made her Dame Commander of the Order of the British Empire. At war's end, when the artworks were returned and the concerts ceased, a great many British citizens expressed a profound sense of loss.

I F ENGLISH PIANISTS subtly reflected their reserved cultural atmosphere, the frothy, rich sauces of Parisian cuisine and the sleek, immaculate fashions of Milan also suggested the pianistic character of those regions. Even before Friedrich Kalkbrenner and Henri Herz introduced to France such techniques as "caressing" the keys (sliding the finger from the middle to the edge of the key with gentle pressure) and producing *jeu perlé*—successions of notes that sound like beaded pearls—French playing was a highly sensual affair, characteristically light and fleet. One of the country's greatest pianists, Marguerite Long (1874–1966), described the sound as "lucid, precise, and slender," one that prized "grace" rather than "force."

Paradoxically, France's most famous piano personality, Alfred Cortot (1877–1962), fit no easy category. His highly polished technique, honed at the Paris Conservatory under Émile Descombes, a disciple of Chopin, was typical of the French. But Cortot's fascination with Wagner's music led him to Bayreuth, where he became a choral coach and then an assistant conductor. Returning to France in 1902, twenty-three-year-old Cortot conducted the Parisian premiere of Wagner's *Götterdämmerung*.

The surface beauty of Cortot's French side took root in that Wagnerian soil, and the result was a pianism that combined Long's lucid and graceful execution with a palpable sense of mood and drama. According to the distinguished American pianist Murray Perahia (b. 1947), Cortot "followed an inner emotional logic . . . He would change tempo if he felt the dramatic context required it, getting faster if the mood became more restless, slowing down if he wanted to show the culmination of a thought." The result was unconventional, yet highly convincing.

Perahia's own training, cemented at Marlboro Music, was in the German analytic and chamber tradition—his recording career was launched, in fact, as a Mozart pianist and conductor—yet he became a huge fan of Cortot. The Frenchman's cross-pollination of styles reflected Perahia's own circuitous journey. In the 1980s Vladimir Horowitz became Perahia's mentor, and the younger pianist began to inject more risk and drama into his playing, which made him especially sympathetic to Cortot's force of personality. Indeed, revealed Perahia, Horowitz had actually studied with Cortot. "He told me that when he left Russia his teacher, Felix Blumenthal, told him that the only person in the West that he really must work with was Cortot," said Horowitz's last protégé. "He studied all the Beethoven Sonatas with Cortot, though Cortot wasn't very nice. Of course, there probably was a touch of anti-Semitism in Cortot," says Perahia. "He had a very dodgy war record."

ITALIAN PIANISTS were not so enamored of Wagnerian drama nor of shimmering surface color. Italian playing tends to be superbly polished, and as reliable as a Swiss clock, but by historical imperative it is driven by the "singing line." The best Italian performers are unfailingly lyrical and elegant, with never a note out of place. In some ways they mirror postwar Italian architecture, such as Rome's Termini Railway Station and Milan's Torre Velasca skyscraper, models of clarity in design and impeccable attention to detail.

Arturo Benedetti Michelangeli (1920–1995), perhaps the greatest Italian pianist of the twentieth century, could "no more hit a wrong note or smudge a passage than a bullet can be veered off course once it has been fired," wrote Harold Schonberg. Yet he was never lacking in emotion: Cortot labeled Michelangeli "a new Liszt," and in some repertoire, particularly Beethoven, he could rally all the forces of darkness. Nevertheless, the surgical precision of his performance was striking, a quality that also characterized the playing of one of his students, piano great Maurizio Pollini (b. 1942).

Still, the Italians, particularly those of today's generation, play even contemporary works with the sweet breadth of an operatic aria, full of phrases that linger.

YOUNG AMERICAN PIANISTS seized the opportunity to study with masters of each of these styles, clamoring to work with such eminences as Cortot, Rubinstein, Hofmann, Serkin, and a host of Russian pedagogues. They adopted what they liked, rejected what didn't suit them, and integrated what remained into a brash, sure-footed style that was infused with America's greatest artistic asset: an inborn improvisatory flair.

Leon Fleisher (b. 1928), a student of Artur Schnabel, was one of the best of that young American school. He made his Carnegie Hall debut at age sixteen with the New York Philharmonic under the direction of conductor Pierre Monteux, who dubbed him "the pianistic find of the century." Throughout the 1950s and early 1960s, he fulfilled every expectation of greatness. Then, at the age of thirty-six, Fleisher developed weakness in two fingers of his right hand; they began to curl involuntarily.

There was no explanation for it, though in time it garnered the official diagnosis of "focal dystonia." "I went from doctor to doctor," he recalled. "I tried everything from aroma therapy to Zen Buddhism and no one had any answers . . . [But] it usually happens to people who use fine muscles under pressure. It hits surgeons in the hands, horn players in the lips, and singers in the vocal cords." The pianist turned to repertoire for the left hand alone (much of it previously commissioned by pianist Paul Wittgenstein, who had lost his right arm in World War I), and pursued other artistic avenues, such as conducting and teaching.

The roster of his students included the phenomenally successful André Watts (b. 1946), whose own electrifying teenage debut took place with conductor Leonard Bernstein; the masterful French-Canadian musician Louis Lortie; and Yefim Bronfman (b. 1958), the Russian-Israeli-American pianist described by Philip Roth in his novel *The Human Stain* as "Bronfman the brontosaur! Mr. Fortissimo!"

Though Fleisher's playing was far less muscular, Roth's account of Bronfman's performance suggests the kind of rapturous response that the teacher himself once inspired:

> Enter Bronfman to play Prokofiev at such a pace and with such bravado as to knock my morbidity clear out of the ring . . . When he's finished, I thought, they'll have to throw the thing out. He crushes it. He doesn't let that piano conceal a thing. Whatever's in there is going to come out, and come out with its hands in the air. And when it does, everything there out in the open, the last of the last pulsation, he himself gets up and goes, leaving behind him our redemption. With a jaunty wave, he is suddenly gone, and though he takes all his fire off with him like no less a force than Prometheus, our own lives now seem inextinguishable. Nobody is dying, *nobody*—not if Bronfman has anything to say about it!

Fleisher's flashes of insight, delivered like poetic lightning bolts, are legendary. Writer Anne Midgette, who co-authored Leon Fleisher's 2010 autobiography, *My Nine Lives,* recalled the advice he gave Bronfman on the proper approach to Rachmaninoff. When playing Rachmaninoff, said Fleisher, the sound must "stay cool, so cool that it's hot, like dry ice. That's the way to generate heat in that music."

Such visceral images are only the beginning of a larger picture for Fleisher. "Your focus is not exactly on the poetry or tragedy or pathos of the phrase you're playing," he says in his book.

> You're thinking about the quality of sound you're getting. You're thinking about how to play the rhythms so they come to life. You're thinking about how to depress the pedal—sometimes only halfway or one-third of the way—so that you support the phrase with the resonance of the strings, and then, when the next thought begins, you release the pedal and stop the haze of sound and start again fresh. What you gradually learn is that focusing on the score and learning to understand it and developing an awareness of the music's structure actually broaden your expres-

sive possibilities rather than limiting them. It's only through that process that you start expressing things that are truly worth expressing.

In recent years Fleisher has been able to return to the piano thanks to various medical treatments, including botox injections to keep his hand muscles from spasming.

In a strange twist of fate, Leon Fleisher's American colleague Gary Graffman (b. 1928) was also struck with a hand ailment in 1977. "We think it happened," he explained,

> when I was playing the Tchaikovsky Piano Concerto no. 1 with the Berlin Philharmonic, using a brand new, totally dead piano. New pianos are often brilliant sounding, but this one wasn't. I had been told (incorrectly) that Richter had just used it, and that he had been happy with the results. In any case, there was no time to make a change.
>
> To get more sound—but also in anger—I hit a key with my fourth finger, and used such force that the knuckle went up and out. When I returned to New York, my doctor said it was a typical "baseball finger"—something that happens to athletes—and that it would hurt for a while and then get better. I was facing lots of concerts, and to get back in the swing, I started re-fingering the music I was playing.
>
> Subconsciously, I was protecting my fourth finger, using my thumb and *third* fingers to play octaves. And there was secretly another reason: when a friend in the audience told me, "Now, I see how you get such a big sound: using fingers 1 and 3 really makes a difference!" I thought, I guess it's a good idea. I was playing with more power. Of course, I was also hurting myself.

His wife, Naomi, had her own take on the matter: pianos, she said, were not designed for humans but for gorillas. Nevertheless, the lessons learned from these cases have spawned educational programs and medical research to prevent future injuries.

PIANO TECHNIQUE

Proper piano technique has always been a contentious subject, and it remains so. Mechanical devices to improve finger dexterity (the kind that ruined Robert Schumann's hand) had a history as far back as John

Bernard Logier's early-nineteenth-century Position Frame, a contraption into which students inserted their hands as far as the wrists. It allowed only horizontal motion, keeping unnecessary movement to a minimum and forcing the wrists to maintain a "correct" level of rotation. (Clara Schumann's father, Friedrich Wieck, endorsed the Logier method.) Somehow, the idea that practicing should feel bad became a popular notion in the nineteenth century. In Germany, there was the vise, built to stretch the fourth finger into obedient submission. In America, the Atkins Finger-Supporting Device used springs attached to overhanging rings for each finger, adding extra resistance to build the strength of each digit.

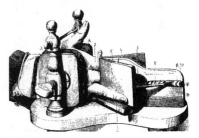

The pursuit of superhuman technical abilities encouraged the editor of *The Etude* magazine to endorse surgically cutting the connective tissue that binds the fingers to each other. More natural methods, like those advocated by Tobias Matthay, stressed the importance of proper touch and arm movement. However, as Juilliard teacher Martin Canin explained, "There are all kinds of approaches, and they each have their cult following. If you believe in something, it works." Canin studied with a disciple of technique guru Demetrius Constantine Dounis (1886–1954). "He had me play exercises while sitting on the floor," Canin reported. It's not a practice routine he recommends.

TOP
The Atkins Finger-Supporting Device

ABOVE
The vise

Two modern-day proponents of natural coordination in piano playing are Dorothy Taubman and her former protégée Edna Golandsky, for whom acolytes claim miraculous results. Taubman even asserted that she could cure Fleisher and Graffman if only they would place themselves in her hands. However, they were informed that it would require

287

abandoning forever their entire learned repertoire and starting afresh. Since for these two pianists that trove of studied music amounted to nearly all the piano masterpieces of the Western canon, neither pursued the matter.

Some inventors have tinkered with the piano keyboard in an effort to reduce the physical stress on players. The Jankó Keyboard, for example, designed in 1882 by Hungarian engineer Paul von Jankó, offered players a complex, symmetrical array of keys (264 in place of the usual eighty-eight), arranged so that all chords and scales follow the same shape, and wide stretches are virtually eliminated. Franz Liszt predicted that it "will have replaced the present piano keyboard in fifty years." He was wrong.

The psychological pressures that musicians face have also come under scrutiny in recent times. Studies show that great numbers of musicians have intense performance anxiety, and a shorter life expectancy than the general population. The plight of child prodigies in particular was revealed in a provocative autobiographical memoir called *Forbidden Childhood* by pianist Ruth Slenczynska (b. 1925). Slenczynska's account stands as a warning against "stage mothers and fathers" in the music world. It's worth noting, for those addicted to the spectacle of young, emotionally undeveloped virtuosos tackling the deepest works of the piano literature, that in its archaic meaning, "prodigy" derives from *prodigium*, the Latin word for "omen" and "monster" (rather than "artist").

Fleisher and Graffman came to represent a generation of American pianists who experienced setbacks at the peak of their careers—the list included William Kapell (1922–1953), Eugene Istomin (1925–2003), and William Masselos (1920–1992)—through injury, physical or psychological fragility, or early death.

YET THE BEAT GOES ON. In the 1950s, the next American generation emerged, spearheaded by an East Texas naïf who unexpectedly changed the course of history. Small-town piano teacher Rildia Bee Cliburn had wanted her son, Harvey Lavan ("Van") Cliburn Jr. (b. 1934), to study with the legendary Olga Samaroff (née Lucy Hickenlooper). But Samaroff had passed away before he arrived at the Juilliard School, and he began studies instead with Rosina Lhevinne. As it turned out, the match between student and teacher couldn't have been better. "His playing touched a deep Russian chord in her," remembered former Juilliard classmate Jeaneane Dowis. "For Rosina, Van was first. Maybe we were all close seconds, but he was always first."

What made Cliburn's playing so singular? There was, in the words of one Texas patron, his "magnolia blossom sound"—warm and full-hearted, a valentine to his audience. And then there was his phrasing.

The Chinese have an expression for movement that is delicately balanced and extremely graceful; they describe it as "like pulling silk from a cocoon." Cliburn's musical lines had an exquisite elasticity that gently tugged in one direction or another without ever breaking the thread. His way with a phrase was like pulling silken melodies from an endless cocoon. "He had a physical genius," explained Dowis. "It was so natural—he didn't have to think about what he was doing. He was unafraid to pick up his hands and drop them from two feet in the air. [Fellow classmate] John Browning was jealous of that. John had a good technique, but he had to work for it. Van did not; for him it came from the birds and the bees and the trees and the air."

In 1958, at a time when America was in the throes of a panic engendered by the launch of the Soviet's *Sputnik* space satellite, Cliburn entered the very first Tchaikovsky Piano Competition in Moscow. His career at home, despite some awards and small-scale management, had not been going well. But when he arrived on the Moscow stage and began to play, the Tchaikovsky jury was completely overwhelmed. Sviatoslav Richter, who was told to rate pianists on a scale of one to twenty-five, gave just a select few pianists,

*Van Cliburn
at the Moscow
competition*

including Cliburn, very high grades, and most others outrageously low scores. He proclaimed the American "a genius." Emil Gilels rushed forward in tears and kissed him. Composer Aram Khachaturian said he was "better than Rachmaninoff." Soviet premier Nikita Khrushchev had to be consulted before the first prize was awarded to this foreigner, but it was nearly impossible for him to refuse.

Cliburn returned home to cheering crowds and a ticker-tape parade. *Time* magazine commented, "He may be Horowitz, Liberace and Presley rolled into one." The West saw it as a political as well as a musical victory, and he sold out sports stadiums playing his signature piece, the Tchaikovsky First Piano Concerto. Yet, before long, critics began to complain about the sameness of his repertoire, and eventually, the seeming depletion of his early "fire." Just one year after his phenomenal win, critic Paul Henry Lang wrote of

Cliburn's failings, noting that he was being "hounded and clobbered by the public and the entrepreneurs."

The pianist, like Augie March's grandma, a character created by the novelist Saul Bellow, had always been "as thin and full of play as fiddle wire." Now he was losing weight and becoming increasingly exhausted, plagued by personal demons as well as public pressures. After Moscow, he had wisely described his own celebrity as not really "a success" but just "a sensation." Now the sensation was fading.

Nevertheless, for a while, his star power continued to attract fans. In 1962, when Cliburn and Igor Stravinsky both performed at the New York World's Fair, the pianist played to a packed, enthusiastic house while the composer conducted his ballet score *The Firebird* to a half-empty hall. Still, his career trajectory followed a long downward slope. Finally, he took an eleven-year "intermission," returning to play only sporadically. Meanwhile, in Fort Worth, Texas, a group of piano teachers created a piano competition in his honor, beginning in 1962. Scheduled to take place every four years, it continues to this day.

Cliburn's ticker-tape parade in New York

THE TCHAIKOVSKY AND CLIBURN competitions weren't the first of their kind, but they arose long before the field became cluttered. Over the decades, such contests have proliferated faster than Fibonacci's rabbits. In 1945, there were only five international piano competitions. By 1990, the number had risen to 114. Today there are at least 750.

Many great artists—Vladimir Horowitz, Rudolf Serkin, Glenn Gould, and Byron Janis among them—never entered one. And early competitions, like the discontinued Leventritt, established in 1939 in memory of lawyer Edgar M. Leventritt, fostered an intimate atmosphere that has by now been lost. "[The Leventritt] was held when Rudolf Serkin and [conductor] George Szell were available," remembered Gary Graffman.

> After their availability was settled, other conductors were invited, along with several pianists, and the powerful manager Arthur Judson. Only performers who might actually win were allowed into the finals. And the jurors could talk openly with each other about their reactions, which is forbidden in most of today's contests.
>
> This was a good thing. I remember getting a phone call from Rudolf Serkin about Van Cliburn; he thought Van's Beethoven was terrible, but he loved the beauty of his playing, and he encouraged me to hear him. Today, Van would get deductions from judges who disliked the way he played a particular composer. And, of course, the Leventritt winners had instant concert bookings through the jury members, which was an immediate career boost.

It was a far simpler time. By now, major competitions—the Cliburn, Leeds, Chopin, Queen Elisabeth, Gina Bachauer, Montreal, Esther Honens, and others—have taken on the attributes of large-scale sports events. Recently, a new trend has emerged: some competition winners—like Alexander Ghindin, who won top prizes in many prestigious competitions, including the Tchaikovsky, Queen Elisabeth, Cleveland International, and, in 2010, the International Piano Competition of Santa Catarina in Brazil—have turned contests into a career, entering new ones as soon as the cash prizes and performing opportunities gained through their last win begin to dwindle.

The Gilmore Prize, established by the Kalamazoo, Michigan, Gilmore International Keyboard Festival, was an attempt to circumvent this trend. Billed as a "noncompetition" competition, a traveling jury selects a winner every four years from a pool of pianists who don't know they are being judged. The idea, almost universally hailed by critics, proved to have a serious downside. The original intent of the prize was to discover an unknown worthy of a major career. But someone with talent who is still unknown might have good reasons for preferring things that way; the first winners of the prize did not relish the life of a concert artist, as the Gilmore had hoped, and in at least one case the pressures proved hazardous. Subsequently, the organization changed the nature of the award and began selecting pianists who had already established reputations to some degree.

Competitions for outstanding amateurs—adults in other professions who have nevertheless achieved a high level of pianistic accomplishment—first sprang up in Paris in 1989, and then at the Cliburn in Texas, in Boston, Washington, D.C., and in other cities around the world. They quickly became rife with the same problems faced by the larger, professional competitions. A circuit of contestants began to surface over and over again, like an inbred tribe. The levels varied wildly, and the results were often contentious.

Of course, controversy has been a mainstay of piano competitions—without it, very little attention would be paid. When Ivo Pogorelich (b. 1958) was eliminated at the 1980 Chopin Competition in Warsaw, the audience—especially young women who swooned over his tight leather pants—was aghast. Juror Martha Argerich, in a display of Latin temperament, declared him a genius and angrily resigned (she later apologized). It brought the young pianist immediate fame and a recording contract. More recently, the president of the Géza Anda competition in Zurich publicly disavowed her jury's decisions after the first round, claiming they were enamored of fast and loud players who had little musical depth. And the Tchaikovsky Competition, reeling from accusations of corruption over decades, hired Richard Rodzinski, former president of the Van Cliburn Foundation, in 2010 to help reorganize the procedures and restore its former prestige.

Despite the drawbacks, however, competitions give pianists a chance to be heard, and the alternatives have grown slimmer. There are still musical soldiers fighting the good fight, however, like

Giselle Brodsky of the Miami International Piano Festival, who has the uncanny ability to find formidable piano talents *before* they win awards at the major competitions. Her discoveries have included pianists Piotr Anderszewski (b. 1969) and Ingrid Fliter (b. 1973), who went on to win the Gilmore Award, as well as the remarkable concert pianist and superb improviser Gabriela Montero (b. 1970).

Back in 1958, when the idea of an international competition was still fresh, the impact of the Moscow event was dramatic. The artistic détente signaled by Cliburn's win gave both the American and Soviet governments an opportunity to establish a cultural exchange program. American Daniel Pollack (b. 1935), who won eighth place, returned repeatedly. Then in 1960, the Soviets sent Richter to the United States, while America's electrifying Byron Janis (b. 1928), a student of Vladimir Horowitz, performed at the Moscow Conservatory—with two strikes against him.

The first was the fact that American pilot Francis Gary Powers had recently been shot down while flying his U-2 spy plane over Russian terrain. The second was the deep affection for Cliburn that remained in the hearts of Muscovites; as far as they were concerned, there was no substitute. When Janis walked out on stage he first heard chanting of "U-2" and then "Kleeburn, Kleeburn." But "by the intermission you could see that I was winning them over," he remembered. At the end, the audience was in tears. "I thought to myself, I don't think these tears are due to the music," Janis said, "but because of something else: When I first walked on to that stage I was literally the enemy. Now they saw I was just a human being, like them, who could please their deep musical spirit."

In a way, the triumph of Cliburn marked a high point for the classical virtuoso. The circumstances that brought him to international attention were unique and unlikely to arise again. Meanwhile, just as Cliburn's career was taking off, a major shift in the piano world was quietly taking place, introduced by an artist whose radical ideas still reverberate. It's not overstating the case to suggest that Canadian pianist Glenn Gould ushered in an entirely new era.

CHAPTER 15

On the Cutting Edge

H E WAS A LITTLE CRAZY. Canadian Glenn Gould (1932–1982) attracted as much attention for his personal oddities as for his brilliant playing. He sat on a rickety old chair that placed him lower at the instrument than any piano bench. He wore hats, gloves, and scarves even in summer. Incessantly fearful that death was just around the corner, he popped pills like candy mints. And at the height of his popularity he made a complete retreat from the concert stage—a place he had come to dread like a Christian facing the lions.

Gould burst on the international scene in 1955 with a recording of J. S. Bach's *Goldberg Variations,* a work that had been little recorded or performed until then. Once considered austere and too academic, in Gould's hands it was suddenly spellbinding, filled with drama, heartbreak, and jauntiness, a mesmerizing kaleidoscope of pianistic color. The recording became a landmark and a best-seller. Impor-

*Pianists
Glenn Gould
and Arthur
Rubinstein,
relaxing together
in New York in
1969*

tant Bach performers like Rosalyn Tureck (1914–2003) suddenly seemed too rarefied in comparison.

Of course, the recording set off heated arguments throughout the music world. Nothing is more contentious in the ivory towers of Baroque specialists than a Bach interpretation. (Harpsichordist Wanda Landowska, who could whip Bach's notes into a swirling maelstrom, famously remarked to Tureck, "Look, you play Bach *your* way, and I'll play Bach *Bach's* way." Gould sided with Tureck. "[Hers] was playing of such uprightness, to put it in the moral sphere," he recalled. "There was such a sense of repose that had nothing to do with languor, but rather with moral rectitude in the liturgical sense.") Since the *Goldberg Variations* were intended for a harpsichord with a double keyboard, the fact that they were played on a modern piano at all was cause for debate. Today, American pianist Christopher Taylor plays them using a specially constructed Steinway piano with two keyboards, conceived by Hungarian composer Emanuel Moor.

"The nut's a genius," remarked conductor George Szell after attending a Gould performance in Cleveland. His deportment was certainly strange: the low chair, the slouching posture, the way he conducted with his left hand when the right one was playing, the swooning, the humming. He had an explanation for the hunched position, which brought his upper back into a downward arch over the keyboard. "I discovered early on," he explained, "that there are certain keys to the kingdom in terms of manipulating the instrument." His ideal carriage, which brought him extremely close to the piano's keys and strings, required an approach that favored finger power rather than arm weight. It also contorted his spine, giving rise to muscular problems that emerged slowly over the years. This technique was limited, he explained, applicable only to the music of Bach, or Mozart, or the pre-Bach era, where the span of the hands is narrow; it was not for Romantic icons like Scriabin, "for the simple reason that the leverage required to support a widening of the hands is such that you have to be further away from the keyboard, you couldn't be that close."

Rosalyn Tureck, Bach specialist and early advocate of synthesizers

His list of reviled composers nevertheless included Mozart, about whom he declared that the problem was not that he had died too early, but rather that he had lived too long. According to Gould, who was a master of personal theatrics, Mozart's late work was tainted by "a theatrical gift [that he applied] not only to his operas but to his instrumental works as well, and given the rather giddy hedonism of eighteenth-century theater, that sort of thing doesn't interest me at all." He proved his point by playing Mozart's music horrendously, turning pearls into clams. And it wasn't just Mozart who suffered under Gould's fingers. As author Peter F. Ostwald wrote of Gould playing Chopin, "One is reminded of a frigid woman being forced to kiss a man she despises."

GOULD'S BENCH

Glenn Gould's chair, a relic from his childhood, became as indispensable to him as his instrument. It was a folding bridge chair, modified by his father in 1953 by sawing four inches off the adjustable legs, which placed the pianist just fourteen inches above the floor (six inches lower than a standard piano bench). He claimed it had "exactly the right contour" for performing, and he clearly didn't mind the creaking noises it made as he swayed to the music (which merely added additional ambient sounds to his own incessant humming). "Official" replicas of the Gould piano chair, endorsed by his estate, have been offered for sale through "the Glenn Gould Chair Project," a collaboration of Italian chair maker Cazzaro and the French designer René Bouchara.

Historically, piano seats have come in all shapes and sizes. They haven't always been needed: the heights of some harpsichords required the player to stand—not a big problem, considering the lack of pedals. Paintings of early pianists often show them seated on a high-back chair, or a stool covered with an embroidered cushion. Geography has been one factor in the design of piano seats. A recent discovery of an early-eighteenth-century Iberian piano included a stool featuring cabriole legs and ball-and-claw feet (one leg was made of mahogany, the other three of walnut), a common design on the Iberian Peninsula.

The convention today is to use a solid wooden bench, an adjustable leather-covered one, or a swivel stool. Unless you are Glenn Gould, the important detail is to be placed high enough for optimum leverage when striking the keys.

Adventurousness and perversity were the twin poles of Gould's art. His interpretations of the big Romantic concertos were especially grotesque. As a result of his distaste for showy display, he decided to suppress the passionate, expressive nature of the soloist's role—essential to the very idea of a concerto—flattening the emotional peaks, and robbing the music of its dramatic narrative. Indeed, his infamous performance of the Brahms Piano Concerto no. 1 under the baton of Leonard Bernstein, for which Bernstein offered a disclaimer to the audience beforehand, was not, as sometimes reported, too slow, but rather too pernicious in its refusal to bring on the musical fireworks. Like a musical vampire, he drew all the lifeblood out of Brahms's throbbing masterpiece and left a pale, cold cadaver in its place. Gould tellingly admitted that his favorite colors were battleship grey and midnight blue: "My moods," he said, "bear an inverse relationship to the degrees of sunlight on any given day." Despite his standing in the piano world, the decision to become an "antivirtuoso" garnered no followers.

"All the critics are really responding to is a denial of a certain set of expectations that have been built into their hearing process," he insisted, as if tradition were really unimportant. The reality was simply that the Romantic legacy with its overblown emotions was not for him. Bach, a composer whose greatness lives in the inventive unfurling of musical ideas, and for whom emotion was expressed not as personal testimony but rather as something to be projected on a celestial scale, was more in keeping with his inclinations.

Gould's adoration of Bach led him to write a piece called *So You Want to Write a Fugue* for four singers and string quartet, a work that, in his words, plugged "one of the most durable creative devices in the history of formal thought." It begins with a bass voice singing, "You've got the nerve to write a fugue . . . so go ahead." But, the clever contralto warns, "never be clever for the sake of being clever, for a canon in inversion is a serious diversion and a bit of augmentation is a serious temptation."

Gould's preference for serene abstraction over messy sentimentality emerged early on. He rejected his piano teacher Alberto Guerrero because, he admitted, "our outlooks on music were diametrically opposed. He was a 'heart' man and I wanted to be a 'head' kid." It's no wonder that his aversion to what biographer Geoffrey Payzant described as sunny Mediterranean activities, like the Spanish bullfight and Italian opera—"He thinks these depend equally upon herd responses to violent spectacle, and upon flashy personal display"—found relief in the isolation of the control room. "As I grow older I find more and more that I can do without [people]," he wrote. "I separate myself from conflicting and contrasting notions. Monastic seclusion works for me." "The idea of north"—of the lonely, frigid landscapes of northern Canada—became his paradigm. He even wrote a work with that title.

Gould's lasting influence actually stemmed from that shift from the concert hall to the recording studio. His motivation was partly the belief that audiences hoped for a spectacular disaster on stage; it made him feel, he said, like a vaudevillian. But the warm confines of the recording studio represented more than simple comfort; from the vantage of that cocoon he could also exercise complete dominance over every aspect of musical sound.

To some degree, he had a point. "I wonder how often Vladimir Nabokov's publisher has pondered a third and not-yet-final draft," he wrote in an article for the magazine *High Fidelity* entitled "The Grass Is Always Greener in the Outtakes," "and declared, 'Volodya baby, I've told you already, let it all hang out. So you dropped a comma, so you split an infinitive, that's truth, man.' " However, his quest for perfection evolved into something monstrous: today, studio recordings often involve hundreds or even thousands of edits, and the music has undeniably suffered.

Gould's rejection of the accepted performing tradition presaged the remarkable changes soon to be ushered in by the digital generation. He even suggested that the listening public might eventually become co-creators in the musical process by reordering and reshaping the material by means of home equipment. (In a sense, he was re-envisioning the concert experience as one that his fellow Canadian, philosopher Marshall McLuhan [1911–1980], might describe as moving from a "hot" media form into a "cool" one. The pianist often visited McLuhan and was certainly influenced by him.) Today, that vision is real: digital "sampling," iPods, and audio editing have become central to the process of making and sharing art.

E VEN BEFORE THE digital revolution, twentieth-century technology had changed the way people enjoyed the piano. The new media of film, radio, and television embraced the instrument

From the film
Gold Diggers of
1935

and made it possible for wider audiences to appreciate its qualities. With the advent of "talking pictures," which began with the revolutionary film *The Jazz Singer* in 1927, keyboardists from all the genres began to populate the Hollywood screen. Pianist Oscar Levant (1906–1972), George Gershwin's highly neurotic friend and champion, became a film star, along with José Iturbi (1895–1980), the Spanish conductor and pianist who appeared as himself in numerous movies and played Chopin's music on the soundtrack of that composer's film biography *A Song to Remember* (1945). (Gary Graffman performed for Iturbi as a young student, and vividly remembered a set of swords mounted on the walls of his studio. "As soon as I finished playing," he wrote, "Iturbi started to pace around the room nervously, exclaiming over and over, 'Kill his teacher! Kill his teacher!' That, plus the swords," recalled Graffman, "made me quite uneasy.") The piano itself became a main character in cinematic celebrations like director Busby Berkeley's *Gold Diggers of 1935*, in which fifty-six showgirls at fifty-six white baby grands danced across the screen in waltz time.

The first classical piano recital on television, in 1939, featured American virtuoso Earl Wild (1915–2010). Famed for his remarkable tech-

Earl Wild

nical ease and stunningly beautiful tone, Wild's Romantic reveries and rapturous accounts of music from Liszt to Gershwin took him on a roller-coaster career that also included five years as music director for television comedy star Sid Caesar, and a stint as staff pianist for the NBC Symphony under Arturo Toscanini.

Caesar had initially enlisted his help in pulling off a mock opera with a nonmusical cast of comedic characters. "I even created an overture," remembered Wild, "and he had [radio announcer] Milton Cross sitting in a box, describing the proceedings. Afterward, he didn't want to let me go, and the money offer kept climbing until it was so high I couldn't afford to say no." To the end, though, the pianist remained dedicated to classical performance, in interpretations that were always highly personal and Romantic in sweep, free of the boring restraints that were symptomatic of what he called "the good taste virus."

American television audiences enjoyed another pianist who was never accused of succumbing to good taste. Liberace (1919–1987), whose real name was Wladziu Valentino Liberace, first appeared in "soundies"—short films that presaged the music video—and then became one of the highest-paid nightclub and television acts in the world. With a candelabrum on the piano, extravagant costumes, and a native flamboyance second to none, he blithely announced that he didn't give concerts, but "put on a show."

Danish-American Victor Borge (1909–2000), a concert pianist suffering from paralyzing stage fright, realized one day during a mishap on stage that he could make an audience laugh, and found his niche, combining both talents to become a musical king of comedy. "I was one of the first to play the Rachmaninoff Second Piano Concerto," he remembered. "In the middle of the third movement, the conductor lost his place, and I stopped because it was clear to everyone that the performance just wasn't working. So I jumped up, turned the pages for him, and said, 'Let's do it from *here*.' On my way back to the piano I looked at the audience and smiled. In my entire career I have never met with warmer applause than I received that night when I took my bow at the end of the piece." His comedic routines—playing a passage across the keyboard and landing on the floor; strapping himself to the bench after being startled by a loud soprano; or chasing a sidekick around the piano while both men played a Liszt Hungarian Rhapsody, executing alternate passages as they each rounded the keyboard side of the instrument—are based on a keen

sense of observation; they merely exaggerated what he saw around him. But they offered the pianist a safety valve: as a serious virtuoso, "my hands would shake," he said. Comedy made him free.

That satiric tradition continues in the hands of Peter Schickele (b. 1935), a gifted composer who invented the character P. D. Q. Bach—allegedly the last and least talented of J. S. Bach's sons—and used him as the centerpiece for highly successful theatrical and musical parodies. This fictional composer's works carry titles such as *The Art of the Ground Round, The Seasonings,* and the *Serenude for Devious Instruments (S. 36–24–36).*

Peter Schickele as P. D. Q. Bach
PETER SCHAAF

A S GLENN GOULD PREDICTED, technology would reshape the instrument itself. In his classic book *Men, Women and Pianos* (1954), Arthur Loesser pondered "why the electronic piano has never caught on . . . Several small companies were experimenting with it during the 1930s, but nothing further seems to have happened." Indeed, *The Musical Times* of February 1934 reported on the first "electrical orchestra" assembled in Berlin, but complained of the casualness of the tuning on the part of the performers, and offered concerns about the future unemployment of musicians who might be displaced by technology. Both were persistent reasons for resistance. Clara Rockmore, a virtuoso performer on the early electronic theremin (played by moving one's body toward or away from the instrument's antennae) performed under the baton of Leopold Stokowski, who, she reported, "wanted to organize an orchestra of twelve electronic instruments" with her as soloist. "But the project was killed by the union," she stated. "They thought that with Stokowski's name and fame, it would have had such a fantastic impact that electronics would replace the symphony orchestra."

It only stalled the inevitable. As computers and audio electronics advanced, several composers updated the role of the acoustic piano by combining it with sonorities never before available. Karlheinz Stockhausen (1928–2007) was perhaps the first with *Mantra* in 1970 for two pianos, amplified and electronically altered during performance. Then Mario Davidovsky (b. 1934), formerly director of the Columbia-Princeton Electronic Music Center, won a Pulitzer Prize in 1971 for his highly successful *Synchronisms No. 6* for piano and electronic tape. Many others followed. Composer Milton Babbitt (1916–2011) wrote *Reflections* for piano and synthesized tape in 1972; and the important Italian composer Luigi Nono (1924–1990) used piano and tape in 1976 in a work written for pianist Maurizio Pollini called . . . *Sofferte onde serene* . . . (. . . *Suffered, Serene Waves* . . .).

By the 1980s, electronic versions of the piano boasted sounds that had been "sampled" from acoustic models, making them seem more authentic than ever. Piano firms like Yamaha, Bösendorfer, and Steinway each had their own updated "player piano" models with mechanisms controlled by digital discs and computerized memory. Yamaha even launched an "e-Competition," in which competitors played on a special digital instrument in one place while the jury, in a distant city, listened as a second piano reproduced each tone and interpretive nuance. American Tod Machover (b. 1953), who worked in Paris with Pierre Boulez at IRCAM (Institut de Recherche et Coordination Acoustique/Musique), a facility for the development of electro-acoustical art music, created what he calls a "hyperpiano," a Yamaha Disklavier (high-tech player piano) whose sound is carefully manipulated by means of computer programming.

A BRIEF HISTORY OF DIGITAL PIANOS *by Alden Skinner*

In 2004, the traditional piano world felt a collective shudder. For the first time, digital pianos had outsold the acoustic version. As of 2008, industry reports show that digital pianos represent 70 percent of all new piano purchases in the United States, and the trend shows no sign of reversal. The digital piano will never completely replace the acoustic piano, yet it has displaced it in many locations. What is it about the upstart digital piano that has allowed it to encroach on the 300-year reign of the traditional acoustic piano?

The digital piano first emerged in 1983 when Yamaha introduced the YP-30 with a digitally synthesized piano and a weighted action to simulate the feel of a typical acoustic instrument. This was followed in 1984 by Ray Kurzweil's K250 digital piano based on digital samples of an acoustic piano—and the race was on. Compare the sound of a mid-range digital piano to that of an entry-level acoustic piano today and the acoustic piano will likely "lose."

For many, the digital piano has a number of advantages over its elder sibling. Digital pianos are maintenance-free; they require no tuning and no regulation. Want to practice late at night? Plug in the headphones. Want to capture the song you've been composing? Connect your piano to your computer and use notation software to print your handiwork. Want to hear what that Scarlatti sonata sounded like back in the day? Change the temperament to a historical tuning, dial the pitch down to A-415, switch to a harpsichord sample or load in an early period piano sample, and history comes alive.

But is it a *real* piano? If you define the instrument by how it works rather than what it does, then no. But if you define the instrument by its role—allowing a player to perform any music written for the piano, with a result that sounds like a piano—then a digital instrument is simply a different kind of piano. No more, and no less.

Indeed, everything was changing. In 1946, the *Musical Times* had carried an article on "The Future of the Piano," posing questions such as "Why must we always make our case of wood?" The forward-thinking author declared, "I can envisage some beautiful designs in metal, cellulose-sprayed in lovely color schemes." Further, "Why should we not have a range of qualities in a single instrument? Why should a facility possessed by the eighteenth-century harpsichord, with its different manuals, be denied to the twentieth-century piano?" Electronics would now make it all possible.

By late in the century, new visions of the instrument were taking root, offering pianists a range of instrumental colors and timbres previously unimaginable. Electronic pianos flourished in the pop, jazz, and rock fields. They even gave birth to a genre known as "prog rock"—progressive rock—developed by rock musicians who pushed song structures into longer forms and greater levels of sophistication; incorporated classical and jazz elements into their music; and created "concept albums" with epic storytelling elements. (Keith Emerson, of Emerson, Lake & Palmer, drew on works by Bartók, Bach, Janáček, Sibelius, and others for his material; Dave Stewart, of Egg, represented a group known as the "Canterbury school," which brought an avant-garde sensibility and surrealist lyrics to the mix.) The genre had its beginnings in groups like Frank Zappa's Mothers of Invention and in the experimental work of The Beatles in the 1960s and reached the peak of its popularity in the mid-1970s. It became a trademark for such bands as Yes, Pink Floyd, Genesis, Liquid Tension Experiment, and Jethro Tull.

In the jazz world, Miles Davis incorporated these new sounds in "fusion" recordings like the landmark *Bitches Brew* (1970), which merged the trumpeter's love of a musical atmosphere rich with mystery with the texture of contemporary, electrified rock. The result was a powerful, multilayered, highly produced concept album using two or three electric pianos, two bassists, and multiple percussionists all playing at once, along with other solo instruments. Its Gould-like application of recording technology, including a huge number of edits and postproduction studio effects such as tape loops, echo, and delay, made it a turning point in the evolution of modern jazz. Traditionalists were outraged, but the recording was Davis's first gold record, selling more than half a million copies.

Some of Davis's piano sidemen, including Herbie Hancock and Chick Corea, turned to electronic instruments as well. Corea even began to use a lightweight keyboard slung over his shoulders as a solo instrument, in imitation of rock guitarists. This was no mere trend, but a major cultural shift; few jazz pianists today restrict themselves to the acoustic piano alone.

And the technological innovations continue. In 2009, the internet company YouTube launched a global online audition for a new orchestra. After thousands of submissions, the YouTube Symphony was formed with more than ninety musicians from thirty countries, culminating in a sold-out performance in New York's Carnegie Hall. There are plans for more auditions, multimedia collaborations, online master classes, and the creation of a digital meeting place for musicians. The project's artistic advisor, conductor and pianist Michael Tilson Thomas, explained its purpose this way: "We're exploring how classical music's 1,200-year-long tradition can enter the realm of high technology and what that will mean for its mission and legacy." It goes to prove that the art so lovingly cultivated by Cristofori, Bach, and Mozart is still very much alive, despite dramatic technological changes. Even Glenn Gould might be surprised.

CHAPTER 16

Everything Old Is New Again

O N A WET OCTOBER NIGHT in 2010, pianist Menahem Pressler (b. 1923) made his way along the concrete tributaries
in New York's Greenwich Village, racing past falafel stands and
coffeehouses, cheap ethnic restaurants and ramshackle taverns as
his taxi traced the twists and turns of the historic neighborhood—
traditionally, the home ground of poets and artists, intellectuals and
provocateurs. This is the place where Bob Dylan first met Allen
Ginsberg; where the folk-music revival of the 1960s was born; and
where the ghosts of Jack London, Henry Miller, James Baldwin,
and Jack Kerouac still haunt the narrow alleyways.

But Pressler wasn't sightseeing. The diminutive, robust eighty-
six-year-old, one of classical music's most revered performers,
was on his way to a gig. That evening, he and clarinetist Richard
Stoltzman were giving a joint recital at the former site of the Village Gate, the legendary club where jazz lovers once marveled at

live performances by Miles Davis, John Coltrane, Duke Ellington, and Bill Evans. Now renovated into the smaller Le Poisson Rouge, a cabaret with the announced intentions of reviving "the symbiotic relationship between art and revelry," it offers music of all genres, from classical to pop to avant-garde. The venue had become the hippest music stage in New York.

Pressler is a bullet train without brakes. Many younger colleagues who perform regularly with him have complained that they simply can't keep up. He has just returned from Europe, performing at Amsterdam's Concertgebouw, one of the finest concert halls in the world; and from Beijing, where he gave a week's worth of master classes. He is in a category all his own, especially when it comes to chamber music (he was a founding member of the legendary Beaux Arts Trio, and remained its leader for nearly fifty-five years). Few others could boast of a lifetime achievement award from *Gramophone* magazine, or a Gold Medal of Merit from the National Society of Arts and Letters. In 2005, he received two of the world's highest cultural honors: the German Cross of Merit and France's Commander of the Order of Arts and Letters.

But now he was on his way to an informal Village haunt to give a program of Bernstein, Brahms, Debussy, Gershwin, and Reich—a trek that brings to mind Mozart navigating the cobblestones of Vienna, past rows of refreshment stands, courtyards, and taverns, to premiere his D minor Piano Concerto before a small audience at the Poisson Rouge of its day, the Flour Pit.

Of course, Mozart didn't have the luxury of color spotlights over the stage, or an electronic sound system projecting and delicately balancing instrumental voices clearly throughout the room. Certainly no one in his time could have pulled off the intricate Steve Reich work for eight clarinets on this evening's program in the way Richard Stoltzman regularly does, performing it single-handedly by playing one part along with seven prerecorded tracks.

But there are also similarities. Le Poisson Rouge represents both the very old and the very new look of classical music, offering relaxed musical celebrations in a space bustling with waiters and buzzing with expectation, where listeners can order a drink, enjoy

*Richard
Stoltzman
and Menahem
Pressler at Le
Poisson Rouge*
PETER SCHAAF

a snack, and put their elbows on the table without fear of a reprimand.

All formality has been stripped away. After a brief introduction, the musicians begin, and as Bernstein's jaunty rhythms and Broadway charm envelop the room, their sounds merge with the clink of ice cubes and the rustle of tableware. Listeners are nodding or tapping their feet. The stage is aglow, and Stoltzman's clarinet, with a wireless microphone that clings to the instrument like a two-headed snake, suddenly looks like it is being squeezed from his face, which has assumed an unearthly grin. His eyes are closed, and Pressler's head is bouncing left and right to the music's syncopated rhythms. Sitting just feet from the stage, a listener feels like part of the ensemble.

In a solo turn, Pressler plays two selections from Claude Debussy's *Estampes*. Even from the small, well-worn piano, his playing is graceful and warm.

Pressler is a musical caretaker, pursuing the exquisite sound at the core of each work, and bringing it to life with the shaping of a phrase or the weighting of a harmony. "The pianist who has a beautiful sound is like a good-looking person," he once explained. "You immediately feel attracted. For many works, it's essential—a reason for being. Someone playing Chopin with an ugly sound will have a very hard time making the form stand out, because in the end what really counts is the beauty that the composer put into the music. Even Beethoven, whose message is so strong it can bear a hard edge, put indications in his music like 'tender.' " Indeed, this evening, each piano phrase sounds like a musical caress. "You know," Pressler told a student, "when you are in love as I am with these pieces, they are always fresh. They are always young. I remember the first time I was thrilled by them, and I am thrilled by them today."

But why would two stellar musicians used to the finest halls in the world be playing in a little Greenwich Village cabaret? "Wherever people want to hear us, that's where we'll go," said Pressler just before walking on stage, and Richard Stoltzman nodded in agreement.

T HE SCENE at Le Poisson Rouge represents the future of classical music, as it resolutely dissolves the distance that has grown between player and listener. It is a replay of musical days gone by. Indeed, it reflects the state of the piano in the new era: Everything old is becoming new again.

Three hundred years after the invention of the piano, the traditionalists and the experimentalists continue on. There are still towering players of the standard repertoire like Hungarian-born András Schiff (b. 1953), who, like his fellow, too-soon-departed countryman Géza Anda (1921–1976), invests the music with remarkable intelligence and flawless technique. And there is France's Pierre-Laurent Aimard (b. 1957), a phenomenal pianist and thinker, who renders Bach, Beethoven, and Debussy and the latest contemporary works with equally stunning artistry. Jazz artists have developed a wider cultural vision, with the emergence of players like Vijay Iyer (b. 1971), who combines American sounds with music of the Indo-Asian diaspora; and Monty Alexander (b. 1944), who bridges the roots of his native Jamaica to the legacy of Nat "King" Cole and Oscar Peterson. As in the past, we have pianists who look forward as well as backward, like Peter Serkin (b. 1947), Rudolf's son, who enlivens the concert scene with newly commissioned repertoire while engaging in various experiments, such as placing a second "lid" beneath the piano's soundboard to help project the music toward the audience, and using historical tunings in mainstream works (something most often done by early-music groups and members of the avant-garde).

The piano's abundant charms have also continued to spread across the world, especially to the Far East, where over the last several decades it has become a rising star. Gary Graffman's transition from concertizing pianist to educator gave him a front-row seat. With his performing career on hold, he assumed the directorship of the Curtis Institute in Philadelphia and began to notice an increasing number of Asian applicants. "Usually we take only between two and four new entrants at a time," he explained, because the school is so small. "In a year when 119 applied for just two slots, we opened our doors to a young man named Lang Lang."

That Chinese-born pianist reignited the phenomenon of the classical piano superstar, attracting adulation and scorn in equal measure. The endless sweep of his balletic arms, the pain and exaltation that register on his face, a torso that rises and pivots at every dramatic moment, all made him seem not merely a pianist but a theatrical sensation. His musical interpretations were often equally over the top.

"He wanted to be the Tiger Woods of the piano world," explained Graffman, comparing his former student to the celebrated golfer, "and he achieved it, with his picture in every magazine and product endorsements for Rolex watches, Nike sneakers, and Mont Blanc pens." Indeed, Lang Lang was the first artist ever to have his name adorn a Steinway piano model.

But he was not alone. Other talents from his homeland were eagerly waiting in the wings. China has come a long way in its mastery of Western music since a Jesuit named Matteo Ricci first brought a clavichord there while visiting in the late sixteenth century. Although Mao's Cultural Revolution put a temporary halt to Western musical practices, today's young Chinese musicians, like Jin Ju, who won top prizes in competitions from China to Brussels before resettling in Florence, are creating a piano renaissance, filling conservatories and winning awards at a remarkable rate.

Other Asian nations—especially Japan and South Korea—have also discovered the instrument's allure. In Japan, Yamaha began building pianos in 1900, and over the course of a century grew to become the world's most prolific piano manufacturer, offering both acoustic and electronic models. In 2007, it acquired Bösendorfer, the venerable Austrian piano company founded in 1828, whose instrument was a favorite of Liszt, Oscar Peterson, and many other great artists.

THE PIANO IN CHINA *by Yundi Li*

I started playing the piano when I was seven. At that time, China had just opened the door to participating in international competitions. By the time I won the Chopin Competition in Warsaw in 2000—becoming, at eighteen, its youngest winner in history—the Chinese government was actively supportive. Today, there are 30 million children studying the piano in China, and about a dozen truly great concert halls.

I had a love of music from the age of four, but my first instrument was actually the accordion. In fact, I won a children's accordion competition when I was five. Then I heard the piano, a tape of Chopin Etudes (we didn't have CDs then), and everything changed. I listened to it every night, and slept between listenings. I lived those Etudes, and I've had a relationship with Chopin ever since. My teacher, Professor Dan Zhaoyi, helped me to deepen it.

Is there a national style of playing? Yes and no. Our piano tradition developed from the Russian "touch," but also from the French approach to Debussy and Ravel. We want to learn as many good things as we can from a variety of sources. Our attitude is like tai chi [yin and yang]—a combination of mixed and free, not moving too far in any one direction. To understand the Chinese personality, you have to study our poets, like Du Fu [712–770], the "poet-sage," and Li Bai [701–762, one of Du Fu's "Eight Immortals of the Wine Cup"]. We draw our inspiration from five thousand years of history.

One reason that Chopin feels so natural to us is that his music contains the spirit of nationalism—it reaches out to his fellow countrymen. This is something we relate to. He is also, of course, a wonderful piano composer–his whole life was focused on the instrument. And he is Classic as well as Romantic, with a deep love of Mozart. That balance is why his music has continued to thrive from generation to generation.

But China's size and population alone have put it in a special category. Along with its mushrooming piano schools filled with millions of students, the nation has become a center of piano manufacturing. Companies such as Pearl River—owner of the largest piano factory in the world—are producing extremely fine instruments at lower costs than their American and European competitors. Indeed, although few Americans realize it, many of the parts in their new and recently restored pianos originated in China, which is now dominating that market. The musical trickle that began at the Curtis Institute with the introduction of Lang Lang turned out to be an impending flood.

A SNAPSHOT of the current piano scene includes skilled keyboardists breathing new life into old practices, like classical improvisation. American pianist Robert Levin (b. 1947) has championed the return of improvised cadenzas (the places in a concerto where Mozart or Beethoven would simply make up something on the spur of the moment, drawing on themes in the musical score as a springboard for instantaneous composition). He even allows audiences to have a part in deciding his choices.

Venezuelan-American pianist Gabriela Montero has gone a step further. While the practice of playing original cadenzas, and of *preluding*—preceding a work with a short improvised introduction—never disappeared entirely, Montero is a modern-day Liszt, accepting melodies from the audience and improvising entire pieces on the spot. Few artists in any genre can muster her sweeping command and technical flair, her ability to sail through myriad stylistic palettes, or generate intricate counterpoint at a moment's whim.

Composer-pianists are also revisiting the subversive world of the early-twentieth-century avant-garde. Frederic Rzewski (b. 1938) is one of them. Described by Nicolas Slonimsky in his *Baker's Biographical Dictionary of Musicians* as an "overpowering piano technician, capable of depositing huge boulders of sonoristic material across the keyboard without actually wrecking the instrument,"

Rzewski's variety of sound and musical fertility is endlessly stunning, especially in works like *Four North American Ballads* (which includes a sonic depiction of a cotton mill) and *The People United Will Never Be Defeated* (thirty-six variations on the leftist political song by Sergio Ortega). Many of the subtle coloristic shadings that Rzewski achieves were derived from the innovative techniques of American pianist David Tudor (1926–1996), a long-time associate of John Cage.

JUST AS in the eighteenth and nineteenth centuries, when oddities such as "giraffes" were rising in popularity, today's piano world is replete with examples of the peculiar and the extraordinary. Many stem from John Cage's interest in revising our conception of what a piano is, turning it into a percussion orchestra, for example, by inserting objects into its strings. Cage paved the way for a new generation, including Singapore-born American pianist Margaret Leng Tan, who commissions and performs works for a variety of *toy* pianos.

"While everyone has heard of the three B's—Bach, Beethoven, and Brahms—how many are aware of the three C's—Cage, Cowell, and Crumb?" she asks. "They constitute what I call the classical avant-garde for the piano. Cage's 'prepared piano' was built on what Cowell had done with the strings inside the instrument. Contemporary composer George Crumb [b. 1929] doesn't 'prepare' the piano, but his approach—strumming, plucking, or running objects along the strings—simply extends the same idea.

"Cage had written a *Suite for Toy Piano* in 1948, and George Crumb used one in his 1970 song cycle, *Ancient Voices of Children*, and again more recently, in his *American Songbooks* cycle," she explains. "It gave me the idea there was potential for it to become a legitimate instrument. Now a great many composers are writing for it, and I've been actively recording and performing these works; I even recently played the toy piano at a Carnegie Hall concert."

Crumb labeled Margaret Leng Tan "the Sorceress of the Piano." There are many modern "sorcerers" as well, like Michael Harri-

son, who creates his own piano tunings in a continuation of the work of Indian raga master Pandit Pran Nath and American maverick piano composer La Monte Young. Harrison sets aside the modern "equal temperament" piano tuning in favor of the mathematically "pure" musical intervals that produce calamitous collisions when used for a keyboard instrument. He embraces both the purity of these sounds and the collisions, and the results—in works like his ninety-minute hypnotic piano solo, *Revelation* (placed by both *The New York Times* and the *Boston Globe* among the best recordings of 2007)—can suggest angelic choirs in one moment and thunderous explosions in the next.

*Margaret Leng
Tan at her toy
piano*
© 1993 JACK
VARTOOGIAN/
FRONT ROW
PHOTOS

THE LOOK OF the piano, for many years as predictable as the seasons, has once again become a creative outlet in the twenty-first century. Just as in the nineteenth century, specially crafted models have placed the piano in the role of objet d'art. Forerunners like the 1883 Steinway painted by noted Victorian artist Sir Lawrence Alma-Tadema (1836–1912) and the heavily decorated first White House Steinway, presented to President Theodore Roosevelt in 1903, serve as inspiration for new designs by such artists as Dale Chihuly, known for his extraordinary glass sculptures. Other designers are working with varieties of woods. (Steinway takes pains to explain that it is environmentally conscious in its use of woods, so as not to deplete natural resources. Similar concerns have for many years forced manufacturers to use plastic rather than ivory for the piano's keys.)

But modernity has taken the idea of the piano as art even further, incorporating the instrument into conceptual and mixed-media works, from German Heiner Goebbels's music-theater piece

Stifters Dinge (*Stifter's Things*), presented in 2007 at the Théâtre Vidy-Lausanne in Switzerland and in 2009 at New York's Park Avenue Armory under the sponsorship of Lincoln Center—in which five pianos moving on tracks become active characters in a dramatic narrative—to Dutchman Guido van der Werve's 2009 "chess piano," which is played by moving chess pieces on a board.

In 2010, a three-actor theater piece in New York called *Three Pianos* employed three movable uprights, which, in addition to being played, became ventriloquist dummies, coffins, triangulated penalty boxes, and piano bars, complete with drinks and cocktail peanuts.

That same year, an art installation entitled *Stop, Repair, Prepare: Variations on "Ode to Joy" for a Prepared Piano* by Jennifer Allora and Guillermo Calzadilla was presented at New York's Museum of Modern Art (it had debuted in 2008 at the Haus der Kunst in Munich). The work features a Bechstein baby grand piano on wheels with a large hole cut into its center, out of which a pianist rises up and hovers over the keyboard (bending forward from behind the keys) to play an arrangement of the fourth movement of Beethoven's Ninth Symphony. As the music unfolds, the pia-

ABOVE LEFT
The Alma-Tadema Steinway

ABOVE RIGHT
Dale Chihuly's Olympia *Steinway*

nist gently maneuvers the instrument around the room and through the crowd of onlookers, parting assembled listeners like a ship moving through cresting waters. Pianist Evan Shinners confessed that the hardest part of performing it was the strain on his back.

Whether *Stop, Repair, Prepare* is, as *The New York Times* claimed, compelling, and "possibly a form of reparation for the regimes the music, in its greatness, has served," or merely a silly parlor trick, history will judge. (As "theater of the absurd," it certainly pales beside John Cage's 1960 *Theatre Piece*, during which a piano is slapped with a dead fish.)

Such applications take the piano a long way from the cypress keyboard that once transformed the musical world simply by playing soft and loud. Yet they demonstrate that even in an age of previously unimagined technical advances, the old-fashioned acoustic piano can still astonish.

Pianist Evan Shinners performing from inside a Bechstein piano in Stop, Repair, Prepare *at the Museum of Modern Art in New York, 2010*
ADRIENNE
ISACOFF

BACK AT LE Poisson Rouge, as Richard Stoltzman is playing Steve Reich's long, intricate *New York Counterpoint*—an endurance test—the exhaustion, heat, and intensity begin taking their toll. Perspiration is pouring down his face. During a brief break in the solo clarinet part, he attempts to remove his jacket. The air has been thick with pulsations moving in endless loops—jaunty thematic permutations, fragmented phrases flying here and there, syncopations moving against other syncopations, and rhythms everywhere—until the sound builds into what seems like a stampeding herd of clarinets. And as Stoltzman, dripping, and using every ounce of breath to keep the momentum going, finally manages to rid himself of the jacket there is a smattering of giggles and a few handclaps. We have all been drawn into the drama.

After a Brahms sonata of riveting emotional gravity, the duo finishes the night by playing a bluesy Gershwin set, sending patrons back onto the street, where the rain clouds have finally dispersed. Reflecting on the experience afterward, Menahem Pressler is upbeat. What did he think of the experience? "It was more intimate, somehow," he says. "It amazed me how they listened. They ate and they drank, and they listened. I was not discouraged by any noise."

No doubt Mozart would have been comfortable too, though he might have been amazed that the simple keyboard instrument he helped popularize still plays so vital a part in music making. It is rather miraculous. Bartolomeo Cristofori couldn't possibly have imagined our world, and we can barely picture his, yet we still find reasons to appreciate that humble Paduan for his remarkable gift. It's a good bet that some form of his keyboard "with soft and loud" will continue to thrill listeners for generations to come.

Appendix: Supplementary Notes

In Mozart's Footprints: Modern Fortepianists

In 1995, two hundred years to the month after Mozart premiered his D minor Piano Concerto, pianist Steven Lubin (b. 1942) performed and conducted it at the Metropolitan Museum of Art in New York, using a period-instrument orchestra with a fortepiano copied meticulously from the one at Mozart's birthplace in Salzburg. Other prominent fortepianists currently active include Malcolm Bilson (b. 1935), Alexei Lubimov (b. 1944), and Andreas Staier (b. 1955).

Steven Lubin JACK MITCHELL

The Jazz Alchemists

Many jazz pianists followed in the footsteps of Debussy, Messiaen, Scriabin, and Evans, while developing highly individual styles. These included several who filled Evans's shoes in various Miles Davis bands—among them, Herbie Hancock (b. 1940), Chick Corea (b. 1941), and Keith Jarrett (b. 1945).

In a ritualized atmosphere shared by the artist and his audience, Jarrett performed long solo recitals, writhing and rising from the piano bench like a fakir's snake serenading itself, as he spun out free-form improvised passages. Many fans found the result powerfully hypnotic. Hancock's musical evolution took him through multiple genres, with forays into rhythm and blues, electric funk, and elegant performances of music by Gershwin, Ravel, and Joni Mitchell. Throughout it all, his subtle tone and exquisite harmonic palette conveyed the sensibility of a first-class alchemist.

All That Rhythm: Novelty and Ragtime Notables

Ragtimer Eubie Blake's musical inventiveness influenced such piano legends as James P. Johnson and Art Tatum, but in his own view the greatest player of the age was "One Leg" Willie Joseph. "Nobody could copy him," claimed Blake. "He knew everything, the heaviest classics and all kind of rags. I learned plenty from just watchin' him."

Women played a largely forgotten role in much of this music, turning out important original rags. There were talents like May Aufderheide

(1888–1972), who wrote *Dusty Rag* and *The Thriller,* mainstays of New Orleans orchestras; and Adeline Shepherd, whose *Pickles and Peppers,* a huge success, was adopted by William Jennings Bryan for his 1908 presidential campaign. In the novelty-piano field, splashy, finger-twisting flurries and bouncy off-kilter fanfares also show up in the virtuoso keyboard workouts of women who saturated the radio airwaves and turned out hundreds of piano rolls: American-born Edythe Baker (1895–1965) and Pauline Alpert (1900–1988), South Africa's dazzling, short-lived Raie da Costa (1905–1934), Australia's Beryl Newell, and Canada's Vera Guilaroff (1902–1976) were among them.

The men who specialized in novelty piano included Billy Mayerl (1902–1959) and Lothar Perl (1910–1975). Perl's playing, as collector Alex Hassan aptly observed, was "athletic, precise [and] hot." Hassan continues to promote their efforts.

Jazz Piano Personalities

Jazz sounded different in the hands of each of its leading players. Horace Silver (b. 1928) unleashed funky harmonies on the keyboard in crisp, percussive bursts (influenced by his father's Cape Verdean roots). His style was once praised by avant-garde jazz icon Cecil Taylor because of "the physicality of it," "the filth of it," the "movement in the attack." Silver's sound was acerbic and edgy, a tribal dance with clumps of notes sprinkled around like spicy peppercorns. By contrast, Oscar Peterson's approach was marked by clarity and gracefulness—jazz as high discourse, its edges burnished to a fine sheen, with unfailingly eloquent lines, like a modern-day Shakespeare's riffing on the human soul. Other jazz stylists with connections to the Western tradition included the hard-swinging Red Garland (1923–1984) and contemporary players like Fred Hersch (b. 1955), his former student Brad Mehldau (b. 1970), Thelonious Monk International Piano Competition winners Ted Rosenthal (b. 1959), Jacky Terrasson (b. 1966), and Uri Caine (b. 1956).

Erroll Garner

Erroll Garner (1921–1977) flaunted spellbinding tremolos and astonishing rhythmic elasticity. ("That's what made you smile whenever he played," says pianist Dick Hyman.)

The 1950s brought the "bebop" revolution, with breakneck tempos and intricately weaving melodic lines, led by the innovative saxophonist Charlie "Bird" Parker, trumpeter Dizzy Gillespie, and pianist Bud Powell. In its wake, pianists like Hank Jones (1918–2010), Lennie Tristano (1919–1978), Billy Taylor (1921–2010), Barry Harris (b. 1929), and Tommy Flanagan (1930–2001), each contributed unique pianistic "voices."

All were subtle innovators. Wynton Kelly (1931–1971) brought a bluesy panache to the bop style. John Lewis (1920–2001), with his group, the Modern Jazz Quartet, spearheaded the "Third Stream" movement (so named by composer Gunther Schuller), which self-consciously melded the classical and jazz traditions. The impetus for the approach came from meetings with Miles Davis and arranger Gil Evans: "We all used to meet in Gil Evans's little apartment on Fifty-fourth Street . . . The whole idea was to try something more sophisticated than just a simple tune and improvising on it. We were a little tired of that routine," remembered Lewis. He decided, he told author Len Lyons, to "make use of this whole two or three hundred years of musical tradition. I don't want just to throw it out."

Ahmad Jamal (b. 1930) became known for his exquisite use of rests and elegant sense of form.

Dick Hyman (b. 1927), a student of Teddy Wilson with extraordinary imaginative gifts and limitless virtuosity, became a living encyclopedia of jazz history with the ability to re-create the styles of any of its legendary performers. He is the soloist on *Century of Jazz Piano*. Dick Wellstood (1927–1987) was a hard-swinging stride pianist with a full, warm-bodied sound and an infectious sense of joy. Dave McKenna (1930–2008) astonished with his left-hand facility, creating what was known as "three-handed swing," a trademark technique that allowed him to play typical two-handed piano while also rendering bass lines that would normally be performed by an additional musician.

The Latin Family Tree

Arturo O'Farrill, Jr., son of Latin music giant Chico O'Farrill (1921–2001), is at the vanguard of a new wave of musicians who combine knowledge of the Latin world with the expertise of a veteran performer of classical music and jazz. His list of the most important contributors to the style includes Cuban pianist Pedro "Peruchin" Justiz (1913–1977), a fixture in the 1950s mambo and *descargas* scene (all-night jam sessions), and Puerto Rican Papo Lucca (b. 1946), who, O'Farrill says, "codified the rules for playing the rhythmic ostinatos [repeating patterns] known as montunos": he outlined "how their syncopations link up, and the parameters for the way one chord can move to another. He is still the chief exponent of how it's done."

Cuban Emiliano Salvador (1951–1992), says O'Farrill, was "the first pianist who experimented with complex European harmonies—the kind of sophisticated jazz chords you would hear in a Bill Evans solo—but in the context of Afro-Cuban rhythms. It was an important marriage of the old and the new." Another extraordinary technician, Gonzalo Rubalcaba (b. 1963), is often regarded as Chucho Valdés's protégé. Other foundational players included Cuban pianist and arranger René Hernández, who developed a melodic style of playing in octaves (in order to be heard above the sounds of a big band); and the aforementioned Puerto Rican pianists Eddie Palmieri and his brother, Charlie. Of these two popular figures, says O'Farrill, "Eddie was the modernist, making use of advanced jazz harmonies."

Cultivated and Vernacular: South of the Border

Many North American jazz artists first turned to the sounds of Brazil through a fascination with the soft, sultry dance rhythm known as bossa nova ("new trend"). Its chief protagonist was Rio de Janeiro's Antonio Carlos Jobim (1927–1994), whose 1963–64 collaborations with jazz saxophonist Stan Getz, performing the seductive tunes at a near whisper above the entrancing bossa rhythms, became international hits.

Ernesto Lecuona

But important styles south of the border had been developing long before. Ernesto Nazareth (1863–1934), "the Scott Joplin of Brazil," composed polkas, sambas, galops, waltzes, and tangos with the particular Latin American rhythmic flavor that developed from Spanish and African sources. Similar elements infuse the music of Cuban pianist Ernesto Lecuona (1895–1963), who composed over six hundred pieces, many for stage and film, including popular melodies like "Siboney," "Malagueña," and "The Breeze and I."

South American women also made their mark. A young Venezuelan who was smitten by Gottschalk followed his lead in becoming one of the era's great touring pianists. Teresa Carreño (1853–1917) was known as the "Walküre of the Piano," and Liszt tried, unsuccessfully, to lure her to Rome to become his student. She made her debut in New York at the age of nine, astounded Gottschalk, and dedicated her first composition to him. She called it *Gottschalk Waltz*.

Carreño played for President Abraham Lincoln at the White House. He asked for his favorite song, "Listen to the Mocking Bird," and she obliged, with improvised variations. In Europe, Anton Rubinstein taught her (and later co-authored a book with her, *The Art of Piano Pedaling*), and Hans von Bülow declared that "she sweeps the floor clean of all piano paraders who, after her arrival, must take themselves elsewhere." Everyone noted the speed and the power of her playing, as well as the storminess.

Her personal life reflected the same turbulent quality. She was married four times, and juggled her musical roles nearly as often. Carreño met her second (common-law) husband, baritone Giovanni Tagliapietra, while switching from the piano to singing; they performed together in Mozart's *Don Giovanni*. But she interrupted her singing career to pick up the baton when a conductor suddenly fled town in the face of a hostile audience (and during intermissions, she continued to entertain with solo piano works). For husband number three, the composer Eugen d'Albert, she returned to her original instrument full-time once again, championing his Second Piano Concerto. "Frau Carreño yesterday played for the first time the second concerto of her third husband in the fourth Philharmonic Concert," wrote a German critic.

The great Chilean piano legend Claudio Arrau found her playing an inspiring "mixture of Latin feeling and German training." "Oh, she was a goddess," he recalled. "Carreño would play Liszt's *Hungarian Rhapsody No. 6* without cuts, and at the end you thought the house would come down, would cave in from the sound."

Other important South American classical

Teresa Carreño at age eight, and as an adult

pianists included Brazilian Guiomar Novaes (1895–1979), who was accepted to the Paris Conservatory in 1909 while still in her teens, at a time when 387 applicants vied for two openings (her performance stunned jury member Claude Debussy); and Martha Argerich (b. 1941), the Argentinean firebrand. Argerich studied in Austria with Friedrich Gulda (1930–2000), a pianist equally adept at classical and jazz performance, and in Italy with piano superstar Arturo Benedetti Michelangeli, among others. Though severely stage-shy and riddled with insecurities, she typically ripped through the technical challenges in the knottiest of works as if they were mere child's play, performing finger-breakers such as Rachmaninoff's Third Piano Concerto at lightning speed (often to the detriment of the music). But at her best, a vitality in her playing sent shock waves through a listener's nervous system.

In Mexico, Manuel M. Ponce (1882–1948) and Carlos Chávez (1899–1978) used native elements to bring to their music what Chávez described as "what is deepest in the Mexican soul." Agustín Lara (1897–1970) also captured the folk sound of the Mexican people. His career spanned teenage years playing in brothels, to later successes that included receiving the keys to the city from the mayor of Veracruz. (His song of that name is still popular throughout South America.) Composer-pianist Max Lifschitz (b. 1948) continued to champion this music in the United States with his North/South Consonance Ensemble, founded in 1980.

Pianist Barbara Nissman (b. 1944) has long been associated with Ginastera, who wrote his final work, the Piano Sonata no. 3, for her. Brazilian-born Sonia Rubinsky has been a champion of the piano music of Villa-Lobos, which she has recorded in its entirety.

National Styles Around the World: A Panoply of Players

The legendary players are like branches on a huge family tree. Josef Hofmann's teacher Arthur Friedheim (1859–1932) had been a pupil of Anton Rubinstein, but eventually turned to Liszt for instruction, apparently feeling that Rubinstein's method was not well organized. Friedheim grew so close to Liszt that he eventually became the great man's secretary, and as a teacher he disseminated the master's secrets of achieving unhampered movement at the keyboard. Hofmann was in turn an important influence on Cuban-born piano virtuoso Jorge Bolet (1914–1990), who specialized in the Romantic repertoire.

Karl Heinrich Barth—an associate of Liszt, Bülow, and Brahms—who taught Arthur Rubinstein in Berlin, was also mentor to the important German pianist Wilhelm Kempff (1895–1991). Modern Polish pianist Krystian Zimerman (b. 1956) continued their restrained approach,

with flawless tonal control (indeed, with a fanatical focus on sound as it changes from one concert environment to another) as well as with an impeccable sense of musical structure.

Czech piano great Rudolf Firkušný (1912–1994), a revered teacher, was a patrician to the core. His playing was imbued with a rainbow of tonal hues as well as a profound classical sensibility. He performed much of the standard repertoire, but also promoted the music of his countrymen, including Bohuslav Martinů (1890–1959), who combined Bohemian and jazz elements, and Leoš Janáček (1854–1928), who was often inspired by Moravian and Slavic folk music.

The modern French tradition was solidified in 1907, when composer Gabriel Fauré appointed Alfred Cortot professor of piano at the Paris Conservatory. And in 1919, Cortot founded his own school, the École Normale de Musique in Paris, where his students included Gina Bachauer (1913–1976), Clara Haskil (1895–1960), Magda Tagliaferro (1893–1986), the short-lived but exquisite Dinu Lipatti (1917–1950), American Jerome Lowenthal, and Vlado Perlemuter (1904–2002).

Today, Italian piano masters include Aldo Ciccolini (b. 1925), who is associated mostly with French repertoire, and a younger brood of artistic lions, including Emanuele Arciuli (b. 1965), a formidable advocate of contemporary American works; Pietro de Maria (b. 1967); Francesco Libetta (b. 1968); and Roberto Prosseda (b. 1975) and his wife, Alessandra Ammara (b. 1972).

Over the decades, many Americans found a welcome in Europe and Japan that eluded them at home. In the 1920s and 1930s, James Reese Europe, Ada "Bricktop" Smith, Josephine Baker, Sidney Bechet, and other jazz artists made Paris a base of operations. After World War II, Billy Strayhorn, Bud Powell, and a host of their compatriots set up shop there for extended periods. Even today, classical and jazz musicians often rely on their tours of Asia to pay the rent. They follow in the footsteps of figures both famous and little known, including Philippa Schuyler (1931–1967)—the product of a black journalist father

renowned as a champion of the Harlem Renaissance and a blond, blue-eyed Texas heiress—who could read and write at the age of two, play piano at four, and compose by five. As a youngster she was compared to Mozart and appeared in the pages of *Time* and *Look* magazines, the *New York Herald Tribune*, and *The New Yorker*. But her search for acceptance, facing the twin disadvantages of gender and race, led her to Asia, where, after performing a concert on South Vietnamese television (which included her transcriptions of Gershwin, Copland's *The Cat and the Mouse*, and her own original compositions), she died in a helicopter crash, ten miles north of Da Nang.
An American pianist with strong ties to Japan, Sara Davis Buechner (formerly David Buechner, b. 1959), continues to hop between continents, presenting elegant interpretations of contemporary Japanese piano works, along with American and Romantic classics.

More About the Russians

The John Field lineage of lilting, nocturnal music extends to the Polish pianist Maria Agata Szymanowska (1789–1831), who moved to St. Petersburg in 1821. Russia's first important opera composer, Mikhail Glinka (1804–1857), was also a Field student.

A long list of important Russians also include a group known as the Mighty Five (consisting of

Mily Balakirev, César Cui, Modest Mussorgsky, Nikolai Rimsky-Korsakov, and Alexander Borodin). Today, the best-known Russian melodists, composers whose music perfectly expressed that country's dark-hued soul with graceful, expansive lyricism, includes Pyotr Ilyich Tchaikovsky (1840–1893) and Nikolai Medtner (1880–1951). Contemporary Russian composers of significance include Rodion Shchedrin (b. 1932), Valentin Silvestrov (b. 1937), and Sofia Gubaidulina (b. 1931).

Russia produced many brilliant pianists who achieved fame in the West, like the gifted technicians Lazar Berman (1930–2005) and Arcadi Volodos (b. 1972) and the romantic sensation Evgeny Kissin (b. 1971). Others, who remained more obscure, include Vladimir Sofronitsky (1901–1961), who married Scriabin's daughter and specialized in the strange, feverishly mystical music of his father-in-law; Rachmaninoff's teacher Alexander Siloti (1863–1945); Alexander Goldenweiser (1865–1961); Dmitri Bashkirov (b. 1931); Vladimir Krainev (b. 1944); and Grigory Sokolov (b. 1950). Heinrich Neuhaus's student Lev Naumov (1925–2005) became a legendary teacher in his own right at the Moscow Conservatory, with a list of prominent students that

Evgeny Kissin

included competition winners Vladimir Viardo (b. 1949), Alexander Toradze (b. 1952), Andrei Gavrilov (b. 1955), Sergei Babyan (b. 1972), and Ilya Itin (b. 1967).

Peter Tchaikovsky

Several Russian masters left home to take teaching positions, passing the tradition on to new generations around the world. Isabelle Vengerova (1877–1956), after instructing students at the conservatory in St. Petersburg, settled in Philadelphia at the Curtis Institute and also taught at New York's Mannes School; her students in the United States included Leonard Bernstein, Gary Graffman, Abbey Simon (b. 1922), and Gilbert Kalish (b. 1935). ("Although not very tall," wrote Graffman, "she was extremely wide and she sailed around her studio like an overstuffed battleship in search of the enemy, cannon loaded and ready to fire.") In New York, pianists Josef and Rosina Lhevinne held court at the Juilliard School, where Rosina taught Van Cliburn, James Levine (b. 1943), and John Browning (1933–2003). It was Cliburn who truly put her on the map.

Germanic Players

Edwin Fischer, who mentored Alfred Brendel, also trained pianist and scholar Paul Badura-Skoda (b. 1927). Brendel, in turn, taught pianists Till Fellner (b. 1972) and Paul Lewis (b. 1972).

Germanic playing of a lyric character imbued the performances of Walter Gieseking (1895–1956), who specialized in the music of Debussy; Wilhelm Backhaus (1884–1969); and Ferruccio Busoni (1866–1924). Busoni, an Italian composer and pianist with a stunning, steel-trap technique, settled in Berlin and there promulgated his vision of a "music of the future," distinguished by its openness to endless possibilities of sound—a theme taken to heart by his adventurous students Percy Grainger (1882–1961) and Edgard Varèse (1883–1965), the father of electronic music.

Other students of Theodor Leschetizky included such formidable talents as Mieczyslaw Horszowski (1892–1993) and Chopin specialist Alexander Brailowsky (1896–1976). American pianist Ruth Laredo (1937–2005), a student of Rudolf Serkin, made landmark recordings of the complete piano works of both Scriabin and Rachmaninoff.

Viennese pianist Rudolf Buchbinder (b. 1946) continues to invest the music of Bach, Mozart, and Beethoven with an individual perspective.

Around the World: Other Nationalists

Spanish pianist Alicia de Larrocha (1923–2009) brought much of her native country's piano repertoire to wider attention, promoting it where it was nearly unknown, especially in America and Japan. American pianist Douglas Riva (b. 1951), who also specializes in Spanish works, discovered, restored, and performed a forgotten Granados masterpiece in 2009—*Song of the Stars*, for piano, organ, and three choruses, which had not been seen or heard since its premiere in Barcelona in 1911.

Chopin remains unmatched in his ability to embody the Polish character, but other composers from that nation have made important contributions to the literature, chief among them Karol Szymanowski (1882–1937), whose music reflected the broad influences of a Europe on the abyss. "He was influenced by many musical trends," explained pianist Piotr Anderszewski, "in a period—especially before the First World War—of incredible turmoil, decadence, and what seemed like the end of the world. Indeed, Chopin, who left home to live in Paris, longed to express his Polishness in every piece. Szymanowski remained in Poland," but became a cosmopolitan European in every way, absorbing the Impressionist shimmer of the French, the sensuality of Scriabin, and acerbic collisions in the mode of Stravinsky, Bartók, and Prokofiev. Perhaps a clue to Szymanowski's thinking can be found in the words of the Persian poet Rumi, cited for his Third Symphony: "Silence binds my tongues with fetters / But I speak though tongueless in this night." This composer searched for a deeper means of expression than a single tongue could afford, since no one language can express the ineffable.

On the other side of the world, Australian-born Percy Grainger, a friend of

Percy Grainger

Grieg's, also created folk-tinged music. He could be as odd as a kangaroo and was known as "the jogging pianist" because of his inclination to run through the streets on his way to a concert and, still overflowing with energy when he arrived on stage, attack the piano without mercy (he might just as well have been dubbed "the banging pianist"). Grainger once walked more than seventy miles to a concert in South Africa, arriving just in the nick of time. Some of his works, like *Country Gardens,* became hits in his lifetime, though he often filled his settings of simple tunes with idiosyncratic, complex figures, cramming layers of counterpoint into the texture (and producing thorny difficulties for anyone who wished to play them). Among other quirks was his tendency to use his own eccentric terminology when creating a manuscript—in place of "crescendo" or "arranged by," for example, he'd indicate, "louden lots" and "dished up by."

Contemporary Pianists

Stars of our time include Argentine pianist-conductor Daniel Barenboim (b. 1942); Norwegian Leif Ove Andsnes (b. 1970); Poland's Piotr Anderszewski (b. 1969); English-born Stephen Hough (b. 1961); and Americans Ursula

Oppens (b. 1944), Garrick Ohlsson (b. 1948), Emanuel Ax (b. 1949), and Jeremy Denk (b. 1970). The chamber-music experience continues to occupy pianists like Marc Neikrug (b. 1946), artistic director of the Santa Fe Chamber Music Festival, and Wu Han (b. 1959), who co-directs, together with her husband, the eminent cellist David Finkel, the Chamber Music Society of Lincoln Center in New York, as well as the California-based Music at Menlo. These artists all continue to bring vibrancy to the concert stage, keeping the tradition alive.

Our era welcomes hybrids, and among them are America's Pulitzer Prize–winning composer William Bolcom (b. 1938) and Russia's Nikolai Kapustin (b. 1937). Both have infused their rigorous, formal compositions with authentic jazz idioms. Pianist-composers Marc-André Hamelin (b. 1961) and John Salmon (b. 1954) have made wonderful recordings of Kapustin's music. American pianist Christopher O'Riley (b. 1956) has dissolved the barriers between classical and pop by recomposing music by rock groups like Radiohead, shaping their songs into haunting and highly virtuosic original works for solo piano.

Though composer-pianist Frederic Rzewski moved beyond the twelve-tone ideology of his teachers Milton Babbitt (b. 1916) and Luigi Dallapiccola (1904–1975), the method continues to have important proponents, including American composers Charles Wuorinen (b. 1938) and Peter Lieberson (b. 1948). Other players of contemporary music on the American scene include Stephen Gosling, Blair McMillen, Kathleen Supové, Gloria Cheng, and Lisa Moore.

The Piano as Art

German Heiner Goebbels's music-theater piece *Stifers Dinge* (*Stifter's Things*) is based on the writings of nineteenth-century Romantic writer Adalbert Stifter. It was described by Goebbels as a composition for five pianos with no pianists, and a play with no actors. The work uses mechanical devices to produce a variety of piano sounds, from sporadic, plucked grunts to clangorous clouds of vibration from the instruments as they float on rails, moving toward and away from the audience to heighten the dramatic effect of a spoken narrative.

Dutchman Guido van der Werve's "chess piano" was used in a chamber music performance at the storied Marshall Chess Club in New York. Instead of sounding by means of a keyboard, this instrument is played by moving chess pieces on a board. The music at the Marshall Chess Club was based on a game created by grandmaster Leonid Yudasin: each move triggered a hammer beneath the board to strike a string. "I asked Yudasin to start the game with the King's gambit accepted, and to end in a stalemate," reported van der Werve. "Each chess move provided me with a

Piece for chess piano and strings by Guido van der Werve performed at the Marshall Chess Club, New York City

GUIDO VAN DER WERVE

note but also with a musical context. I wrote the whole piece in three movements, following the triptych structure of the chess game: opening, middle game, and end game."

Even stranger than the chess piano was the "speaking piano," created by Austrian composer Peter Ablinger. Using advanced digital filters, Ablinger found a way to utilize a computer-controlled player piano to replicate the human voice. He premiered his invention in Vienna and Graz, Austria, in 2004, where it mimicked a speech recited by a young boy.

Final Thought: The Piano Is Good for Your Brain

Recent breakthroughs in the field of neuro-science have shown that playing the piano is good for your brain. Dr. Gottfried Schlaug of Beth Israel Deaconess Medical Center and Harvard Medical School spoke in 2009 at the Library of Congress in Washington, D.C., on the brain's "plasticity"—its capacity to change—and announced that even nine- to eleven-year-old musicians show more brain activity than nonmusicians when performing tasks that require high levels of perceptual discrimination. Playing the piano, it turns out, is especially effective in enhancing skills in such important areas as pattern recognition and memory. To your health!

Contributor Biographies

PIOTR ANDERSZEWSKI was born in Warsaw in 1969. He received the Gilmore Prize in 2002, the Szymanowski Prize in 1999, and the Royal Philharmonic Society's Best Instrumentalist Award in 2001. He has been the subject of two award-winning films by Bruno Monsaingeon.

EMANUEL AX was born in Lvov, Poland, in 1949 and moved to Winnipeg, Canada, while still a small boy. He won the first Arthur Rubinstein International Piano Competition in Tel Aviv in 1974, followed by Lincoln Center's Avery Fisher Prize. He records extensively and is considered one of the premier pianists of his time.

ALFRED BRENDEL, an Austrian pianist now residing in the United Kingdom, was born in Czechoslovakia in 1931. His performances, recordings, and writings have made him one of the most influential pianists of his generation.

YEFIM BRONFMAN, a pianist of exceptional power and musicality, was born in Tashkent in the Soviet Union in 1958. His family moved to the United States in 1973, where he studied with Rudolf Firkušný and Leon Fleisher. He has one of the busiest careers in the world.

BILL CHARLAP is one of the most active jazz pianists and recording artists of his generation. Born in New York City in 1966, he is the product of a musical family: His mother, Sandy Stewart, is a singer, and his father, Moose Charlap, was a Broadway composer.

CLAUDE DEBUSSY was one of France's greatest composers.

VLADIMIR HOROWITZ, born in Kiev, was a legendary piano virtuoso, the most famous pianist of the twentieth century.

ALDOUS HUXLEY (1894–1963) was an English writer and cultural philosopher. Author of such classics as *Brave New World* and *The Doors of Perception*, he exerted a significant influence on the counterculture of the 1960s.

ILYA ITIN was born in Ekaterinburg, Russia, studied at the Moscow Conservatory with Lev Naumov, and currently resides in New York City. He won top prizes at the William Kapell Competition, the Casadesus Competition, and the Leeds International Piano Competition.

BILLY JOEL, born in 1949, is an American pianist, singer, and songwriter. He is a six-time Grammy Award winner who has sold over 100 million records worldwide.

WANDA LANDOWSKA (1879–1959) was born in Poland and became a French citizen. She was an extraordinary harpsichordist and played an important role in reviving the popularity of the instrument in the twentieth century.

YUNDI LI was the youngest pianist ever to win the International Frédéric Chopin Competition, in 2000, at the age of eighteen. Born in Chongquing, China, in 1982, he now resides in Hong Kong.

MIKE LIPSKIN, born in New York in 1942 and now transplanted to San Francisco, was a protégé of Willie "the Lion" Smith, and also studied with stride masters Luckey Roberts, Cliff Jackson, and Donald Lambert. For thirteen years he was a producer at RCA Records, where he worked on historical reissues as well as new albums by the likes of Gil Evans, Cedar Walton, and Duke Ellington.

MIKE LONGO, originally from Cincinnati, now lives in New York City. Born in 1939, he worked with jazz legend Julian "Cannonball" Adderley while still in his teens, studied with the great Oscar Peterson, and spent many years as a member of trumpeter Dizzy Gillespie's ensemble.

GABRIELA MONTERO, born in 1970 in Caracas, Venezuela, now lives in Massachusetts. She gave her first public performance at the age of five. Montero has always improvised, and despite reservations about whether doing so would detract from her classical career, this aspect of her talent has taken on increasing importance, due especially to the urging of her friend pianist Martha Argerich.

GARRICK OHLSSON in 1970 became the first American to win the International Frédéric Chopin Piano Competition in Warsaw. He also won the Busoni Competition and the Montreal Piano Competition. He received Lincoln Center's Avery Fisher Award in 1994.

MURRAY PERAHIA is an American pianist transplanted to London and Israel. He was the first North American to win the Leeds Piano Competition. After establishing a career with a series of Mozart recordings, he worked with Vladimir Horowitz in the 1980s at the older pianist's invitation. His recordings of Bach have been especially stunning.

OSCAR PETERSON, the world-renowned Canadian jazz pianist, was called the "Maharaja of the Keyboard" by Duke Ellington.

MENAHEM PRESSLER, born in Magdeburg, Germany, is a founding member of the Beaux Arts Trio and considered by many to be the preeminent chamber musician of our time. His list of awards would take up an entire book.

ANDRÁS SCHIFF, born in Budapest in 1953 and now living in Great Britain and Italy, is considered one of the greatest classical artists of his age. His recordings and performing legacy include the major works of Bach, Haydn, Mozart, Beethoven, Schubert, Chopin, Scarlatti, and Bartók.

ALDEN SKINNER spent many years with Yamaha Corporation of America before switching to the telecommunications industry. He is the digital-piano editor for Larry Fine's *Acoustic & Digital Piano Buyer,* an annual guide.

BILLY TAYLOR was known as the dean of American jazz. As house pianist at Birdland, he performed with such legends as Charlie Parker, Dizzy Gillespie, and Miles Davis, and became a protégé of Art Tatum. He worked in both television and radio to promote the art form he loved, and founded New York's Jazzmobile, which still provides educational and concert programs in neighborhoods around the city.

ANDRÉ WATTS, born in Nuremberg, Germany, was introduced to a national audience when, at the age of sixteen, he played Liszt's Piano Concerto no. 1 with the New York Philharmonic conducted by Leonard Bernstein on a televised Young People's Concert. Three weeks later, Bernstein asked Mr. Watts to fill in for an ailing Glenn Gould. He is one of the most popular pianists on the concert circuit. He holds the Jack I. and Dora B. Hamlin Endowed Chair in Music at Indiana University.

Acknowledgments

Thanks must go first to my editor, Jonathan Segal of Alfred A. Knopf, whose idea this project was; his assistant, Joey McGarvey, who helped launch it into production; and Maggie Hinders, for her beautiful book design. Throughout the process, my wife Adrienne's advice and support were indispensable.

Many musician friends were invaluable sources of information and inspiration. They include especially two walking encyclopedias of the piano, David Dubal and Joseph Smith, and the many stellar artists who contributed commentary to this book, as well as Emanuele Arciuli, Ed Berlin, Andy Bloch, Joseph Bloch, Bradley Brookshire, Sara Davis Buechner, Noah Creshevsky, Jacob Greenberg, Michael Harrison, Peter Hoyt, Dick Hyman, Andy LaVerne, Steven Lubin, Max Morath, Peter Mintun, Roberto Prosseda, Nancy Reich, Charles Rosen, Riccardo Scivales, Jeremy Siepmann, and Amanda Villepastour. I remain forever indebted to my late friend Nicolas Slonimsky. Of course, any misjudgments or errors in the book are entirely mine.

I am also grateful to the following people for many kindnesses: David Botwinik, Maxine and Dr. Frank Brady, Douglas di Carlo, Liam Comerford, Michael Cuscuna, Larry Fine, Kathy Geisler, Eric Gibson, Herbert Goldman, Peter Goodrich, Richard Halpern, Alex Hassan, Josephine Hemsing and her husband, Dan Cameron, Nat Hentoff, Tad Hershorn, Valeska Hilbig, Todd Kamelhar, Stacey Kluck, Laura Kuhn, Cem Kurosman, Christina Linsenmeyer, Ron Losby, Len Lyons, Loraine Machlin, Eileen MacMahon, Holly Metz, Anne Midgette, Jocelyn Miller, Bruno Monsaingeon, Nell Mulderry, Stewart Pollens, Stephen Russo, Eva Rubinstein, Alina Rubinstein, David Sachs, Peter Schaaf, Zach Schwartz, Tyler Tadej, J. W. Whitten, and Ed Young.

Notes on Sources

CHAPTER I *A Gathering of Traditions*

Comments by Menahem Pressler were made to the author in an interview in 2009. Comments by Piotr Anderszewski are excerpted from the film *Piotr Anderszewski: Unquiet Traveller* by Bruno Monsaingeon. Comments by Mike Longo were made to the author in an interview in 2009.

Comments by Oscar Peterson were made to the author in an interview, likely the last one he gave, conducted in 2006. Elements of it first appeared in the *Wall Street Journal* on August 29, 2006.

Leonard Feather's Oscar Peterson spoof appears in *From Blues to Bop: A Collection of Jazz Fiction*, edited by Richard N. Albert (New York: Anchor Books/ Doubleday, 1992).

On the subject of the relationship between African, African-American, and European music, one indispensable scholarly resource is the brilliant article "Open Letter about 'Black Music,' 'Afro-American Music,' and 'European Music' " by Philip Tagg, in *Popular Music*, Volume 8/3, 1989, pp. 285–298, published by Cambridge University Press (also available at www.tagg.org/articles/opelet.html).

Books drawn on for this chapter include:

Ragtime: A Musical and Cultural History by Edward A. Berlin (Berkeley: University of California Press, 1980); *I Really Should Be Practicing* by Gary Graffman (Garden City, NY: Doubleday & Company, 1981); *A Romance on Three Legs: Glenn Gould's Obsessive Quest for the Perfect Piano* by Katie Hafner (New York: Bloomsbury, 2008); *Dvořák* by Kurt Honolka, translated by Anne Wyburd (London: Haus Publishing, 2004); *Classical Music in America: A History of Its Rise and Fall* by Joseph Horowitz (New York: W. W. Norton & Company, 2005); The *Piano Teacher* by Elfriede Jelinek, translated by Joachim Neugroschel (New York: Weidenfeld & Nicolson, 1988); *Chicago Jazz: A Cultural History, 1904–1930* by William Howland Kenney (New York: Oxford University Press, 1993); *Oscar Peterson: The Will to Swing* by Gene Lees (Toronto: Lester & Orpen Dennys, 1988); *The Piano Tuner* by Daniel Mason (New York: Alfred A. Knopf, 2002); *Is Jazz Dead? (Or Has It Moved to a New Address)* by Stuart Nicholson (New York: Routledge, 2005); *Oscar Peterson: A Jazz Odyssey* by Oscar Peterson, editor and consultant Richard Palmer (New York:

Continuum, 2002); and *Music on My Mind: The Memoirs of an American Pianist* by Willie "the Lion" Smith with George Hoefer (London: MacGibbon & Kee, 1966).

Also cited were the articles "A Piano Is Born, Needing Practice" by James Barron, *New York Times*, April 2, 2004; "Time-Travelers from a Golden Age" by Nat Hentoff, *Wall Street Journal*, August 7, 2010; and "Three Piano Misereres" by Joseph Smith, *Journal of the American Liszt Society* 59–60 (2008–9), 10–23.

CHAPTER 2 *The Piano Is Born*

For historical material on the Medici family and Florence, I consulted *The Last Medici* by Harold Acton (New York: St. Martin's Press, 1958); *Florence: The Golden Age, 1138–1737* by Gene Adam Brucker (New York: Abbeville Press, 1984); *The House of Medici: Its Rise and Fall* by Christopher Hibbert (New York: William Morrow & Co., 1975); *Florence: A Portrait* by Michael Levey (Cambridge: Harvard University Press, 1996); and *Medici Money* by Tim Parks (New York: W. W. Norton & Company, 2005).

For information on the earliest piano and its predecessors, I am indebted to the work of my friend Stewart Pollens, including his book *The Early Pianoforte* (Cambridge: Cambridge University Press, 1995) and "The First 300 Years of the Piano," a public lecture sponsored by Sotheby's Institute of Art and delivered by Stewart at the World Financial Center on September 25, 2003.

In addition, I drew on *Music in the French Royal Academy of Sciences: A Study in the Evolution of Musical Thought* by Albert Cohen (Princeton: Princeton University Press, 1981); *French Musical Thought, 1600–1800*, edited by Georgia Cowart (Ann Arbor: UMI Research Press, 1989); *Early Keyboard Instruments* by Philip James (London: Tabard Press, 1970); *The Clavichord* by Hanns Neupert (Kassel: Bärenreiter, 1965); *Harpsichord Manual* by Hanns Neupert (Kassel: Bärenreiter, 1968); *The Cambridge Companion to the Piano*, edited by David Rowland (Cambridge: Cambridge University Press, 1998); and *French Pianism: A Historical Perspective* by Charles Timbrell (Portland, OR: Amadeus Press, 1999).

The following scholarly articles were particularly helpful: "Pantaleon's Pantalon: An 18th-Century Musical Fashion" by Sarah E. Hanks, *Musical Quarterly* 55, no. 2 (April 1969), 214–227; "The Capture of the Chekker" by David Kinsela, *Galpin Society Journal* 51 (July 1998), 64–85; "The Myth of the Chekker" by Christopher Page, *Early Music* 7, no. 4, Keyboard Issue 1 (October 1979), 482–489; and "Keyboard Scholarship: Letter from Nicolas Meeùs and reply by Christopher Page," *Early Music* 8: no. 2, Keyboard Issue 2 (April 1980), 222–226.

CHAPTER 3 *The First Piano Superstar*

The quote about Mozart from Josef Krips was first conveyed to me by pianist André Watts, to whom Krips used the line when they were performing together. I heard it again in a lecture by András Schiff. Apparently it was one of Krips's favorite sayings.

The comments from Alfred Brendel appear in "A Mozart Player Gives Himself Advice," from *Alfred Brendel on Music* (Chicago: A Cappella Books, 2001).

I was made aware of Borgato and its ongoing production of pedal pianos through Italian pianist Roberto Prosseda. The reference to Chopin's playing of the pedal piano is from *Music in Chopin's Warsaw* by Halina Goldberg (New York: Oxford University Press, 2008).

Sources used for the material on late-eighteenth-century Vienna and Mozart's life and work there included, in addition to Mozart's letters, the books: *W. A. Mozart* by Hermann Abert, translated by Stewart Spencer and edited by Cliff Eisen (New Haven: Yale University Press, 2007); *Mozart in Vienna, 1781–1791* by Volkmar Braunbehrens, translated by Timothy Bell (New York: Grove Weidenfeld, 1989); *Haydn, Mozart and the Viennese School, 1740–1780* by Daniel Heartz (New York: W. W. Norton & Company, 1995); *Concert Life in Haydn's Vienna: Aspects of a Developing Musical and Social Institution* by Mary Sue Morrow (New York: Pendragon Press, 1989); and *Mozart: A Life* by Maynard Solomon (New York: Harper Perennial, 1995). For information on Muzio Clementi I turned to *Clementi: His Life and Music* by Leon Plantinga (New York: Oxford University Press, 1977).

Particularly helpful articles included: "Mozart's Viennese Orchestras" by Dexter Edge, *Early Music* 20, no. 1 (February 1992), 63–65, 67, 69, 71–88; "Mozart's Keyboard Instruments" by Richard Maunder, *Early Music* 20, no. 2 (May 1992), 207–219; "Mozart's Pedal Piano" by Richard Maunder and David Rowland, *Early Music* 23, no. 2 (May 1995), 287–296; "Mozart in the Market-Place" by Julia Moore, *Journal of the Royal Musical Association* 114, no. 1 (1989), 18–42; and "Clementi, Virtuosity, and the 'German Manner' " by Leon Plantinga, *Journal of the American Musicological Society* 25, no. 3 (Autumn 1972), 303–330.

CHAPTER 4 *Piano Fever*

The Vladimir Horowitz comments come from *Talking About Pianos* (Long Island City, NY: Steinway & Sons, 1982).

Sources used for this chapter include: *Inside the Victorian Home: A Portrait of Domestic Life in Victorian England* by Judith Flanders (New York: W. W. Norton & Company, 2004); *Giraffes, Black Dragons, and Other Pianos: A Technological History from Cristofori to the Modern Concert Grand* by Edwin M. Good (Stanford: Stanford University Press, 2001); *After the Golden Age: Romantic Pianism and Modern Performance* by Kenneth Hamilton (New York: Oxford University Press, 2008); *Chopin at the Boundaries: Sex, History, and Musical Genre* by Jeffrey Kallberg (Cambridge: Harvard University Press, 1996); *Music at the White House: A History of the American Spirit* by Elise K. Kirk (Urbana: University of Illinois Press, 1986); *The Sight of Sound: Music, Representation, and the History of the Body* by Richard Leppert (Berkeley: University of California Press, 1993); *Art and the Victorian Middle Class: Money and the Making of Cultural Identity* by Dianne Sachko Macleod (Cambridge: Cambridge University Press, 1996); *American Writers at Home* by J. D. McClatchy, photographs by Erica Lennard (New York: Library of America and the Vendome

Press, 2004); *Player Piano Treasury: The Scrapbook History of the Mechanical Piano in America* by Harvey Roehl (New York: Vestal Press, 1961), brought to my attention by Dick Hyman; *Chambers Music Quotations* by Derek Watson (Edinburgh: W & R Chambers, Ltd., 1991); *A History of the Wife* by Marilyn Yalom (New York: Harper Perennial, 2002); and the article "J. C. Bach and the Early Piano in London" by Richard Maunder, *Journal of the Royal Musical Association* 116, no. 2 (1991), 201–210.

CHAPTER 5 *Performers on the Road*

The Yefim Bronfman quote came from two interviews conducted by the author, the first of which appeared in the *Wall Street Journal*, February 26, 2008; the second took place in 2010.

I am grateful to scholar and author Nancy Reich for making an English translation of Clara Schumann's diaries available to me.

Books used in the preparation of this chapter include: *Mozart's Women: His Family, His Friends, His Music* by Jane Glover (New York: HarperCollins, 2005); *Notes of a Pianist* by Louis Moreau Gottschalk, edited by Jeanne Behrend (New York: Da Capo Press, 1979); *After the Golden Age: Romantic Pianism and Modern Performance* by Kenneth Hamilton (New York: Oxford University Press, 2008); *From Paris to Peoria: How European Piano Virtuosos Brought Classical Music to the American Heartland* by R. Allen Lott (New York: Oxford University Press, 2003); *Vladimir de Pachmann: A Piano Virtuoso's Life and Art* by Mark Mitchell (Bloomington: Indiana University Press, 2002); *A Life in Letters* by Wolfgang Amadeus Mozart, edited by Cliff Eisen, translated by Stewart Spencer (New York: Penguin Classics, 2007); *Virtuoso* by Harvey Sachs (London: Thames and Hudson, 1982); *The Social Status of the Professional Musician from the Middle Ages to the 19th Century*, edited by Walter Salmen, translated by Herbet Kaufman and Barbara Reisner (New York: Pendragon Press, 1983); *Dr. Burney's Musical Tours in Europe, Volumes I and II*, edited by Percy A. Scholes (London: Oxford University Press, 1959); *The Great Pianists* by Harold C. Schonberg (New York: Fireside, Simon & Schuster, 1987); *French Pianism: A Historical Perspective* by Charles Timbrell (Portland, OR: Amadeus Press, 1999); and *The Musician as Entrepreneur, 1700–1914: Managers, Charlatans, and Idealists*, edited by William Weber (Bloomington: Indiana University Press, 2004).

Articles used in the preparation of this chapter include: "Westward to the East" by Joseph Bloch, *Juilliard Journal*, May 1960; "Counting European Slaves on the Barbary Coast" by Robert C. Davis, *Past & Present* no. 172 (August 2001), 87–124; "Public Performance and Private Understanding: Clara Wieck's Concerts in Berlin" by David Ferris, *Journal of the American Musicological Society* 56, no. 2 (Summer 2003), 351–408; "Mozart's Transitory Life," a paper presented by musicologist Peter A. Hoyt at Lincoln Center for the Performing Arts in 2005; "Beethoven's Pianos," a paper written by Stewart Pollens; and "W. F. E. Bach's Six-Handed Flower" by Joseph Smith, *Piano Today*, Fall 2002. The report on the battle between Herz and de Meyer appeared in *Musical World* (London) 22, no. 1, January 2, 1847. The circumstances surrounding Alkan's death are explored in "More on Alkan's Death" by Hugh MacDonald in *Musical Times* 129, no. 1741 (March 1988), 118–120.

CHAPTER 6 *The Four Sounds*

The Murray Perahia quote comes from *Talking About Pianos* (Long Island City, NY: Steinway & Sons, 1982). Additional comments by various pianists were taken from personal correspondence to the author.

Also used were the books *Physics of the Piano* by Nicholas J. Giordano Sr. (New York: Oxford University Press, 2010); *A History of Pianoforte Pedalling* by David Rowland (New York: Cambridge University Press, 1993); and *Performing Beethoven*, edited by Robin Stowell (Cambridge: Cambridge University Press, 1994).

CHAPTER 7 *The Combustibles*

The Aldous Huxley excerpt is from his novel *Point Counter Point* (Garden City, NY: Doubleday, Doran & Co., 1928). The Wanda Landowska excerpt is from *Landowska on Music* by Denise Restout and Robert Hawkins (New York: Stein and Day, 1964). The contribution by André Watts is from an interview conducted by the author in 2009. The contribution by Alfred Brendel is excerpted from "Liszt Misunderstood," in *Brendel on Music* (Chicago: A Cappella Books, 2001). The excerpt by Ferdinand Ries was taken from *Beethoven Remembered: The Biographical Notes of Franz Wegeler and Ferdinand Ries*, translated by Frederick Noonan (Arlington, VA: Great Ocean Publishers, 1987).

The following books were also used as research for these chapters: *Stravinsky Dances: Re-Visions Across a Century* by Stephanie Jordan (Alton, UK: Dance Books Ltd., 2007); *The World of Earl Hines* by Stanley Dance (New York: Charles Scribner's Sons, 1977); *Striders to Beboppers and Beyond* by Leslie Gourse (New York: Franklin Watts, 1997); *Stravinsky: The Rite of Spring* by Peter Hill (Cambridge: Cambridge University Press, 2000); *The Free Fantasia and the Musical Picturesque* by Annette Richards (New York: Cambridge University Press, 2006); *Beethoven's Piano Sonatas: A Short Companion* by Charles Rosen (New Haven: Yale University Press, 2002); *The Romantic Generation* by Charles Rosen (Cambridge: Harvard University Press, 1995); *The Great Dr. Burney: His Life, His Travels, His Works, His Family and His Friends, Volume I* by Percy A. Scholes (London: Oxford University Press, 1948); *Remembering Franz Liszt, Including "My Memories of Liszt" by Alexander Siloti and "Life and Liszt" by Arthur Friedheim* (New York: Limelight Editions, 1986); *Lexicon of Musical Invective* by Nicolas Slonimsky (Seattle: University of Washington Press, 1978); *Late Beethoven: Music, Thought, Imagination* by Maynard Solomon (Berkeley: University of California Press, 2003); *Performing Beethoven*, edited by Robin Stowell (Cambridge: Cambridge University Press, 1994); *Beethoven Remembered: The Biographical Notes of Franz Wegeler and Ferdinand Ries*, translated by Frederick Noonan (Arlington, VA: Great Ocean Publishers, 1987); and *Portrait of Liszt, by Himself and His Contemporaries* by Adrian Williams (Oxford: Clarendon Press, 1990).

CHAPTER 8 *The Alchemists*

The excerpt by Claude Debussy on Mussorgsky is from *La Revue blanche,* April 15, 1901, translated by Richard Langham Smith. The Garrick Ohlsson contribution on Liszt and Scriabin is from an interview conducted by the author in 2009. Herbie Hancock revealed his harmonic ideas to the author in an interview that took place in the 1980s. The Bill Charlap contribution on Bill Evans is from an interview conducted by the author in 2009. The Noah Creshevsky comments were made to the author in 2010. Observations about Steve Reich stem from an interview with him conducted by the author in 1981. I am grateful to pianist Menahem Pressler for his insights on performing Debussy's first prelude. The quotes from Baudelaire are from his collection of poems *Les Fleurs du mal.*

I am grateful to the John Cage Trust and to its executive director, Laura Kuhn, and to Michael Grace and Stormy Burns of the Colorado College Music Press for the essay by Cage on his first prepared piano.

The following books were used in the preparation of this chapter: *Scriabin: A Biography* by Faubion Bowers (New York: Dover, 1996); *The Well-Prepared Piano* by Richard Bunger (Colorado Springs: The Colorado College Music Press, 1972); *Composers on Music,* edited by Josiah Fisk (Boston: Northeastern University Press, 1997); *Paths to the Absolute* by John Golding (Princeton: Princeton University Press, 2000); *The Art of French Piano Music* by Roy Howat (New Haven: Yale University Press, 2009); *Debussy in Proportion* by Roy Howat (Cambridge: Cambridge University Press, 1989); *Kind of Blue: The Making of the Miles Davis Masterpiece* by Ashley Kahn (New York: Da Capo Press, 2001); *The Technique of My Musical Language* by Olivier Messiaen (Paris: Alphonse Leduc, 1966); *Writings About Music* by Steve Reich (New York: New York University Press, 1974); *Arnold Schoenberg: The Composer as Jew* by Alexander L. Ringer (Oxford: Clarendon Press, 1993); *Claude Debussy* by Paul Roberts (London: Phaidon Press, 2008); *Image: The Piano Music of Claude Debussy* by Paul Roberts (Portland, OR: Amadeus Press, 1996); *Early Jazz: Its Roots and Musical Development* by Gunther Schuller (New York: Oxford University Press, 1968); *Arnold Schoenberg's Journey* by Allen Shawn (New York: Farrar, Straus and Giroux, 2002); *Lost Chords: White Musicians and Their Contribution to Jazz, 1915–1945* by Richard M. Sudhalter (New York: Oxford University Press, 1999); *The Cambridge Companion to Debussy,* edited by Simon Trezise (Cambridge: Cambridge University Press, 2003); *Satie the Bohemian* by Steven Moore Whiting (New York: Oxford University Press, 1999); *Portrait of Liszt, By Himself and His Contemporaries* by Adrian Williams (Oxford: Clarendon Press, 1990); and *Bach and the Meanings of Counterpoint* by David Gaynor Yearsley (Cambridge: Cambridge University Press, 2002).

The following articles were also used: "Scriabin's Octatonic Sonata" by Cheong Wai-Ling, *Journal of the Royal Musical Association* 121, no. 2 (1996), 206–228; "Notes on John Cage, Eric Satie's *Vexations* and Andy Warhol's *Sleep,*" by Gary Comenas, *Warholstars.org,* 2009; "Ligeti in Fluxus," by Eric Drott, *Journal of Musicology* 21, no. 2 (Spring 2004), 201–240; "Was Scriabin a Synesthete?" by B. M. Galeyev and I. L. Vanechkina, *Leonarda* 34, no. 4 (2001), 357–361; "Skryabin and the Impossible" by Simon Morrison, *Journal of the American Musicological Society* 51, no. 2 (Summer

1998), 283–330; "Skryabin: Summer 1903 and After" by Alexander Pasternak, *Musical Times* 113, no. 1558 (December 1972), 1169–1174; and "Scriabin's Self-Analyses" by George Perle, *Music Analysis* 3, no. 2 (July 1984), 101–122.

CHAPTER 9 *The Rhythmitizers*

Eudora Welty's *Powerhouse* appears in *From Blues to Bop: A Collection of Jazz Fiction*, edited by Richard N. Albert (New York: Anchor Books/Doubleday, 1992). Material on Louis and Lil Armstrong can be found in *Pops: A Life of Louis Armstrong* by Terry Teachout (New York: Houghton Mifflin Harcourt, 2009).

Some of the material on New Orleans pianists and an interview of Henry Butler by the author appeared in *Piano Today*, Spring 2005. The commentary by Mike Lipskin was adapted, with permission, from his writings from his Web site, mike lipskinjazz.com. The sidebar by Oscar Peterson is taken from "In Memoriam—Duke Ellington, 'The Man': Reflections by Oscar Peterson" in *Sound Magazine*, November 1974. The Billy Joel quote about synthesizers appeared in the *Independent*, May 23, 1990; Billy Joel's comments on composing and his quotes about rock music were taken from an interview conducted by the author for *Piano Today*, winter 1997. The sidebar by Gabriela Montero is from an interview conducted by the author in 2009. The comments on "Afro-Cuban Piano Style," as well as much of the information about Latin music and its pianists, were provided by Arturo O'Farrill Jr. during an interview conducted by the author in 2010.

The following books were also used in the preparation of this chapter: *The City in Slang: New York Life and Popular Speech* by Irving Lewis Allen (New York: Oxford University Press, 1992); *All Shook Up: How Rock 'n' Roll Changed America* by Glenn C. Altschuler (New York: Oxford University Press, 2003); *Five Points* by Tyler Anbinder (New York: Free Press, 2001); *Music in Latin America: An Introduction* by Gerard Béhague (Englewood Cliffs, NJ: Prentice-Hall, 1979); *Ragtime: A Musical and Cultural History* by Edward A. Berlin (Berkeley: University of California Press, 1980); *The Harlem Reader*, edited by Herb Boyd (New York: Three Rivers Press, 2003); *Striders to Beboppers and Beyond* by Leslie Gourse (New York: Franklin Watts, 1997); *Jelly Roll, Bix, and Hoagy: Gennett Studios and the Birth of Recorded Jazz* by Rick Kennedy (Bloomington: Indiana University Press, 1994); *Chicago Jazz: A Cultural History, 1904–1930* by William Howland Kenney (New York: Oxford University Press, 1993); *Too Marvelous for Words: The Life & Genius of Art Tatum* by James Lester (New York: Oxford University Press, 1994); *From Paris to Peoria: How European Piano Virtuosos Brought Classical Music to the American Heartland* by R. Allen Lott (New York: Oxford University Press, 2003); *The Great Jazz Pianists: Speaking of Their Lives and Music* by Len Lyons (New York: Quill, 1983); *A Left Hand Like God: A History of Boogie-Woogie Piano* by Peter J. Silvester (New York: Da Capo, 1988); *Lexicon of Musical Invective* by Nicolas Slonimsky (Seattle: University of Washington Press, 1978); *Music on My Mind: The Memoirs of An American Pianist* by Willie "the Lion" Smith with George Hoefer (London: Jazz Book Club by arrangement with MacGibbon & Kee, 1966); *Lost Chords: White Musicians and Their Contribution to Jazz, 1915–1945* by Richard M. Sudhalter (New York: Oxford University Press, 1999); and *Chambers Music Quotations* by Derek Watson (Edinburgh: W & R Chambers, Ltd., 1991).

Articles used include: "The Use of Habanera Rhythm in Rockabilly Music" by Roy Brewer, *American Music* 17, no. 3 (Autumn 1999), 300–317; "Percussion and Petticoats" by Henry G. Farmer, *Music & Letters* 31, no. 4 (October 1950), 343–345; "Social Dance Music of Black Composers in the Nineteenth Century and the Emergence of Classic Ragtime" by Samuel A. Floyd Jr. and Marsha J. Reisser, *The Black Perspective in Music* 8, no. 2 (Autumn 1980), 161–193; "The Nineteenth-Century Origins of Jazz" by Lawrence Gushee, from *Black Music Research Journal* 14, no. 1 (1993); "Defining Ragtime Music: Historical and Typological Research" by Ingeborg Harer, *Studia Musicologica Academiae Scientiarum Hungaricae*, T. 38, Fasc. 3/4 (1997), 409–415; "Why They Call American Music Ragtime" by J. Rosamond Johnson, *The Black Perspective in Music* 4, no. 2 (July 1976), 260–264; "Eugene Stratton and Early Ragtime in Britain" by Michael Pickering, *Black Music Research Journal* 20, no. 2 (Autumn 2000), 151–180; "Three Piano Misereres" by Joseph Smith, *Journal of the American Liszt Society* 59–60 (2008–2009), 10–23; "Ben Harney: The Middlesborough Years, 1890–93" by William H. Tallmadge, *American Music* 13, no. 2 (Summer 1995), 167–194; and "Chicago's Jazz Trail, 1893–1950" by Dempsey J. Travis, *Black Music Research Journal* 10, no. 1 (Spring 1990), 82–85.

In addition, references from nonprint media include the DVD *Jerry Lee Lewis: Killer Piano* (2007) and the following CDs: *Fidgety Digits: Rare Syncopated Piano 78's from Collectors' Archives* (Shellwood Productions); *The Ragtime Women*, Max Morath and the Ragtime Quintet (Vanguard); and *Jazz Nocturne: The Collected Piano Music of Dana Suesse*, Sara Davis Buechner, piano, E1 Music: Port Washington, New York, 2009.

CHAPTER 10 *The Melodists*

The András Schiff contribution is from an interview conducted by the author in 2009. The Garrick Ohlsson quote on Chopin is from an interview conducted by the author in 2009 for Lincoln Center's *Stagebill*. The Emanuel Ax quote is from an interview conducted by the author in 2009.

Although parallels between Gershwin and Schubert may seem odd, Gershwin was a devotee of Schubert, especially of his great String Quintet in C Major, and it is worth noting that Gershwin's sidekick Oscar Levant, the pianist, found evidence of direct influences of that piece in Gershwin's show *Let 'Em Eat Cake*.

The following books were used for this chapter: *Better Than It Sounds* by David W. Barber (Toronto: Sound and Vision, 1998); *Virtuosity of the Nineteenth Century* by Susan Bernstein (Stanford: Stanford University Press, 1998); *Schumann Piano Music* by Joan Chissell (Seattle: University of Washington Press, 1972); *Music in Chopin's Warsaw* by Halina Goldberg (New York: Oxford University Press, 2008); *World of Our Fathers* by Irving Howe (New York: Harcourt Brace Jovanovich, 1976); *Chopin at the Boundaries: Sex, History, and Musical Genre* by Jeffrey Kallberg (Cambridge: Harvard University Press, 1996); *Nineteenth-Century Romanticism in Music* by Rey M. Longyear (Englewood Cliffs, NJ: Prentice-Hall, 1973);

Erik Satie by Rollo H. Myers (New York: Dover, 1968); *Mendelssohn Remembered* by Roger Nichols (London: Faber and Faber, 1997); *Ravel Remembered* by Roger Nichols (London: Faber and Faber, 1987); *Oscar Peterson: A Jazz Odyssey* by Oscar Peterson, editor and consultant Richard Palmer (New York: Continuum, 2002); *George Gershwin: His Life and Work* by Howard Pollack (Berkeley: University of California Press, 2007); *Schubert Piano Sonatas* by Philip Radcliffe (Seattle: University of Washington Press, 1970); *Clara Schumann: The Artist and the Woman* by Nancy B. Reich (Ithaca, NY: Cornell University Press, 2001); *Romantic Poets, Critics, and Other Madmen* by Charles Rosen (Cambridge: Harvard University Press, 1998); *The Lives of the Great Composers* by Harold C. Schonberg (New York: W. W. Norton & Company, 1970); *Lexicon of Musical Invective* by Nicolas Slonimsky (Seattle: University of Washington Press, 1978); *Chopin in Paris: The Life and Times of the Romantic Composer* by Tad Szulc (New York: Scribner, 1998); *Frédéric Chopin: Profiles of the Man and the Musician*, edited by Alan Walker (New York: Taplinger Publishing Company, 1966); *Schubert Chamber Music* by J. A. Westrup (Seattle: University of Washington Press, 1969); *Satie the Bohemian* by Steven Moore Whiting (New York: Oxford University Press, 1999); *Robert Schumann: Life and Death of a Musician* by John Worthen (New Haven: Yale University Press, 2007).

Also used were the articles "Gabriel Fauré, a Neglected Mastery" by Aaron Copland, *Musical Quarterly* 10, no. 4 (October 1924), 573–586; "Fired! Because He Could Not Play Jazz!" by A. L. Wallace, *Popular Songs* 1, no. 5 (April 1935); and "Chopin in London" by Iwo and Pamela Zaluski, *Musical Times* 133, no. 1791 (May 1992), 226–230.

CHAPTERS 11, 12, 13, AND 14 *The Cultivated and the Vernacular; The Russians Are Coming; The Germans and Their Close Relations; Keys to the World*

The comments by Ilya Itin were made to the author in an interview in 2009. The comments by Yundi Li were made to the author in an interview in 2010. The reference to Augie March's grandmother is from *The Adventures of Augie March* by Saul Bellow (New York: Penguin, 2006). Comments by Alfred Brendel were made to the author in the fall of 2010.

The following published materials were used in the preparation of these chapters: *Prokofiev's Piano Sonatas* by Boris Berman (New Haven: Yale University Press, 2008); *Alfred Brendel on Music* (Chicago: A Cappella Books, 2001); *The Roots of Texas Music*, edited by Laurence Clayton and Joe W. Specht (College Station: Texas A&M University Press, 2003); *Hitler's Piano Player: The Rise and Fall of Ernst Hanfstaengl, Confidant of Hitler, Ally of FDR* by Peter Conradi (New York: Carroll & Graf, 2004); *Reflections from the Keyboard: The World of the Concert Pianist* by David Dubal (New York: Schirmer, 1997); *Ignaz Friedman: Romantic Master Pianist* by Allan Evans (Bloomington: Indiana University Press, 2009); *My Nine Lives: A Memoir of Many Careers in Music* by Leon Fleisher and Anne Midgette (New York: Doubleday, 2010); *Famous Pianists and Their Technique* by Reginald R. Gerig (Washington, D.C.: Robert B. Luce, 1974); *I Really Should Be Practicing* by Gary

Graffman (Garden City, NY: Doubleday, 1981); *Piano Playing, with Piano Questions Answered* by Josef Hofmann (New York: Dover, 1976); *Music at the White House: A History of the American Spirit* by Elise K. Kirk (Urbana: University of Illinois Press, 1986); *Myra Hess by Her Friends*, compiled by Denis Lassimonne, edited and with an introduction by Howard Ferguson (London: Hamish Hamilton, 1966); *Life and Culture of Poland* by Waclaw Lednicki (New York: Roy Publishers, 1944); *Richter, the Enigma*, a film directed by Bruno Monsaingeon (NVC Arts, 1999); *Sviatoslav Richter: Notebooks and Conversations* by Bruno Monsaingeon, translated by Stewart Spencer (Princeton: Princeton University Press, 2002); *Beyond Frontiers* by Jasper Parrott with Vladimir Ashkenazy (New York: Atheneum, 1984); *The Human Stain* by Philip Roth (Boston: Houghton Mifflin, 2000); *My Many Years* by Arthur Rubinstein (New York; Alfred A. Knopf, 1980); *Music and the Line of Most Resistance* by Artur Schnabel (New York: Da Capo, 1969); *History of Italian Architecture, 1944–1985* by Manfredo Tafuri, translated by Jessica Levine (Cambridge: MIT Press, 1989); *Composition in Black and White* by Kathryn Talalay (New York: Oxford University Press, 1995); *The Oxford History of Western Music, Volume 3: The Nineteenth Century* by Richard Taruskin (New York: Oxford University Press, 2005); *French Pianism: A Historical Perspective* by Charles Timbrell (Portland, OR: Amadeus Press, 1999); and *Schnabel's Interpretations of Piano Music* by Konrad Wolff (New York: W. W. Norton & Company, 1979).

Articles used include: "The Future of the Piano" by S. Montagu Cleeve, *Musical Times*, July 1946; "Looking Ahead—II" by Feste, *Musical Times*, February 1934; "More Play for Prizes" by Corinna da Fonseca-Wollheim, *Wall Street Journal*, September 20, 2010; "The Great Piano War of the 1870s" by Cynthia Adams Hoover, *A Celebration of American Music: Words and Music in Honor of H. Wiley Hitchcock*, edited by Richard Crawford, R. Alen Lott, and Carol J. Oja (Ann Arbor: The University of Michigan Press, 1990); "The Great Chicago Piano War" by Paul and Ruth Hume, *American Heritage*, October 1970; "Catching Up to the 21st Century" by Stuart Isacoff, *Keyboard Classics*, May/June 1986; "The Rise and Fall and Rise of Van Cliburn" by Stuart Isacoff, *Ovation*, September 1989; "Van Cliburn Then & Now" by Stuart Isacoff, *Piano Today*, Summer 2001; "Vladimir Ashkenazy: Pianist of the Straight and True" by Stuart Isacoff, *Piano Today*, Spring 2007; "Another Early Iberian Grand Piano" by Beryl Kenyon de Pascual and David Law, *Galpin Society Journal* 48 (March 1995), 68–93; and "His Cold War Concerts Helped Break the Ice" by Barrymore Laurence Scherer, *Wall Street Journal*, June 11, 2008.

CHAPTER 15 *The Cutting Edge*

Martin Canin's comments on technique were made to the author several years ago. Some of the quotes from Gary Graffman were given during an interview with the author in 2009. I am grateful to Italian pianist Riccardo Scivales for his insights into the world of prog rock. The comments from Earl Wild are from an interview conducted by the author and published in *Musical America* for their Instrumentalist of the Year Award in 2006. The Victor Borge comments were derived from an interview conducted by the author and published in the magazine *Keyboard Clas-*

sics, November/December 1984 in the article "They Laughed When I Sat Down To Play . . . Victor Borge at 75."

Books used in the preparation of this chapter include: *Conversations with Glenn Gould* by Jonathan Cott (Boston: Little, Brown, 1984); *A Romance on Three Legs: Glenn Gould's Obsessive Quest for the Perfect Piano* by Katie Hafner (New York: Bloomsbury, 2009); *Men, Women and Pianos: A Social History* by Arthur Loesser (New York: Simon & Schuster, 1954); *Glenn Gould Variations,* edited by John McGreevy (New York: Quill, 1983); *Glenn Gould: The Ecstasy and Tragedy of Genius* by Peter F. Ostwald (New York: W. W. Norton & Company, 1997); *The Glenn Gould Reader,* edited and with an introduction by Tim Page (New York: Alfred A. Knopf, 1984); and *Glenn Gould: Music & Mind* by Geoffrey Payzant (Toronto: Van Nostrand Reinhold, 1978).

CHAPTER 16 *Everything Old Is New Again*

The comments by Margaret Leng Tan were made during a conversation with the author in 2010. The explanation of the chess piano was sent to the author by its creator, Guido van der Werve; I am grateful to author and chess master Frank Brady, president of the Marshall Chess Club, for alerting me to Mr. van der Werve's work.

Appendix

Resources for this chapter included *A Woman's Gaze: Latin American Women Artists* by Marjorie Agosin (Fredonia, NY: White Pine Press, 1998).

Index